# FACE TO FACE *with* COUNTRY

# FACE TO FACE
## *with* COUNTRY

*A Diary of Interviews
with Country Superstars of the
70s, 80s, and 90s*

# WILLIAM L. TURNER

BRANSON PUBLISHING COMPANY
*1994*

*Branson, Mo • Tucker, Ga*

Branson Publishing Company
Distribution Center
P.O. Box 1232
Tucker, GA 30085

Manuscripts dealing with country music are solicited. Materials will not be
returned unless sufficient postage is enclosed in the package.

Manuscript editor: Greg Angelo
Sketches: Gayla Pankey
Cover and text designer: Gary Gore
Project co-ordinator: Marte Johnson
Pre-press production: Graphic Composition, Inc., Athens, GA.
Printing and binding: BookCrafters, Virginia division.

*To my family and friends*
*who believed in and supported*
*this project.*

Charles
Thank you for your
support and friendship.
I hope you enjoy the
book.

Best Wishes,
William [Turner]
1994

# Contents

# Preface

I HAVE OFTEN BEEN ASKED FOR REPRINTS OF
my newspaper columns or permission to listen to my audiotaped interviews of country music entertainers. Realizing a need to make these
materials available to my readers, one of my editors urged me to com-
pile a book/diary of my interviews. Determining the format and contents
of a book of this nature was not easy. After reviewing each interview, I have
chosen thirty-six to comprise *Face to Face with Country: A Diary of Interviews with Country Superstars of the 70s, 80s, and 90s*. The interviews were
chosen on the basis of their warmth, content, and readers' responses to my
newspaper columns. Each interview required only minor editing of re-
peated sentences or sentence fragments. At no time was material taken out
of context or altered to change the intent of the interviewees. Pauses in the
conversations are indicated in text by ellipses (. . . ).

Country music is believed to be the only true American art form in
existence, so it is important to look at responses of the past and of the
present to give substance to this theory. The goal of the project is to present
a book that the reader will find informative, entertaining, and interesting.

# FACE TO FACE *with* COUNTRY

*I believe our music has roots. A basic, simple quality that a lot of people can identify with, what we are saying in our music.*

*— Teddy Gentry (Alabama)*

A S THEIR NAME SAYS, most of the members of Alabama are from that state, specifically Fort Payne and the Lookout Mountain area.

Except for the group's drummer, Mark Herndon, from Springfield, Massachusetts, all the members are related. Cousins Randy Owen, Jeff Cook, and Teddy Gentry grew up near each other, and first met musically in Fort Payne, where Jeff was working for Western Electric, Teddy was laying carpet, and Randy was going to school. In 1969, they assembled to make music together for the first time.

The cousins moved to Anniston, Alabama where they became roommates. Closeness came through more than family ties. At night, the musicians pushed their beds together into the biggest room in the house so they could continue singing until they went to sleep.

In 1973, they struck out for Myrtle Beach, South Carolina where they started playing in clubs six nights a week. Stardom came in 1980 when they had their first hit in the top twenty.

# Alabama

TURNER:  How did you get the name Alabama?

COOK:  Well, in 1977 after being "Wild Country" for several years, we had a one-shot single release on GRT records, and they thought we should change our name. We had sorta been thinking about it for some time. So we made up a list of names and eliminated them until we got down to Alabama. Also, people knew what state we were from, but they could not remember "Wild Country." They would say, "Hey! there goes Alabama." It's also a nice place to be in the record line-up in the album store.

---

I think our music is a combination of every kind of music that we have ever come in contact with.

---

TURNER:  That's true when you go by alphabetical order.

GENTRY:  We didn't think about that at the time. Actually, it is because three of us are from Alabama.

COOK:  It has worked out real good that way, though.

TURNER:  Where do you see yourself on the music spectrum?

GENTRY:  We see ourselves as doing what we feel like doing. I think our music is a combination of every kind of music that we have ever come in contact with. Jeff has a background in rock and country. I have played mostly bluegrass, a little gospel, and a little rock and roll—really a little bit of everything. I think we apply all techniques of music to our individual songs. I don't think you can put us into a category because our songs don't sound alike.

TURNER:  Today there seems to be a trend away from labels per se—you know country music, and rock singles. Do you feel this has unleashed a lot of talent, and a lot of creativity that would have never been discovered had this not have happened in the industry?

TEDDY:   Yeah, I think so because if we run into a good song and we like the song, we go in and cut it. We don't care where it comes from or who wrote it or who has publishing on it. If we think it's a good song, we want to cut it.

COOK:   Or if we think we can perform it the way we feel it should be.

TURNER:   Who has been the greatest influence on your career?

COOK:   That is a very hard question. Of course, there are the legends like Ernest Tubb and Hank Williams who influenced our music. More recently, the Beatles, the Eagles, and Creedence Clearwater, which was a four-piece group which made a lot of music with four pieces.

GENTRY:   Mostly we were influenced by each other!

TURNER:   South Carolina—more specifically Myrtle Beach—played a big part in your career, did it not?

GENTRY:   Yeah, it really gave us a chance to earn a living for a few years during the summer time as well as a chance to work on a lot of original material—they didn't care if we wrote the song or who wrote them, as long as we were making some kind of music on stage. It was really a good opportunity to play a lot of the original material.

TURNER:   Why South Carolina over Alabama?

COOK:   We were from a dry county—actually we were from a damp county, but there were no clubs there for us to play in. So we had to get out of town, and it just happened that the drummer we had at that time, our original drummer, had played in Myrtle Beach with another band and he had a contact there.

GENTRY:   It was the only place that offered us a job.

COOK:   That's the best way to put it.

TURNER:   You were not an overnight success then?

GENTRY:   We were a ten year "overnight" success.

TURNER:   During those ten years, what factor or factors kept you going and believing in yourselves?

COOK: I guess . . . the love of playing music, entertaining people, and producing something we felt was a good sound.

TURNER: You are enjoying tremendous success now. Why do you think your sound has been so widely accepted?

COOK: I don't know—I am just thankful for it.

GENTRY: I believe our music has roots. A basic, simple quality that a lot of people can identify with, what we are saying in our music.

TURNER: Country music is enjoying phenomenal success right now. Why do you think country music is so popular?

COOK: Because of movies like *Urban Cowboy, Bronco Billy,* and what's the Rose picture?

TURNER: *Honeysuckle Rose.*

COOK: That's it. Movies like that have had an impact on it. The sound tracks, and songs that were featured in those movies did real well on the charts. I hope its popularity continues.

TURNER: Do you think this is a fad and will pass like disco did?

GENTRY: I certainly hope not because this is the way we make our living.

COOK: I think the people who are truly turned on to country music will find out, "Hey, we really like this type of music; this is really where the heart is and a lot of the basics and a lot of the truths in country music." I feel that a lot that are turned on to it will always be country music fans. The ones who are out in the new boots and hat because it is the hip thing to do and don't care for country music, probably don't care about any kind of music. They probably only care about fads, so you know it will probably be a passing thing for them. I still think the people who really find out what country is all about and where we are coming from will continue to like country music.

TURNER: Where do you want your music to take you in the future?

GENTRY: As long and as far as we can go—something we touched on earlier—this is my personal opinion that it is getting harder and harder to tell country now from say pop music of ten or twelve years ago. A lot of old pop songs have turned to country.

TURNER:   Do you feel that there are a lot of people who are not inter-ested in country music in the industry, who are into it for the business sake only and not for the creativity?

---

It is getting harder and harder to tell coun-try now from say pop music of ten or twelve years ago. A lot of old pop songs have turned to country.

---

COOK:   Well, there are people who like to make money, but most of them know where it's coming from—they know what's buttering their bread.

TURNER:   What do you look for when you are selecting material for a new album?

COOK:   Good harmony lines, original thoughts, story lines. There are a lot of good songs, but they would not be good songs for us.

GENTRY:   Number one, I think you gotta look for a hit song. If you are going to cut something of somebody else's. We have many songs we have written over the years, but we feel that they are just not right for our group—you know!

TURNER:   Do you pitch them to someone else?

COOK:   Yeah . . . if we can.

TURNER:   What kind of song do you feel most comfortable with: a bal-lad, up tempo, or whatever?

GENTRY:   It doesn't matter as long as we can apply our—what we do best—style to it.

TURNER:   If you were an interviewer doing an interview with Alabama, what question would you ask them that I have not asked?

GENTRY:   Well, I would ask anything except, "Are you really from Alabama?"

TURNER:   Entertainment business means a lot of traveling and hectic schedules, and you are on the road a lot between concerts. How have you been able to entertain yourselves for those long hours?

GENTRY:   We got a sheep and bay horse.

COOK:   No, don't say that. Well, we got us a video recorder and we are building up our library of tapes, and we have audio tapes and we have a good sound system in the bus. We sleep a lot.

GENTRY:   Some of us play backgammon; some of us play cards.

COOK:   We sleep a lot.

May 1981

*The country music of today has no western aspect. We used to be country and western artists but now we are just country artists. . . . Marty Robbins and I were the only two country and western artists in the business, and when Marty died I was the one left to carry it on.*
*—Rex Allen, Jr.*

Rᴇx Aʟʟᴇɴ, Jʀ. has consistently recorded hit after hit for the past several years. Allen works alongside wife Judy in selecting hit recording materials. Their combined efforts include "Goodbye," "The Great Mail Robbery," "Two Less Lonely People," and "No, No, No." Rex, Jr., son of the singing cowboy movie star of yesterday, is determined to preserve his heritage and western music. In a time when many songwriters are concentrating on wrong-hearted romances, trains, trucks and jails, they have forgotten the prairies, the camp-fires, cattle drives and outlaws. But not Rex Allen, Jr. Each stage show includes a western segment devoted to such songs as "Can You Hear Those Pioneers," "Tear Drops in My Heart," and "Streets of Laredo." Allen is an entertainer, and his show has something sure to please the most discriminating audience.

# Rex Allen, Jr.

TURNER:  Where do you see yourself on the music spectrum?

ALLEN:  Today in country music there are both the hardcore country acts and the crossover acts coexisting. Up until recently I think the best description of Rex Allen, Jr. would have been "fence straddle" music. Rex Allen, Jr. straddles the fence. I do everything from songs like "With Love" to "Lonely Street," one of the more aggressive country or pop country or cosmopolitan country songs. By the way I won a BMI award for writing "With Love." I was on that side but yet I did things like "No, No, No." I also did some hardcore things like "It's Over." If you had to look at my career, it would be one of trying to straddle the fence, and what we have done has taken almost a year to do. We came off the fence recordwise, and we have decided to go in the direction that I always wanted to go—which was more country. The reason why I was not able to do that earlier is real simple to understand. I have a two and a half to three octave range in full voice. Producers have a tendency to produce me like, "My God, we have a singer here who can do anything we want." They want more of avant-garde country, if you want to call it that. Gary Morris is a victim of the same problem.

TURNER:  Your father is a living legend; what advice did he give you when you decided to toss your hat into the music arena?

ALLEN:  The only real advice that my mom and dad (both were entertainers) gave me was to always be humble and be the same on stage as you are at home and let the person you really are come out. I think that everybody that comes and watches us work sees the real me on stage. There are certainly tricks that I use to try and get the audience involved. Basically, when I stand up and tell you a story about something, it is true. That is me and that is humble.

TURNER:  I often hear your voice described as being articulate, deep, and mellow. How did you develop your voice?

ALLEN:  I majored in theater arts in college. I will be honest with you; I had six voice lessons as a child and I stopped on the sixth lesson. I learned the right kind of techniques; I learned how to breathe. The range and the pipes came from the genes. I feel that you are born with the pipes. I don't think you can really develop the pipes. I learned how to use the pipes properly by learning how to breath and resonate properly.

Live theater was great for me. I started live theater when I was 12 and 13 years old. I played every Rhett Butler part there was to play. I learned how to sing and project from singing on stage in live theater. When I was in the service, I did eight major theater productions. I did everything from *Funny Thing Happened On The Way To The Forum* to *Wildcat*. I wrote and directed eighty-six variety shows while I was in the service and I also worked with the troops. I did shows in Madigan General Hospital in Washington. I did four of those shows a week. I got my training by not singing in front of a microphone. A lot of entertainers eat the microphone and that is the only way they can work. I know real well how to work the microphone. That came with experience. Another thing is the band and musicians have worked with me for a while and they know me pretty well and I know them real well.

TURNER:   You have had vast experiences in the theater and you hosted the television series *Nashville On The Road*. How did this add depth to your career?

ALLEN:   There are people who look good on television and people who don't. I am fortunate enough to look good on television, and I like TV. A lot of people are scared when that "eye" is looking at them. They think that behind that eye are three to five million people but it does not bother me at all. I work a camera just like I am working you. You look the camera in the eye and do the job. You sing to the camera or make love to the camera or whatever you want to call it. I would like to have the opportunity to go back someday and do more television. I would like to have a daily late-night show. A working title would be *The Late Rex Allen, Jr.* I would open the show by coming out of a casket every night. It would be a cross between *David Letterman* and *Johnny Carson*.

TURNER:   You have the reputation of being one of the classiest acts in country music; how important is packaging and image development?

ALLEN:   I think it is terribly important. I think you are alright as long as the packaging does not conflict with what the artist really is. Hank Williams, Jr. is a prime example. I had been on Warner Brothers for three or four years when they first signed him and they came to me and said, "We are going to sign Hank, Jr. and I hope you are not upset about that." I told them I thought it was a great idea. I also told them that Hank was a wonderful man and a great talent. However, I said promote Bocephus, not the Hank Williams, Jr. who recorded "Eleven Yellow Roses." I said, "Do Hank a favor and let him be what he is, not what his mother and his father's fans want him to be." I feel that if a record company thinks an individual has talent and can entertain people, then their job is to take that person into a recording studio and record that individual. They should try to sell that

---

> If nobody likes me and the public does not like me then I will get out of the business and pump gas.

---

individual, not try to change that individual. Sell the person on the record. If the public does not buy it, they could probably go on to someone else. Please don't try to make Rex Allen, Jr. into the next Jim Reeves. There was a Jim Reeves but I am Rex Allen, Jr. and I will do my songs and I want to sing my way. If you can't sell it and it is not working for your particular company, go on to somebody else. If nobody likes me and the public does not like me then I will get out of the business and pump gas.

TURNER: To really showcase the talents of Rex Allen, Jr., what song would you perform?

ALLEN: That is a toughy. "A Better Memory Comes Along" probably showcases me better than any song I have ever cut. The reason I like it so much is because it has the soul that I have always wanted to be able to do in a country song and it also showcases me vocally. "A Better Memory Comes Along" was produced by Ron Chaney. He is an extremely nice man and a tremendous producer. Ron is known to a lot of people as probably the biggest-selling producer in Nashville. Out of the current stage work that we do, the song that most epitomizes the way I feel inside and the way I think I am vocally is not a country song. It is a rock and roll song called "Cool Chains." "Chains" is probably above the heads of a lot of people in audiences because they are not familiar with rock and roll. It appeals to me because it symbolizes the way I feel. I like the ocean. My goal in life is to have enough money someday to buy a fifty-five- to sixty-foot yacht and live down in the Marathon Keys in Florida. I would love that. Also, I want a ranch in Texas.

TURNER: In the past country music was known as country and western music; what happened to the western aspect of it?

---

> Marty Robbins and I were the only two country and western artists in the business, and when Marty died I was the one left to carry it on.

---

ALLEN: The country music of today has no western aspect. We used to be country and western artists but now we are just country artists. I am the only country and western artist in the business today. Riders in the Sky are tremendous western artists and I am fans of theirs. They do great western music. Marty Robbins and I were the only two country and western artists in the business, and when Marty died I was the one left to carry it on. I am the one that has the heritage and I have the background to go ahead and do it and I will always do it. What I said on stage, I believe is true. I firmly believe that western music is the only true form of American music.

TURNER: Marty passed the torch to you. Is there anyone currently in the field of country music that you will pass the torch to?

ALLEN: Not yet!

TURNER: Kenny Rogers once told me that any music form needs to step back and take a good look to see where it has been and where it is going. Do you feel that it is time for country music to take a step back and look around?

ALLEN: There are two statements that I will make about country music today. I think that country music is the most creative music around because there are so many people involved in the business today. That makes it very creative. The second point is that country music very confused. Listeners are confused. They don't know what country music is anymore and radio doesn't know what country music is. They don't know what to play and they are a little bit worried. I think that more than anything we need to let the public define country music and not a group of record executives. I think that is the job of the general public. The biggest argument I ever had with a radio programmer was a few years back. I became

---

❖

I think that country music is the most creative music around because there are so many people involved in the business today.

❖

---

enraged when he told me he played the records he wanted to hear. At the time Ray Stevens had a record in the top twenty and he was not playing it because he didn't like it. I said, "Your job is to play what the public wants to hear." I think the country music business has a tendency to sign acts that will appeal to the eighteen-to-twenty-six-year-old market. The last time I checked my demographic studies, country music appealed to people twenty-six and older. If you have not been hurt, been fired from a job, had a relationship that died, gone through a divorce, or watched somebody die, you don't know what life is yet. Country music is life. It is a life experience; it has been, it is now, and always will be. The sooner the powers that be understand that the better off country music will be. I can't understand why record companies will spend $250,000 promoting a new act while at the same time they will not spend $250,000 promoting a veteran act that is selling ten times more records than the new country act. If you look at who went gold or platinum over the last year, it is Ricky Skaggs, George Strait, and Reba McEntire. They are not pop crossover acts; they are country acts. It is like, "Let me be a country act; I don't want to be a crossover act." I loved playing the Palladium, but I would rather go to Oklahoma any day of the week because those folks are going to get up and dance and have a good time. That's what we are out here for.

TURNER:   What are you most proud of in your life?

ALLEN:   I think there are probably two things, not necessarily in this order: the first thing that I am most proud of is a song that I did not perform here tonight called "Can You Hear Those Pioneers." I wrote it about my experience as a child. Had it not been for that song I would not be here before you tonight. For years people have said to me it would be nice if someone could put a little more western music back into our lives. I wrote a song about that. I think it is time we put western back into the country sound. I wrote it about heroes like Roy, Gene, and, more than anyone else, the person that taught me about music: my dad. If you really sit down and listen to my song, you will find that what really sticks out in Rex Allen, Jr.'s music is the background vocals. Though they may be modernized and sound like a modern version of The Sons of the Pioneers, I didn't do that intentionally. That just came from the past. The second thing that I am really proud of is my son who at age 6 ½ earned a yellow belt in Tae Kwon Do. The kid is doing good.

TURNER:   What role do you see for Rex Allen, Jr. in the future?

ALLEN:   I see a lot of things. My dad always told me that if you reach your goals, you didn't set them high enough. I have set my goals for several things. I want to have a platinum-selling record and I think I will someday. I would like to see crooners come back, and I want to be that crooner. I think that it is time for an individual like me who can go out and rock and roll with the best of them, sing a hillbilly song, sing a western song or turn right around and sing bluegrass for you if you want, to have a platinum-selling record. I majored in theater arts in college; therefore, I would like to do motion pictures. I would like to see westerns come back. I may get too old to do it, but maybe my little boy will do it. I think there is nothing new in our business. Everything comes around in cycles. The movies today are nothing but an old film done in color. I think singing cowboy musicals will come back. I think musical comedies will come back and I would like to be a part of that because they were fun films. The last thing is the television aspect of it. I think that right now my future lies in television. I feel that music is a stepping stone to where our business is going and where entertainment in general is going. I was told by somebody that by the year 2000 there will be eight hundred television stations available to the public on a satellite. Obviously that is where we need to go. That is where entertainment will be in the future. Television is where we will all be eventually. In the future I don't think that there will be anybody going on the road— maybe occasionally.

TURNER:   Has your correct enunciation and pronunciation been a barrier in Country Music?

ALLEN:   Yes, they have been at times. In the past I've told people there are three or four different Rex Allen, Jr.'s. There is the Rex Allen, Jr. who sings on the record, there is the Rex Allen, Jr. who is on stage, there is the Rex Allen, Jr. who signs autographs, and there is the Rex Allen, Jr. who goes home. Four different people. You can't perform in a studio. Recording is a separate career and a separate kind of medium from onstage work. Working a microphone is a lot different from working a live audience. I change what I do and I put more emphasis on enunciation when I'm on stage than I do when I'm in a studio because it is harder for people to hear me from the stage. On stage you don't have the technical ability to boost the vocals in just the right places therefore you have to enunciate properly so people can hear you.

   I learned to enunciate at the University of East Oregon. Also, my dad had a great influence on my enunciation. I can remember when I was about fourteen years old I was sitting in my room playing the guitar and my dad walked into the room. He had a Craig tape recorder with him and he turned to me and said, "My business is changing; I am moving from being a road performer to being a narrator." He said, "I have done five Disney narrations, and I have just signed a contract today for twenty more of them, and I just got the Ralston-Purina account." I did not really understand what he was talking about. He told me that if I were going to be successful and have longevity in the business, I needed to learn how to speak correctly. He handed me the tape recorder and a copy of the L. A. *Times* and said, "Read this into the tape recorder." I started out saying, "Yesterday—afternoon—on—the—Ventura—Freeway—at—5—0—5—there—was—an—accident—involving—sixteen—people." He told me to stop and play it back. I did and thought it was awful. He said that I needed to learn how to speak so I could say, "yesterday afternoon at 5:05 on Ventura Freeway in Los Angeles, 14 people were killed and 435 were injured." He told me to learn to enunciate correctly and that I would always be able to get jobs as an announcer. My dad was right because I have done lots of announcing work.

TURNER:   Which aspect of your career is the most fulfilling?

ALLEN:   The studio work definitely! From a creative standpoint, studio work is the most fulfilling. I also like working with the general public. I enjoy making people laugh and cry.

TURNER:   Is there a difference between an entertainer and a singer?

ALLEN:   You are (expletive) right there is! As a matter of fact, there are not too many singer/entertainers in this business as far as I am concerned. The greatest compliment anyone could pay me would be to say that I am a singer and an entertainer. Mel Tillis is an entertainer; Barbara Mandrell is an entertainer; she is a singer as well as an entertainer. Don Williams is a singer; he may mesmerize you with his material but he is a singer. I think that if we do have a definite problem in our business it is that we are trying to develop people who are singers and not entertainers.

---

The greatest compliment anyone could pay me would be to say that I am a singer and an entertainer.

---

TURNER:   Is the current craze in videos going to eliminate a lot of performers who cannot make the transition from singer to entertainer?

ALLEN:   Several years ago when videos first came out I said, "Country music will have to start looking for acts that look good on camera and they will have to produce concept albums." I think "Oklahoma Rose," "Cat In The Cradle," and "The Singing Cowboy" are good concept-oriented albums. I feel that in time there will be a tremendous market for videos for the home player. The fans can put an album on and either watch it or listen to it on the stereo. That's why I think all albums in the future will have to have some kind of story. In my opinion an album not being concert-oriented is a crime. Most rock and roll albums are concert-oriented, yet country albums are not. In the past albums would have three or four good singles on them and the rest would be a bunch of fillers. Fans would buy the album for one or two of the singles. That's (expletive)! Now country music will have to be concerned with the video. I was one of the founding members of a video company. We started out with over seventy-eight thousand album titles. We sold everything from country, to gospel, to new wave through 1–800. Videos sold like crazy. The point is that we are all going to end up in the video business therefore all acts are going to have to look good on camera. The acts are going to have to be more creatively involved in the process. I think that is even more fun. You look at it and that opens whole new fields and whole new creative outlets for country music. I think that is neat. Country music will not deal with blowing up or (expletive) like some of the rock and rollers do. Country music will not do that. Country music deals with the heart and soul. Personally I think that country music will be more successful on a video level than it has ever even thought of being on a radio level.

TURNER:   If you were an interviewer doing an interview with Rex Allen, Jr., what question would you ask him that I haven't?

ALLEN:   What is the life goal of Rex Allen, Jr.? I want to be in a position to turn down gigs when they conflict with my family. I want to be able to say, "No, I am not going to go," or "I can't go today because my son is going through karate championship or my daughter is graduating from high school or my wife is having a baby today and I am not going to be there." The question is, what does Rex Allen, Jr. want? Rex Allen, Jr. wants life and times with family, good friends, and a sixty-foot yacht on Marathon Key.

September 1987

HOWARD AND DAVID BELLAMY were reared in the wilds of North Florida by a cowpoke father and a pioneer mother. Howard was influenced by traditional country music, but David was raised on rock and roll. When their musical interests blended together, the Bellamys produced a style popular with both country and contemporary rock fans.

Their hit, "If I Said You Had A Beautiful Body, Would You Hold It Against Me" was followed by other suggestive songs such as "Lovers Live Longer" and "Do You Love As Good As You Look?"

The Bellamy Brothers have continued to record several successful albums and have had many top-of-the-chart hits.

*. . . we're not trying to jump on the* Urban Cowboy *trend; we're not into that at all. In fact, we hope that all of that passes us by without grinding us up. . . . We're trying to keep an even pace rather than just a flash in the pan.*

*—David Bellamy*

# The Bellamy Brothers

TURNER:  How has the Bellamy Brothers' sound changed since the sixties when you were in Atlanta?

DAVID:  Who told you about that?

HOWARD:  We're going back a long way.

DAVID:  You know what? We haven't changed drastically. We know a lot more now than we did then.

HOWARD:  We have a lot more material than we did then.

DAVID:  We've gained a lot of knowledge, but as basic people, I don't think we've changed a great deal. We have more money.

HOWARD:  We're not quite as wild as we used to be.

DAVID:  No, we're not as wild as we were, that's true.

TURNER:  How about the style approach to a song since the sixties; has it changed?

HOWARD:  Not really. We kind of separate when we talk about vocals and then talk about music. Our vocal style really can't change 'cause we can't do anything other than what we do very well. It just blends naturally what we do very well. Musically, we always end up surrounding ourselves with kind of a drive and acoustic rhythm and pumping drums and bass and the kind of feel we always treated our songs with. It really hasn't changed that much.

TURNER:  What are the Bellamy Brothers doing today to insure that there will be a Bellamy Brothers act ten years from now?

HOWARD:  Well, we took out insurance with New York Life.

DAVID:  We write a bank of songs so we try to keep quality. We have sort of our own high standards for material, what we consider a high standard, and we're working for longevity in our career and in our career moves that we're doing. Like I was saying earlier about the trend, we're not trying to jump on the *Urban Cowboy* trend; we're not into that at all. In fact, we hope that all of that passes us by without grinding us up. We've got an old Brahma Bull that we ride down at the ranch that wouldn't even buck y'all. We're trying to keep an even pace rather than just a flash in the pan.

TURNER: If you were doing an interview with the Bellamy Brothers, what question would you ask them that I haven't asked you?

HOWARD: Are we real brothers?

DAVID: That's the most asked question. I don't know. I couldn't conduct an interview. I mean, I could sit down with somebody and talk to them. Maybe somebody that I wanted to talk to.

HOWARD: That was a good question—I would have to think about that.

DAVID: I'd probably come up with the same dumb questions that everybody has asked everybody since the beginning of time.

TURNER: What do you think has brought country music the success that it is now enjoying?

DAVID: Ah, well, that's a tough question. You know, country music's been strong for a long time. There has been a lot of, I hate to use the term, but a lot of hype in country music lately. That kind of took over a vacant spot, I guess, when disco and whatnot went out, and there was not a whole lot left and country kinda filled that gap. Our personal opinion about it is we're a little afraid of the hype, and that it might be a trend and trends only last for a little while. So, we personally are trying to stay away from all that—trying not to get involved in the trend that's happening so much.

TURNER: Your background in music has been very different in that you sang with black groups, folk type groups, rock groups, etc. How has this helped you in today's music?

HOWARD: I think probably the main thing it has done is that it has given us a broad base in what we do, 'cause we don't just draw from country influence. And that's given us a pretty broad base 'cause we've been interested in rock and roll, R & B, the classics, and everything for a long time. We still listen to all different types of music. I think that's the main thing it's done.

TURNER: How would you describe the Bellamy Brothers' sound?

DAVID: I don't know—it took a long time to develop. I don't know how we'd describe it. As far as the vocal sound, it's something that kind of felt natural.

HOWARD: Somebody in the band the other day called it "Bumper Billy!" I guess that's a pretty good title.

DAVID: I don't know—it's sort of a natural sound. It's fairly simple, really. It's simple and it's complicated at the same time. We have worked hard to develop the sound that we don't think sounds like anybody else in particular. Something we've tried to do is to be ourselves, and not sound like anybody so that we wouldn't be compared to any other artist. And it's a hard thing to do this day in time: not to sound like somebody because there are so many groups. But we still strive to do that.

---

What's good about country music fans is that they're not fickle. If you prove to them that you're for real, they'll stick with you.

---

TURNER: What has been the greatest influence on your careers? Would it be a person, an individual, or an event?

HOWARD: I don't think we'd pick out one single person or event. We have people that we greatly admire in the business. I guess we admire Merle Haggard in country as much as anybody. And in the rock end we like . . . ah, James Taylor, Paul Simon, those types, you know. And of course, we've been in this a long time. We've been in it almost as long as some of them. We just happen to surface around 1975. We've been at this thing a pretty good while, really.

TURNER: You know, we hear so much about the crossover bit. Do you think country bands are easier or more willing to accept pop artists, people like James Taylor, their influence coming into the country field as opposed to a country artist going out into the pop field?

HOWARD: To me, country people will accept anything that's genuine, and that they can understand and relate to—if it's genuine. What's good about country music fans is that they're not fickle. If you prove to them that you're for real, they'll stick with you.

TURNER: The Bellamy Brothers' dress is not real traditional. You have the long hair and yet I've read somewhere and I thought it interesting: "We have more cowboy in us than most cowboys." What did you mean by that statement?

HOWARD: I think that's right. Well, we are not only country singers, but we're cattle men. We raise cattle. We have registered Brahman cattle on a farm. Matter of fact, we bought two head yesterday. We just did a little cattle trading.

DAVID: Our family, our whole family, were cattle people. They were orange pickers and grew cattle in Florida. Every year we round up cattle and castrate and brand and mark and do the whole works. We've done it all of our lives. So I don't know many people in this business who have done all of that.

TURNER: What aspect of your career do you find the most fulfilling?

DAVID: I guess you could hang yourself on that question.

HOWARD: It's a combination of a lot of things. You know, a good show's fulfilling, a good recording session is fulfilling, and hit records are fulfilling. It's a lot of different areas. I guess some people are into one area and another person is into another area. We like to do it all. We like the studio, and we like to play live and of course we like to have hit records. It would be a lot of things. A lot of things in this business could be really fulfilling, or they could be the other extreme.

DAVID: Yeah, it has a lot of rewards and a lot of downfalls, both. You just have to kind of balance out between the two.

TURNER: I read somewhere that songwriting plays an important part of your life. When you write, do you start with a lyric or with a sound to develop the song?

HOWARD: You can start with a lyric idea or just a musical lick or feel.

DAVID: It comes in different ways. The songs all have different personalities. You can't treat any one the same way; they deserve different treatment so you just have to . . . whatever one deserves, treat it at that time.

TURNER: Do you write for the times?

DAVID: Not necessarily.

HOWARD: Not so much. I think we do without knowing it. But I think a lot of writers do without knowing it. A lot of writers set the times as far as music goes.

DAVID: A lot of the more commercial radio material is more current. Writing is a combination of things, really.

TURNER: The seventies were described as the period of music explosion. How do you think the eighties are going to go down?

DAVID: I wish we knew. I think the seventies were sort of stale music. I liked the sixties much better. After the sixties, the seventies were quite conservative, musicwise. They were . . .

HOWARD: They were slick. The sixties really were creative.

DAVID: Yeah, there were no real artists evolved out of the seventies. You look at the sixties and see people just came out of nowhere—these great artists. But the seventies didn't have a whole lot to offer after the sixties. The eighties, I don't know, the trend seems to be going conservative—obviously, look what's happening . . .

HOWARD: Along with President Reagan.

DAVID: Yeah, so who knows, maybe the music will follow. A lot of times when a trend starts in a particular direction, people get tired of that and go to the other extreme, just to be different, so it would be hard to say.

TURNER: Do you think people in Nashville and the record industry in general are more receptive to creativity today than they were in the past?

DAVID: I think in one way they were more receptive to creativity, but I think in another way that a lot of music or the music capitals sort of emulate themselves over and over. You know, they become a little redundant. They copy themselves over and over and over. That's one thing I don't like about, quote "musical capitals" like Nashville, L. A., New York, and that scene, is that everybody does the same old thing over and over. Not everybody, I shouldn't say that, but in a lot of cases it's rehashed over and over.

TURNER: You know, it's almost an unwritten code in Nashville that the older people rule the industry.

DAVID: Well, it's a very tight clique.

TURNER: This is destroying a lot of creativity that could be on the scene today.

HOWARD: Yeah, it's not only there, it's in this business, period. There is a lot of creativity being destroyed in the history of music. 'Cause the people in the business, they naturally want to control the artists because if they don't, there's no money in it for them so they like to keep control. And there are a few artists who battle their way through and don't get control. I don't know, I hope we are with one of those artists.

TURNER: What has success given you?

DAVID: Well, I believe we've both built new homes in the past couple of years; that's something we thought would never happen. It's given us financial freedom. We came from a kind of rags-to-riches story. I mean, we always had plenty to eat, but we came from a poor family—we never had any money. We had land and cows. You've heard of being land poor; that's about the way we were. And we still have a ways to go, but we're better off than we have been. And that's for sure.

TURNER: What has it taken away from you?

HOWARD: Little privacy.

DAVID: Yeah, privacy is it. That's the one thing that we have less of today.

HOWARD: As we get a little bigger, it is a little harder to get privacy, even when you're home. There is always something to be done.

DAVID: It seems like there's always someone coming up with something that they have to talk to us about.

TURNER: You all seem to be unchanged by success. How have you managed to be able to keep your life in perspective?

HOWARD: Well, I think it is a combination of the good and bad things that have happened to us. Since the beginning of our career, we've had some hard luck and some good luck, and to both extremes. One as big as the other. So I think we learned quite early that we couldn't get too high over any of this or too low, we just try to maintain a balance and go on. Hopefully, we can keep doing that. It gets a little harder sometimes.

TURNER: You've had some really good records and I have enjoyed them. Some of them have suggestive lyrics and I can see how some people could interpret them as chauvinist. How have you been able to counter this?

HOWARD: Well, you know, I'd say the majority of the ladies don't feel that way, or they don't let us know.

DAVID: Also, country music almost, ah . . . well, I shouldn't say it thrives on male chauvinism, but I mean the songs of country music are just really . . . they are chauvinistic. And I think country people are a little bit, men and women country music fans, are more inclined to be that way.

HOWARD: I think the country fans end up looking at it as a sense of humor rather than chauvinism. I thing country fans have a better sense of humor than the normal people. We like to think we have a better sense of humor. I think if we didn't, we would not have survived in this business. That's what we kinda look at ourselves as.

March 1981

T GRAHAM BROWN defies all musical labels. Brown is a product of many southern influences that were cultivated in Athens, the classic city of Georgia. A lifelong dream of becoming a baseball player led Brown to the University of Georgia. His musical talents lay dormant as he struggled to fulfill this dream, but when it became apparent that baseball was not his major talent, Brown was readily accepted into the musical fraternity of the college town.

The move to Nashville, music's major league, was prompted by a friend's advice: "*Get out of Athens if you want to be a star.*"

The country music industry appeared to be waiting for an individual with "country soul." T. Graham Brown found his niche.

*The day I moved to Nashville was a glorious, sunny day—a great day! It was like I had finally graduated from the local scene and now I was going to grad school with the big time.*

*—T. Graham Brown*

# T. Graham Brown

TURNER: You once said that Coach Jim Whatley at UGA directed you to a career in the music industry. How could a coach have that much impact on a young man's career choice?

---

The day I moved to Nashville was a glorious, sunny day—a great day! It was like I had finally graduated from the local scene and now I was going to grad school with the big time.

---

BROWN: That's so funny! I wanted to be a baseball player so bad. That's all I ever wanted to be. I was a sophomore at the University of Georgia. I had this friend I went to high school with who said, "Man, you ought to get a couple of songs together and come over to the Holiday Inn and play for our manager." So I thought, "What the hell!" We put together four, five, or maybe six songs, some Burt Bacharach and B. J. Thomas songs. So we hauled this antiquated junk of ours into the lounge and played our songs. The manager said, "I'll hire you!" We got three hundred dollars a week. We played Tuesday through Saturday. I thought, I'm in show business! That was in the afternoon, so I went back to baseball practice. I saw Coach Whatley there. I said, "Coach, I've got to figure out what I'm going to do. This man over at the Holiday Inn has offered me three hundred dollars a week to sing, but I can't sing and play baseball, too. I've got to figure out what to do." Coach was about sixty-two years old. He said, "If I were you, I'd go for the singing!" He was letting me down easy. It was like he was saying, "You're never going to play for me." So that's how he helped me make the choice.

TURNER: Was it difficult making the transition from being a star in the Athens area to being one of many in Nashville?

27

BROWN: No man! The day I moved to Nashville was a glorious, sunny day—a great day! It was like I had finally graduated from the local scene and now I was going to grad school with the big time. I had to go back to school once I got to Nashville. I had to start all over. It was good! It was like I had a new life. It was a great experience. I did my graduate work! I got a record contract with Capital and as you know I recorded five albums

---

Had I been discovered singing at some honky-tonk I would have been scared to death and if I had been offered a record deal when I first came to Nashville I would have blown it.

---

for them. Now I'm with Warner Brothers. I am trying to get back on the radio. The more records I put out, the further I'm leaning to R & B. Therefore, I've gotten less country airplay in recent months. I've got to figure out a way to do things my way and get more country airplay at the same time. The guy who discovered me knows the kind of "soul" guy I am. He's trying to guide me back to the arms of country radio. I've never had any problems with anybody saying I'm too black. I need to find a way to bridge the gap.

TURNER: Do you feel that a career as a demo singer helped to develop the T. Graham Brown style, or did T. Graham Brown style help to develop the demo style?

BROWN: Oh, I think it's probably a little bit of both. The bad part about demos—they don't pay any money, maybe twenty to thirty dollars a song. You might get two songs a day. However, I got some good experience. I did twenty or thirty albums of demos. Had I been discovered singing at some honky-tonk I would have been scared to death and if I had been offered a record deal when I first came to Nashville I would have blown it. But I had been studying and I was ready for my turn.

TURNER: Did you ever demo a song that you said, "Gosh, if I had a chance to do this I could take it to number one on the charts"?

BROWN: Yeah, and I did, too. "Tell It Like It Used To Be" was one I put on the shelf. There were a few, too, that I sang that I knew were hits that other people went ahead and recorded before I had the chance to record them. They were hits too—but that happens with every demo singer. You're usually the first guy to sing the song. The reason you're hired to sing them is because usually the writer can't sing worth a flip. So he has to hire somebody who can sing to showcase his song in the best possible light.

TURNER: In your opinion, what is the relationship between baseball and entertainment? So many country stars were once aspiring baseball players, such as Charlie Pride, Conway Twitty, and Billy Ray Cyrus.

BROWN: I think probably the reason I played baseball and not football or basketball was that baseball was the only sport that was organized in the little town in which we lived. We barely had enough kids to do that. I guess because when you live out in the country you can at least get up a game of baseball with a bunch of guys—everybody knows how to play baseball. I grew up in South Georgia. We moved to Athens in 1970 and I graduated from high school in 1972. A funny thing happened tonight: some people just brought me a clipping from the Cordele *Dispatch*, and it said, "Twenty-five years ago today (May 27) in sports: Tony Brown got the win on the mound and he also hit a double—leading his team to a 13-two victory over the Braves." This was when I was in Little League, even before junior high. I was twelve years old then.

TURNER: Journalists are always looking for words to describe an artist's style. How do you describe the T. Graham Brown style?

BROWN: George Jones meets Otis Redding.

TURNER: Athens has helped to spawn the careers of some very successful acts. What is it about this town that harbors or promotes such creativity?

BROWN: Athens is just a great music town—always has been. Athens is a college town and you have all of these creative people who bring their talents with them to college. I've been told that back in the forties and fifties that a guy by the name of Terry Melton, a former big-timer, fostered the creative atmosphere of Athens. Athens is a college town and is a melting pot for all of the creative people, artists, and etcetera. who come to college. I think that happens in college towns. It happened in Austin, Texas and various other towns around the United States. I think it's just that "cool atmosphere" Athens has. It's such a laid-back place. It's a wonderful town.

TURNER: How important is timing in the music business?

BROWN: Oh, it's very important. Timing is everything.

TURNER: Had you gone to Nashville in the seventies, would you have been as successful as you are now?

BROWN: I don't know! I don't know! Boy I was as wild as a buck in the seventies. I probably would've self-destructed. I was burning it down back then, for sure. I was in trouble.

TURNER: You began to hit at about the same time as Randy Travis and Dwight Yoakum—what impact did their careers have on your career?

---
❖
---

## Boy I was as wild as a buck in the seventies.

---
❖
---

BROWN: Didn't affect me one way or another.

TURNER: Entertainers talk about getting their big break. In your opinion what was the big break in your career?

BROWN: It was the night Randall Bramblett told me to get my (expletive) out of Athens, Georgia and to go to Nashville, Tennessee and never ask him how to be a star again. Randall was the only star I knew back then. I used to ask him, all the time, how can I become a star. That's the stupidest question you can ask. Looking back I can't believe I was so naive as to ask him that, but that's what he told me. That was my big break, the night he told me to get out of Athens. I went to Nashville about six weeks after graduation. Nowadays, guys are asking me the same question.

TURNER: Do you use record sales or record responses as a barometer for determining your musical direction?

BROWN: Well, I haven't up to this point. I think the record company would like for me to. I don't know. No, I don't really look at it that way. My manager does. Everything is fine as long as you're selling enough records to make the record company a profit.

TURNER: How much control does T. Graham Brown have on his career?

BROWN: Well, I've got veto power. I've worked with the record companies and I always will. We sit down and listen to songs together. They tell me what they like. We go over the ones I like. We work together.

TURNER: What parameters do you work with when you sit down to write a song?

---

❖

people believe that if somebody has success in country music, it is at someone else's expense. I don't believe that.

❖

---

BROWN: I don't have any. I may write anything from gospel songs to rhythm and blues to honky-tonk.

TURNER: Do you write topical songs or do you write for the times?

BROWN: No, well, you know—if you can do it—writing topical songs is a cool way to write. One way to do it is write like the Hank Williams, Jr. Which I don't necessarily like—I like Hank Williams, Jr. all right, it's just some of the songs he writes. But, hell, he makes more money than I do.

TURNER: You do not wear the traditional country entertainer costume. What influences the way you dress?

BROWN: There used to be a black store right across from The Varsity in Athens, called Sanford and Son, and I liked their style of clothes. I used to enjoy shopping there. Do you remember that place?

TURNER: Yes, as a matter of fact I do. Where do you find your clothes today?

BROWN: I just seek them out or either have them made.

TURNER: What aspect of your career do you find the most rewarding?

BROWN: Helping folks, I think. Having the power to pick up the phone and help somebody along the way—anything from recommending somebody for a job in somebody's band or helping a new songwriter in town get his song cut. Just helping folks. Because I've had people help me like crazy. In Athens, people were always helping me. In Nashville, people have continued to help me.

TURNER:   Isn't that what country music is all about: one big family pulling together?

BROWN:   Yeah! You know people always try to make something controversial out of things. Somehow people believe that if somebody has success in country music, it is at someone else's expense. I don't believe that. Tanya (Tucker) is a perfect example. I've been knowing Tanya for six or seven years now. When we get together, Tanya bitches about not getting the CMA Vocalist of the Year award. It didn't matter who got it—she would say, "Why not me? I've been working here twenty years, blah, blah, blah." And I always told her, "You're in a class by yourself. There's Tanya Tucker and then there's everybody else. You don't fit in any mold at all and don't you realize that you don't have to worry about that kind of stuff." In country music it's not like if I have success somebody will have to miss out on something. When we all get together, I consider myself T. Graham Brown and I don't have any competition. A lot of people think that Randy Travis, Alan Jackson, Doug Stone, and Travis Tritt are competitors, but the thing about it is everybody can prosper. When we all get together, it's great! Not long ago we all got together for a tribute to Minnie Pearl. Everybody in Nashville was there for the special. It was a lot of fun. Next Sunday we're all playing a softball game for a hospital there in Nashville. We do it all the time. Country music is like one big fraternity.

TURNER:   They say every great performer has to have a great backer behind him, and yours has been Sheila. How has she helped you?

BROWN:   Oh, man! She's been like a rock. She's been wonderful. She has two master's degrees from the University of Georgia: one in dairy science and one in nutrition. She had just gotten admitted to vet school when Randall Bramblett told me to move to Nashville. She was quick to say, "Let's give it a try because I can always come back to vet school." Thank goodness we never had to go back to vet school. And my brother Danny Brown takes great care of me. He's his brother's keeper. He takes great care of me.

TURNER:   If you were an interviewer interviewing T. Graham Brown, what question would you ask him that I have not asked him?

BROWN:  I don't know. I guess I would ask him his motto to life. My answer would be I think you have to be true to yourself. Live your life asking what Andy would do.

TURNER:  Do you mean Andy Griffith?

BROWN:  Yes, the thing of it is, see, if you ever get in a situation when you don't know what to do, ask yourself, "What would Andy do?"

May 1992.

*I think country music makes you aware that the common man is great and it glorifies that, as opposed to glorifying the singer. I think that's what makes country music great.*

*—Lionel Cartwright*

LIONEL CARTWRIGHT is not new to country music but his approach to country music is new. In the past, country music has drawn its power from painful experiences. Cartwright's power is positive. He brings to country music a wealth of experience and knowledge gained from his varied musical background.

The West Virginia native is a gifted singer/songwriter and an accomplished multiinstrumentalist. He began to display his talents in local radio stations while he was still in high school. After he graduated, he worked as feature singer and musician on the *Country Cavalcade* on WMNI in Columbus, Ohio. From there, he moved to the famous Wheeling (West Virginia) Jamboree where he was feature singer. He left to take a job as performer and musical director of the television series *Into Paradise* on the Nashville Network. It was during this time that he became associated with Felice and Bondreux Bryant, who encouraged him to contemplate on his songwriting talents.

Cartwright's good looks and gifted talent soon had record label representatives knocking at his door offering national exposure.

# Lionel Cartwright

TURNER: You've been a successful songwriter for sometime now. Did you ever get to a point and think, "Well this is as far in the music industry as I want to go"?

CARTWRIGHT: No! That's easy. No, I've always tried to keep setting my sights higher and higher and, gosh, there are a lot of things that I've got in the back of my mind that I'd like to do. The music industry is like a set of stair steps for me. I just want to keeping climbing.

---

❖

> The music industry is like a set of stair steps for me. I just want to keeping climbing.

❖

---

TURNER: What step are you on now?

CARTWRIGHT: We're still at the bottom. I don't know, we have a lot more stairs to go.

TURNER: There seems to be different schools of songwriters. Some seem to be able to pull songs out of the air. Then there are other songwriters who put it together piece by piece; they construct a song. Which school can you identify with?

CARTWRIGHT: My best ones have just fallen out of the sky. I mean that doesn't happen every time I sit down, but the ones that have really worked, like "Leap Of Faith," just fell out of the sky. It's really weird—it's like you are not even thinking them up yourself. They are like coming through you almost. "Leap Of Faith" was written a day before our last session. We had one more session for the album and I just couldn't resist writing one more song for the album and, boy, I'm glad I did.

35

TURNER: So you didn't get a chance to test "Leap Of Faith" in a show?

CARTWRIGHT: No, Tony Brown and Barry Beckett produced that song and they both wanted to cut it and I was nervous because I do like to test them, and even if you can't test them I like to live with them for a little while. Within the space of two weeks "Leap Of Faith" was written, recorded, mixed, and mastered—this process usually takes a lot of time. A lot of songs are left lying around a long time before they are cut. To top that off, it was the first single released off the album. The label instantly said, "We want 'Leap Of Faith' to be the first single released off the album." You know you like them yourself but as far as what other people are gonna like, who knows; nobody can ever guess that, so I was thrilled.

---

I'm definitely an exception to the rule as far as my appearance goes, but I'm a hillbilly from West Virginia

---

TURNER: Have you ever written a song that you have labored over and thought, this is a number-one hit and then it wasn't such a big hit?

CARTWRIGHT: I thought "Say It's Not True" was really gonna do great; I still like it. It was a top-twenty record but it didn't do as well as I thought it would. So I tell you what, on the next album, I'm gonna do a lot less thinking and just kind of go with the gut feeling and go with the flow and just write them more from the heart and less from the head. The best ones I have written have definitely come from the heart. But boy, "Leap Of Faith" has really taught me a lot. I taught me not be afraid to just write what's coming through you and through your spirit; just put it down and go with it.

TURNER: Was it Harlan Howard who said he would much rather write a song that was a standard than to write a successful record?

CARTWRIGHT: That is interesting; that is funny. I just spent a night talking with him last week; that's a good comment.

TURNER: You neither wear a hat nor rhinestones; how have you been able to make it in country music today?

CARTWRIGHT: Well I'm definitely an exception to the rule as far as my appearance goes, but I'm a hillbilly from West Virginia and I think hats are great but they don't look good on me. Something different sometimes takes a little longer to get a handle on, and I feel like people are finally getting a handle on who I am—you know it's taken a little while.

---

I think Lionel Cartwright is gonna stick to writing songs from the heart and whatever people label them is OK; they may come out hardcore traditional or they may come out contemporary.

---

TURNER: The editor of *Billboard* magazine recently said that there seems to be a trend away from traditional country music as witnessed by the success of today's young artists. If this trend continues, what impact will that have on your career?

CARTWRIGHT: Boy! I don't know! I think Vince Gill does real traditional country music. "When I Call Your Name" is as traditional as you can get. I think Lionel Cartwright is gonna stick to writing songs from the heart and whatever people label them is OK; they may come out hardcore traditional or they may come out contemporary. That's part of my new songwriting plan: less thinking about a song, because I think sometimes you can over-think things. I don't think when Hank Williams, Sr. was writing songs he thought, "I want to write it and I want it to sound right." He was just writing out of his heart and that's what made him great. That's what makes all great songwriters and singers great: it's really coming from the heart. So I would rather do that than say, "Well I want it to sound like this." I'm gonna try to come a little more from the heart. "Leap Of Faith" was certainly like that. That works, and I think country music audiences and most people in general can tell when something is real. More than anything else I wanna to be real—so you know that's my goal.

TURNER: Rodney Crowell recently said we need to get a shot at the younger generation's minds because we have a lot to give them. What does country music have to give younger audiences?

CARTWRIGHT: I believe it has reality to give them. I believe it has real human things to give them. I think country music does not put the artist on a pedestal like a god. I think country music makes you aware that the common man is great, and it glorifies that, as opposed to glorifying the singer. I think that's what makes country music great. It writes about very common everyday experiences and it lets you feel great. I think that's a real worthy thing to sing about: just everyday things and being a good person.

TURNER: Is that what attracted Lionel Cartwright to country music or turned him on to it?

---

country music speaks in very simple terms about a vast array of subjects, deep subjects, but in very simple terms that can be understood by both young and old

---

CARTWRIGHT: Yeah, I started listening to it when I was about ten years old. The beauty of it is—it's not always great—but when it is great, country music speaks in very simple terms about a vast array of subjects, deep subjects, but in very simple terms that can be understood by both young and old. Take Merle Haggard, I was hooked on that guy when I was about ten—hearing songs like "Momma Tried" and "Hungry Eyes." You don't have to have a Ph.D. to understand those lyrics. But when it's great there is a wisdom in it that's really good. I think country music has a lot of good things about it. I think being down to earth is really important, because we live in such a high-tech world. Oftentimes we need reminding that we're just human beings—let's kind of chill out a little bit.

TURNER: Who were the biggest encouragers of Lionel Cartwright when he started out?

CARTWRIGHT: Well let's see, my mother and father were tremendously encouraging. My family has really been a source of encouragement professionally. Ricky Skaggs has been encouraging to me for quite some time. Encouragement is not easy to come by in a business like this, and when you do find people that really believe in you, you really hold on to that because it's rare. Tony Brown is another big believer in me.

TURNER: How do you view yourself? How would you describe yourself for a press kit?

CARTWRIGHT: Very down to earth. Someone who would like to use his talents in a positive way to have a positive effect on other people. That doesn't mean I will always sing positive songs. I think you can get positive things out of sad songs, but that's what I'm about. I feel like I've been given a God-given talent in music. I've tried to cultivate it a little bit. I think music can be a great communication tool; it can be a healing kind of tool for people. It can bring people together. I've seen it bring my family together and break down the barriers and some of the ice that exists. There is a lot of ice in the world today. It's a cold place and I think music, especially country music, sounds more human, less programmed, and less synthesized. You know there's something about that. I really like listening to it.

---

❖

I think music, especially country music, sounds more human, less programmed, and less synthesized

❖

---

TURNER: What are your feelings when you drive up to a gig and you see women and men screaming—how do you handle this?

CARTWRIGHT: I'm always kind of surprised. I'm flattered, but I think the image of the person gets blown up and I think this is a bit heavy. It's very flattering that people like what you do, but I think the fame side is very deceiving; it makes it bigger than life, and it is bigger than life. Real life is completely different.

TURNER: Is there a difference between the gentleman I'm sitting next to as opposed to the gentleman I see on the stage?

CARTWRIGHT: Yes, there is; off stage I'm a little more laid back, a little more calm. I love to be on stage—there is this surge of adrenalin. Everything has to be fast on the stage. Sometimes I'll listen to a tape after the show, and I'll think my gosh, that ballad sounds like an up-tempo song. We have a very good drummer that keeps me back. I would say I'm different—I'm much more out-going on stage.

TURNER: What are the down sides to singing?

CARTWRIGHT: The first thing that comes to mind is time away from your family. Traveling and time apart from your spouse can take a toll and if you're not careful it can take a toll on your relationship. We've tried to be careful and balance it out, but that's the first downside. The other is if you do tend to be a private person, oftentimes people recognize you and they will always come up. I'm flattered by that. You have a spotlight on you but there are ways to balance it out. I don't buy this thing that if you are in the business you've got to say goodbye to a lot of things that you enjoyed before. I think there are ways to balance it out; you just have to think about it and sometimes there are hard decisions to be made.

TURNER: I recently read an article about you and it said you were one of the top new stars. Does that put a lot of pressure on you?

CARTWRIGHT: Well, I'm really thrilled to be an up-and-comer. Right now in country music it's incredible at what's happening. When I was in high school, country music was not cool at all. Now I go out on stage and there are kids in the audience and it's hard to believe. There is definitely pressure to win them over. You know, I wish entertainment wasn't so competitive; it's such an award-centered thing. Now there is a lot of emphasis on competing. I wish the fans could see us out at the big shows, where you have a bunch of acts; they could see that we aren't competitive. I mean everybody is really friendly to each other. Everybody has come up in the ranks; no one is an overnight success. It takes a lot of determination and a lot of hard work. I'm happy to see anybody make it. The competition definitely comes from the corporate side of things. They've got to make money. I understand that, but it kinda puts pressure on me, but it's really not that bad. I can deal with it!

TURNER: What do you want for yourself in the nineties?

CARTWRIGHT: I'd just like to write and record some truly great songs— it would be wonderful to be able to do that. I would like to establish a niche for myself in country music. I definitely consider it a blessing to be in country music. Just to be able to make a living at entertaining is a great blessing. I've tried to make a living at it for a long time; it's a tough thing to do. I'd also like to have records out on a national basis and to tour around the country and actually make a living and not have to do other things. I would like to enlarge our audience and appeal to a wider audience. However, I don't want to water down what we're doing. Hopefully in time we can make better records and widen our audience and just have fun doing it.

TURNER: If you were an interviewer doing an interview with Lionel Cartwright, what question would you ask him that I haven't asked?

CARTWRIGHT: Is that really your name? And yes it is. Everybody asks me that question. I've put up with jokes about that my whole life. I really love that question.

March 1992

H E  I S  T H E  O N L Y  member of Nashville's Grand Ole Opry who "don't pick or sing." But when you're Jerry Clower, the number one stand-up comedian in country entertainment, there's not likely to be many places you can't talk your way into.

Clower's career actually got its start when he traveled Mississippi as a fertilizer salesman. Clower found that weaving a few tall tales into his sales pitch helped move the goods. Before long, he was being sought out for Farm Bureau meetings, 4-H Club banquets and civic club functions.

To his fans, he is the master of yarn-spinning slapstick. To the less impressed, he is downhome cornpone. But to Clower, where there is laughter there is life.

*I'm a very simple fellow. The first thing I do every morning when I get up is to pray. I say, "Lord, I'm on your side and you ain't never made a mistake. You ain't going to make a mistake with me. So what-ever happens in my life today, I'll praise your holy name and keep going."*
*—Jerry Clower*

# Jerry Clower

TURNER: How did you become affiliated with the radio show *Country Crossroads?*

CLOWER: Well, I backed into show business and *Country Crossroads* interviewed me one time to be a special guest on the show. I was pleased to be interviewed, and during the interview I gave my Christian testimony. They found out that I was a Christian and as I grew in stature in show business, they asked me if I would be a regular on *Country Crossroads* with Leroy Van Dyke and Bill Mack each and every week. I accepted the offer and I consider it a place of Christian service. I look forward to being on *Country Crossroads.* I enjoy doing it because I have complete liberty to say whatever I want to say about my Christian convictions. Another thing, I don't reckon I could prove this, but it's classified and probably is the largest syndicated radio show in the world. It's in over a thousand stations in America now and the armed services overseas. From what I understand, about forty million people a month hear it.

TURNER: Can your success be partially credited to your Christian beliefs and doing shows like *Country Crossroads?*

CLOWER: Well, yes. I'm a very simple fellow. The first thing I do every morning when I get up is to pray. I say, "Lord, I'm on your side and you ain't never made a mistake. You ain't going to make a mistake with me. So whatever happens in my life today, I'll praise your holy name and keep going." If I sell a million albums, I'll praise the Lord the same. This is the way I live. I don't go through life biting my fingernails. I don't go through life making life miserable for my friends. I have been asked to be on *Country Crossroads,* and a lot of Christian publications have written about me. I've written a book, *Ain't God Good,* that was a bestseller. I'm a little sensitive about some people thinking that I may be a Christian because it helps me financially. That's not so. I was paying my bills before I went into show business. The thing I'm trying to say is that the Lord works in mysterious ways. A lot of the times I have done something and didn't have a dollar mark in mind at all. I was just doing it as a place of Christian service and ended up making money off of it. So I'm not saying that my book didn't make some money, I'm not saying that doing a lay preaching album didn't

43

make some money. Certainly *Country Crossroads* gives me exposure. Certainly the Southern Baptist Convention putting my Christian testimony on the bulletin one Sunday gave me tremendous exposure, but I didn't try to get it done, it just happened.

TURNER: What do you do to unwind when you get depressed?

CLOWER: Well, I cut show business off when I'm not on stage. I go home and I go down that tall, long hill at Yazoo City, Mississippi, and when I get with Mama and them children, I'm Daddy. I don't pick up on show business again until I get back on the road and on stage. Naturally I'm called on by the press or there may be some press in Yazoo City, but when I'm in Yazoo City, I'm myself. I put 'em in my Dodge pickup truck and ride 'em through the cotton fields while they interview me. Or I may take 'em to the catfish pond. I literally lean on God; I do have a strong faith—it's hard for me to foul up. A man who claims to be a Christian and then when a tragedy hits his life, he acts like a pagan. I *cannot* follow individuals in doing that. If rain falls in your life, you need to give thanks and keep going. I guess the biggest disappointment in my life and in some people have been folks that I thought were devout Christians, who claimed to love God, and then when rain would fall in their lives, they would go all to pieces and act like a pagan; they would not act like a Christian.

TURNER: Do you still make your home in Yazoo City?

CLOWER: Right. I didn't move to Nashville. My four children have all attended public schools in Yazoo City. That's my home, I'm a deacon in the Baptist Church there. I can fly out of Jackson, Mississippi as easy as I can fly out of Nashville. I'm a member of the world-famous Grand Ole Opry. I have to do twenty performances a year to stay a regular member, but I can do that in seven weeks. I think one thing me and my manager have going for us is that we're 400 miles apart. I never second-guess him, but I might be tempted to if I was close to him.

TURNER: Does your being on the road so much put extra pressure on your family?

CLOWER: It puts a little extra pressure on my wife, because when I'm home, me and Katy go riding. Well, if Katy is out riding with me, Mama's sitting at the house relaxing, not wondering if Katy is in the street with her bicycle. It puts extra pressure on my home life, but me and Mama have been married over thirty years. We've got a Christian home where love is.

If God gave me the ingredients and told me to make a woman, I'd make her exactly like my wife. On our thirtieth wedding anniversary, my friend Paul Harvey opened his newscast by saying, "If you don't think the entertainment knot stays tied, let me assure you that Jerry Clower put his eyes on at age thirteen and never took them off of her." A lot of people heard that newscast. By the time dark came, I had more flowers and fruit in my house than I could tote.

TURNER: When you're sitting around relaxing, do you completely disengage music or do you still listen to music?

CLOWER: I completely disengage music unless I'm in my car. I've got my knobs fixed on 'em stations where I can punch 'em to see if they are playing my records. That way I keep up with the latest country music and other kinds of music.

TURNER: Do you have any favorite artist that you like to listen to?

CLOWER: Yeah. I'd have to admit that Larry Gatlin completely turns me wrongside outwards. I think he has got one of the better voices in show business right now. I like Conway and Loretta and people like that. I also like Mel Tillis. I was a country music fan before I backed into show business.

TURNER: Do you have one event or moment which stands out as a special moment in your career life?

CLOWER: Well, being inducted into the Grand Ole Opry and being the only member of the Grand Ole Opry that don't pick or sing would be an outstanding event in my show business career. And for the President of the United States to hold a town forum in Yazoo City in a high school gym on national network television and right in the middle of a question, stopping and saying, "Jerry Clower is here tonight; he is a great entertainer and I admire him very much," and then the townspeople applauded. Then he comes back and says, "Yazoo City should be commended that Jerry Clower would live here," they applauded again. Next, he said, "Jerry met me at the airport a while ago. It was raining and he held my raincoat." Well, I got plumb emotional. I cried—it really got to me. I wonder how many artists of any stature, regardless of who they are, have ever stood in a public place and had the President of the United States point to them and say, "He's a great entertainer and I admire him very much." That had to be one of the highlights of my life.

TURNER: Do you have any hobbies?

CLOWER: Watching sporting events on television. My hobby is working.

TURNER: Do you still try to keep a close working relationship with Mississippi State University?

CLOWER: Yes, I'm a Bulldog. My personal, close working relationship would just be supporting them. But I try to help them academically and any other way I possibly can. I gave 'em a little money and set up a scholarship. And when the vet school was in jeopardy and it looked like the politicians weren't going to fund it, I went to Jackson and done some lobbying for the school. Mississippi State has been good to me. I went there as a poor boy and played football. I worked my way through college, and I got a college degree. My son went there, and I love Mississippi State. I have proven that you can love Mississippi State and not have to hate Ole Miss or some other school. Some people think that if you love one school you've got to hate somebody else's school. That's not necessarily so. I buy season tickets to every football game. I very seldom ever go because it's unfair for me to tell my manager I ain't going to work on weekends in the fall, because that's the busy season in the fairs and all. I might block out one weekend a season to go to a game with Mama.

TURNER: How many fair dates do you work a year?

CLOWER: Probably twenty-five to thirty. But I do two hundred shows each and every year. I'm very diversified. I don't know how to say this, but if I was farming and planted several crops, I would be a diversified farmer. Well, I could do one album a year and make a good living, or I could just do personal appearances and make a good living. I do over two hundred appearances a year. Or I could just do commercials, or I could just write a book a year. I'm never in a rut, so I'm never bored. If I went to a coliseum every night and that was all I ever done, I can see where maybe it would be the same thing over and over and I would get bored. But in January and February, I may do thirty Chamber of Commerce banquets by myself all over the country—great big banquets; they pay good.

TURNER: You tell a joke, and you have to repeat it so many times. Do you ever get bored telling the same jokes or stories over and over again?

CLOWER: No, I never do. I marvel at the people, like these country music fans right out here tonight, they might have heard the coon hunting story on the radio while they were driving down here, but they want to hear me tell it. It's unbelievable that you could get a few classics that people want to hear you tell—they don't care how many times they've heard you tell it. It's a challenge to come up with new materials and have enough good material to have a hit album every year. I've been fortunate enough that I've always had a chart record every year. But it doesn't bore me to continue to tell the same story. Because if people enjoy it, that's where I get my enjoyment.

TURNER: You were already on the banquet circuit to a certain extent when you worked for a fertilizer company were you not?

CLOWER: Yes, I used storytelling to help my sales techniques with Mississippi Chemicals, and it got to where the Farm Bureaus and County Agent Associations and folks like that were asking me to come and speak at 4-H banquets and such. It got to taking up a lot of my time. I did this for a long, long time. Then in 1971 a fellow said, "Jerry, why don't you do an album." He had heard me make one of those talks. I said, "You're crazy," but he taped the next time I talked and he pitched it to MCA and they put it out on an album. In two months it sold a million dollars worth. So I served an apprenticeship while doing speeches for nothing.

TURNER: When you are looking for new material, do you draw on past events or people you have known in the past?

CLOWER: I contend that the funniest things in the world actually happen. A lot of comics have full-time writers who write materials for them. That's all right, but I think if they would just sit around an airport or just sit at a country story and listen and observe, they could come up with better material, because the funniest things in the world do happen. About all my material are things that I see happen. I embellish it. Then I involve my characters in them. I have never had a staff or writers. Some friends may write me and say, "Jerry, why don't you tell about the time we done so and so, or did you hear about this?" I may get an idea from that.

TURNER: Do you have any other future plans you would like to tell me about?

CLOWER: Well, I'm sold out for the rest of the year. I don't have any more dates that I can work, and everything's beautiful. I praise the Lord; I don't have any complaints. I enjoy working and I'm just the luckiest guy in the world.

August 1977

*I am a singer/songwriter or maybe a hillbilly poet.*
*—Mark Collie*

**M**ARK COLLIE'S MUSIC defies labels. However, Collie admits he has roots deeply seated in hillbilly music but that he is no cowboy.

Collie was born and raised in Waynesboro, Tennessee, a small town located between Nashville and Memphis. Mark's proximity to two diverse musical meccas afforded him the influence of the rockabilly rhythms of Memphis and the country sounds of Nashville. Collie successfully fused the two sounds and created a unique style for himself, which enhances his songwriting and performing abilities.

It was his songwriting skills that landed him his first job in Nashville as a staff writer with a large publishing company. After several months he became disillusioned with "factory" writing and decided to write tunes that he felt comfortable with and could sing.

To showcase his material, he performed at the Douglas Corner Cafe. His emotionally packed songs soon attracted the attention of record company officials and Collie was signed to a recording contract.

# Mark Collie

TURNER: Where do you see yourself on the music spectrum?

COLLIE: Oh, I don't know. That is a hard question for me to answer because I am looking at the whole picture from the inside out. It depends on where you fit in and what your music is like or how you describe your music. I don't know. I make the music and it is up to people to interpret what it sounds like and what it is or where I fit in. That is a question that I have made the mistake of trying to answer in the past. I don't have an answer for it.

---

> I try not to write or make music that I would not listen to or that I would not want to own.

---

TURNER: Some people feel that you have been able to make the bridge between artistic and commercial appeal. Did you consciously work in this direction or did it just come naturally?

COLLIE: I think it probably just happened. I don't know. I just have a great respect for the music and for the really great music and songs that have come from the country music industry. I try not to write or make music that I would not listen to or that I would not want to own. That is about the best way to put it. I am glad that the critics have been very kind to me up until now. However, that could change tomorrow. I could lose my integrity with the release of my next record, but I hope that doesn't happen. I guess it is a conscious effort on my part just to make music that I can feel good about. It is important to me to keep having hits because you don't keep doing this unless you have a certain amount of commercial success. I don't ever sit down and write a song thinking that I am writing a hit record. When I sit down to write, I try to think I am going to write the best song I can write.

TURNER: Garth Brooks recently said "A song is three minutes to give the world a message." What message do you want to deliver to the world?

COLLIE: Maybe, that is true. I don't know if that is true or not. Sometimes that is true. I don't know if it is my place to be bringing the world a message. I think it is just a matter of sharing emotions, and the most positive of those emotions is love. I think that is what songs are about. They are

---

## Music is a way to communicate love to everybody.

---

an expression of love. Music is a way to communicate love to everybody. A song is one more way of expressing love. There are millions of ways to express love. Some people go through life and never discover one of those. Maybe, I have found a way to express that love—that is through my music.

TURNER: A lot of people feel that an effective songwriter must keep one foot on the street in order to make music that people want to hear. How do you keep one foot on the street?

COLLIE: I have lived on the street for so long. I am kinda on the outside of the picture, in the trenches of music row and the music business. I have worked and still do work bars and nightclubs and roadhouses. The people

---

## I think some people get real successful and they isolate themselves from the things that made them successful.

---

get up close and you can tell what they are thinking. Well, country music fans are pretty open about what they are thinking. They will let you know what they are thinking. If they do not like it, they will let you know right off. If they do like it, you will know right off. I think some people get real successful and they isolate themselves from the things that made them successful. I try not to do that. I try to stay pretty much open to the people around me and to my fans. I try not to get caught up in the "star" trip and everything that goes with it. It is not easy to do. I have seen a lot of people who let it happen to them. You always hate to see that because that is usually the beginning of the end to a real creative career. If that starts happening, let me know.

---

❖

---

People come to country music to find a bit of comfort. Sometimes it is a healing process to hear somebody express a real sad emotion that they have felt.

---

❖

---

TURNER: Which is most important in country music, the words or the melody?

COLLIE: I think the lyric has to be there, and that is why country music is so strong. We have the best love songs and more of them. We have songs that deal with issues that are more relevant to day-to-day life. People come to country music to find a bit of comfort. Sometimes it is a healing process to hear somebody express a real sad emotion that they have felt. The melody has to be there to make people want to hear it. It gives it staying power. What is the most important? I don't know. I wish you would ask someone who knows, but unfortunately Stephen Foster is not around. Who knows which is most important? I don't know.

---

❖

---

When I was a little kid I found that when I had something on my heart I could express myself through music.

---

❖

---

TURNER: Are you a composer who sings or a singer who composes?

COLLIE: I don't really know. It is hard for me to think of myself as a composer. When I hear the word *composer*, I think of much greater and grander names than I could even list right now. I am a singer/songwriter or maybe a hillbilly poet. I don't know what I am. When I was a little kid

I found that when I had something on my heart I could express myself through music. I started out doing that when I was ten or eleven years old. Writing songs was a bit of an escape for me and a way to find reality within the music. It brought me lots of happiness and inner peace. When I grew up, I wanted to share that with other people. I guess that is why I got into country music.

TURNER: What events in your life steered you toward a career in the music industry?

COLLIE: I wanted to share something that made me feel so good and gave me so much joy. I wanted to return that feeling and share it with people. I found out that people were entertained by what I did and that made me feel good. I wrote songs because it was a way for me to communicate. Many times it is hard to say what you are thinking. Even now if I am trying to communicate with my family, friends, or closest loved ones and I am not able to find the right words or the way to say what is on my mind or heart, I sit down with a guitar and write it into a song. I think if you look at the works of any songwriter—good, great, bad, or whatever—you can find out a lot about them by listening to their songs. You can find out things that they would not tell you otherwise. Sometimes we will write songs just for fun: songs that make you get up, party, have a happy feeling, and celebrate. Sometimes they are meant to do other things, like communicate other thoughts and emotions. That is the beautiful thing about songwriting: when you sit down to write you have nothing, but when you finish you have something that could last forever.

TURNER: You give so much in your music. What do you get back in return?

COLLIE: Well, all I need is for people to come out to the shows and let me know how they feel by their applause. That is all I need. I work real hard because I don't know how to give anything less than a hundred percent. That is the way I have been all my life, whether it was playing music or doing other forms of work.

TURNER: If you were introducing Mark Collie on stage, how would you introduce him?

COLLIE: Well, I don't know. I would just say, "Here is Mark Collie." The bottom line is that the music has to speak for itself. If the music is not communicating, then nothing I could tell you about myself or anybody else could tell you would amount to a hill of beans. People will come up and ask me, "What is this song about?" If they listen to the song and still don't know what it is about then, I have obviously failed in my endeavor to write a song. I tend to stay away from telling people what the song is about or what I am about. I am just a guy who is learning how to write songs and doing my best to communicate the ones I have on record.

October 1992

*We spend very little time reveling*

*in our accomplishments.*

*—Danny Shirley*

CONFEDERATE RAILROAD is the hottest group in country music today. They are burning up the record charts with their debut album, *Confederate Railroad,* which has produced five number-one releases and has been certified platinum by Atlantic Records.

The Georgia based quintet brings to country music a unique sound: a combination of southern rock fused with traditional country. Legions of rock and roll fans have been brought into the country music fold by this refreshing new sound. Danny Shirley and his fellow band members developed this new sound while playing in the legendary David Allen Coe band, and in house bands alongside Travis Tritt.

Shirley recently sat down and reflected on his roller-coaster musical career.

# Danny Shirley
# (Confederate Railroad)

TURNER: Where do you see yourself on the music spectrum?

SHIRLEY: A lot of people think we're doing a different kind of music—a new kind of music—but it's the kind of stuff we've been playing for ten or twelve years. We could have gotten record deals back in the eighties had we been another George Strait or another Randy Travis, but that just wasn't what we wanted to do. So we decided to stick with the kind of music we did naturally and hoped it would come back in style—which it did! Everybody says, "Boy! That's great that you'll come up with all this stuff." I'm quick to say, "Man, we've been doing this for ten or twelve years."

> I've spent my entire adult lifetime playing night clubs and I had no idea that little kids were into our type of music.

TURNER: How would you describe the Confederate Railroad sound to someone who had never heard your music or seen you in concert?

SHIRLEY: Versatile. We've been real lucky, because you see everybody from preschoolers to grandparents at our shows. All our shows are like that. I never realized that little kids went to concerts until we played fairs and festivals this summer. It's made a big impression on me. You know I grew up in bars! I've spent my entire adult lifetime playing night clubs and I had no idea that little kids were into our type of music. On the new album we took out all the hells and damns simply because of those little kids. It means so much to me that they are coming to the shows. I feel a responsibility to them and they shouldn't have to hear that kind of language. I'll see them standing out there singing every word to every song. On the first album we've got a couple of "off" words. And I noticed that when they got to the off word they would stop singing. Evidently their parents had told them they could not say those words. This bothered me. So on the new album they can sing any word they want to.

TURNER: For years you were a staple on the club circuit in the southeast. Could you have been happy just being a regional star had you not been tapped for national stardom?

SHIRLEY: I had a good time doing it—I was very happy doing it! I think eventually it would have gotten to the point where I would have thought, "Well, it's not going to happen. What I do is not going to be back in style, so I need to think about something else." I would have always played music. I'd probably been seventy years old playing in honky-tonks. Even the years we were with David Allen Coe—that was *HIS* band. That was a lot of fun and a good learning experience, but it wasn't what I wanted to end up doing. It wasn't my goal to be the David Allen Coe band or the Johnny Paycheck band or anybody's band.

TURNER: What lessons did you learn from David Allen Coe?

SHIRLEY: David and I were talking the other day and he said, "I read an interview you did. It kinda made me mad at first until I thought about it." I said, "What did I say, David?" He said, "You said you learned more about what not to do than you did what to do from me. Then I got to thinking about it and realized that you were probably right." They say that making mistakes is a good teacher—which it is—and I was fortunate in that I was able to learn from some of the mistakes they had made so that I could avoid them in my career. David used to tell me, "When I was confronted with this situation, I decided to go this way, and this was the outcome of it. If I had it to do over again, I think I might have tried this and hoped for this." So he taught me a whole lot of stuff like that. I told him the other day, "So many things that I thought you were crazy for thinking back then, I understand today."

TURNER: What measures are you taking today that will insure longevity for Confederate Railroad?

SHIRLEY: The first thing we have to do is to make sure the recorded material is right. Without radio we can't keep growing, and they have to stay behind us. We have to make sure these albums are right. Basically, right now the only thing we can do is to keep trying to make the live show better. We have some of the best management in the world—our management company handles Alabama, Dolly Parton, Michael Jackson,

Bon Jovi, The Pointer Sisters, Neil Diamond, and us. That's heavyweight management—they obviously know their job. Our producer, Barry Beckett, is a legend. We know we've got that covered. Atlantic Records have been real good! We've sold over a million albums, mainly because of their efforts. All that's pretty much covered. I still like overseeing everything but basically all we can do right now is to keep trying to get better on stage.

TURNER: What appealed to you about working with a group as opposed to going solo?

---

❖

I have the best of both worlds—I've got my solo career and I've got my band career all in one.

❖

---

SHIRLEY: Well, actually, we had always been solo even though the band has been together for so many years. It was my road band. I signed the deal with Atlantic Records as a solo artist and I recorded a Confederate Railroad album as a solo artist. Right before we were ready to release, I went to the label and I said, "Look, there's so many new male artists out right now you can't even keep up with everybody, so why don't we rename ourselves as a band, because none of the new groups coming out have the edge or do the type of music we do." I have the best of both worlds—I've got my solo career and I've got my band career all in one.

TURNER: Are all of you of the same mind when it comes to the direction for your music?

SHIRLEY: Pretty much; it's not just the band and the group, it's management, the label, and Barry—we all see things pretty much eye to eye.

TURNER: Do you ever stop and look back on all the crooks and turns that your life and career have taken?

SHIRLEY: Not really. I have a theory; as a matter of fact I have several theories. One of them is that if you spend too much time thinking about what you've done, then you're spending too much time thinking about what you've done instead of what you've got left to do. I'll give you a perfect example: one day when "Trashy Women" was going up the charts and it

made like an eight or nine spot jump. That's just unheard of! We were at
a show in Washington, D.C. Management and the band came backstage
at a show in Washington, D.C. and told me, "Man we jumped nine spots
on the charts." I said, "Good!" and that's all I said and they said, "What?
We thought you'd get excited." My mind was already thinking, "Ok nine
spots—that moves us up to number so-and-so; that means we've got so

---

❖

if you spend too much time thinking
about what you've done, then you're
spending too much time thinking about
what you've done instead of what you've
got left to do.

❖

---

many adds and so many conversions. So that means there are this many
stations not playing it—why aren't they playing it? Will they play it? How
many's in heavy rotation? How many can we get up to heavy rotation? I
just automatically think that way. We spend very little time celebrating in
this band. When the album went platinum, the label called and said they
wanted to have a platinum party and I told them, "Well, I've got one Sunday in December." They said, "No, you need to come to Nashville now
and bring everybody up and have a big party." I said that it would cost us
$10,000 a night to come up there and party. I thought, "We can take a
night off on the road and I'll pitch a party and send you the bill." We
spend very little time reveling in our accomplishments.

TURNER: What makes an ideal Confederate Railroad song?

SHIRLEY: Honesty! It has to be something that I believe in. I want to be
able to stand up there and sing so that when the show's over you will be
able to say, "I know something about that guy." For example it might be,
"I know what he thinks is funny, I know what he thinks is offensive, what
he likes, what he doesn't like," or it might be something spiritual. It has to
be something like that! I sit here talking to you telling you the truth about
me, and I hope the fans can feel that same thing from my music.

TURNER: There are these people in management in Nashville—record
executives—that believe that a young entertainer cannot effectively deliver

a song because he/she hasn't experienced enough of life. How do you feel about this rationale?

SHIRLEY: I think it's true. Of course, I don't have that problem. It's been fifteen years since I was young. It's kinda hard for me to sit and have some twenty-year-old kid sing to me trying to tell me about life. I think, "Kid, you've got another seventeen or eighteen years to catch up with me. Let me tell you a little something about life!" Maybe that's why so many young people are in music right now, or at least listening to country music. Maybe they are talking to the people who are younger than them. I don't know.

TURNER: Is there one particular song that was the turning point in your career?

SHIRLEY: We noticed a big difference after "Queen of Memphis." The crowds, the excitement of the crowds, energy of the crowds, our t-shirt sales, and everything went way up with this song. This is a good indication of the effect you're having on the market. Then of course everything tripled after "Trashy Women."

TURNER: Your songs are all different styles and sounds—Is this a conscious effort on your part to design each one of them differently?

SHIRLEY: Yes! Nowadays the audience is so quick to stereotype you. You take a group like the Head Hunters. They came out with two back-to-back songs that had them so typecast that they could never have pulled off a "Jesus and Mama" or "When You Leave That Way". The public would just refuse to hear it from them. I intentionally released "She Took It Like a Man" first because from that medium point I could go left or right. We went right with "Jesus and Mama" and then came back with a dance song, followed by another really heavy ballad and then "Trashy Women". It's now to the point where any song that I put out, as long as it is a good song, a good honest song will be legitimate.

TURNER: Is a career built on change?

SHIRLEY: I think so. You hear so many people talking about artists whose songs all sound the same. It seems that they wear out a little quicker than those who go for diversity.

TURNER: What appealed to you about "Trashy Women"?

SHIRLEY: Anyone in particular? (laughs) Well, there's this little blonde in Florida. (laughs) Actually, my wife and I were driving back from Ocala,

Florida late one night—three or four in the morning. We were picking up Tallahassee radio stations which were kinda fading in and out, and this song "Trashy Women" came in by Jerry Jeff Walker. We were both really listening as it was fading in and out, trying to make out the words. At the end of the song she looks at me and said, "That song is about you—you have to sing that song." I thought to myself, "She knows me better than I thought she did." It was just a fun song. It is something I can relate to. I'll be honest—you take one of these girls and put her in a business suit and walk her across the floor, I might notice her and I might not. But dress her like one of the Trashettes she's going to catch my eye. I like my women a little on the trashy side! The song was all done in humor—it was a fun song. The line that brings it all together is, "I want a woman just as tacky as me." That way I'm picking on myself. The same thing goes with "She Took It Like A Man." That's the way I behave when I lose my temper. I'm still making fun of myself in a roundabout way. That puts the humor in it. That keeps it from being offensive to feminists and a chauvinistic song.

TURNER: Chet Atkins once told me that a hit song is one that can be whistled as well as sung. Do you think that is part of "Trashy Women"'s success?

SHIRLEY: Could be, could be. I hadn't heard that, but yeah. I have never tried to whistle that one, but I do whistle on my new album. I've always wanted to whistle on a record, and I got to do it! We cut this song called "Elvis and Andy." It talks about a boy from down south who always knew he would marry a good southern belle. But he falls for this blonde up north. However, she likes Elvis Presley and Andy Griffith; therefore, she's OK. At the end the guitar player does the *Andy Griffith* theme and I got to whistle it on the record.

TURNER: Are you a fan of Andy Griffith?

SHIRLEY: Oh, yeah, oh yeah! Half the band used to call me Andy or Ange all the time. It's just southern logic, I guess. A lot of the time when I've got a problem I handle it the same way Andy did on the *Andy Griffith* TV show. They used to say I was just like him.

TURNER: That's exactly what T. Graham Brown told me about himself.

SHIRLEY: All right!

TURNER: In the video "Trashy Women," you cast Jeanie Sealey and Stonewall Jackson. Why did you choose to cast these Opry greats in this video?

---

❖

There's not a me that walks on stage and then changes to another me when I walk off stage.

❖

---

SHIRLEY: Well, I wanted some Opry stars because we're talking a dangerous zone here. I wanted to eliminate all the negative I could. We had to make a fun video so that people would know that it wasn't serious—it is a fun song. I wanted the older Nashville establishment to accept the song, and what better way than have a couple of Grand Ole Opry stars in it? Stonewall Jackson was a natural because of his Georgia base and his name and all. Jeanie Sealey, she was just perfect—I just about fell in love with that lady. She was great, so much fun. The video turned out to be a monstrous hit. However, it could have gone just the opposite—it could have really set my career back.

TURNER: Please fill in and make a complete sentence. My friends like me because . . .

SHIRLEY: I'm trying to think of a friend! (*laughs*) Ask some of my friends—I don't know. I'm pretty much the same way, twenty-four hours a day. There's not a me that walks on stage and then changes to another me when I walk off stage. I'm pretty much "take it or leave it."

TURNER: Where do you want your music to take you in the future?

SHIRLEY: I don't really set long-range goals as far as things like that. I know a couple of things I want to accomplish in '94. I tend to set goals that I know that, with the proper amount of work and a little luck, I can accomplish. I don't set things like, "By the end of my career I want to have sold ten million records," or anything like that. In '94 I would like to see the new album go platinum. I would like to win another major award. And I'm working real hard on getting my publishing company back to making money. I really want to build on it. I'm planning to hire a couple of staff writers. I own some old Alabama songs—they pay some dividends all along. But as far as what I want to do before I'm done, I don't think about it.

TURNER: If you were an interviewer doing an interview with Danny Shirley, what questions would you ask that I haven't asked?

SHIRLEY: You know what I'm thinking, but I can't say it! (*laughs*) "What's the true story about you and Tanya Tucker?" Let's see, what would I have liked for you to have asked?

TURNER: That's a good way to put it.

SHIRLEY: Actually about my son. He's on my mind more that anything else on the face of this earth.

TURNER: What makes him the light of your life?

SHIRLEY: He's real mean—like his mama. I don't know. I guess you have to have a son and hold him for the first time before you realize what you mean to your parents.

TURNER: Let me phrase it this way. Your dad is probably your biggest cheerleader. What would you like to pass on to your son that your dad passed on to you?

SHIRLEY: That you accomplish success by hard work. I worry about him a lot. The way my career is going, he should have very few financial strains in his life. There were times when I was working two forty-hour-a-week jobs just to make ends meet. He'll never have to do that. I hope that I can raise him to know that to really amount to something he has to work hard. There's some things that I can't give him. My dad and I are real close. My parents divorced when I was five years old, and I was raised by my dad, and it's amazing the friendship we've always had. I remember one day, out of the blue I decided I was going to buy a new pickup truck, so we went to the Ford place, and we sat there and laughed and cut up while I was buying this truck. This guy said, "Man, do you two always get along like this?" I said, "Yeah," and he said, "Me and my dad could never sit and talk for ten minutes because we'd have nothing to say." Me and my dad hang out all the time and I try to get my son to hang out with me some, too. It is real strange; you know a kid can tear your heart out quicker than anything. He's in kindergarten this year and he had to write a thing for "why he loves his family" or "what he loves about his family." In his little book it says, "Why I love my Dad. I love my Dad because he takes walks with me." Anybody can take a walk with a kid—it doesn't matter if you're a plumber, a garbage man, or president. It's just the fact that me and him take walks—that's what he likes about our relationship. Since I'm gone all the time, I try to make up for that by buying him a little something extra. I know you can't do it, but I do anyway, because I can't be there and give him the time that he really needs, so I try to make up for that with material things.

TURNER: You sound so much like Loretta Lynn. I asked her that question several years ago. Her family was her main concern.

November 1993

*It takes a lot to impress me, and it takes an awful lot to get my attention, so I take it for granted that everybody is like that. Sometimes this gets me in trouble.*

*—Earl Thomas Conley*

EARL THOMAS CONLEY is painting a bright future for himself in country music. However, Conley's first artistic endeavors were directed to sculpting and painting. Conley, an outstanding high school art student, was awarded an art scholarship upon graduation. But the desire for adventure and self-control forced him to decline the scholarship.

The Portsmouth, Ohio native's appreciation for country music surfaced while serving with the U.S. Army in West Germany. His conceptual artistic abilities were evident in his early songwriting and won him the title "thinking man's poet". Soon his material was being recorded by such artists as Mel Street and Conway Twitty.

Conley's recording career did not meet with commercial success and as a result he was bounced from label to label until he recorded "Silent Treatment" for Sunbird Records, a small independent label. After joining RCA Records, Conley's career escalated with several number-one hits, and he made music history by being the first entertainer to have four number-one hits from a single album—a feat no other entertainer had achieved, not even Elvis or The Beatles.

# Earl Thomas Conley

TURNER You have long been described as one of the best of the new breeds to come along in a long, long time, and your voice is adapted to doing pop, rock, blues, and country. Why did you choose country?

---

❖

---

I was born and raised in the country, and my first influence in music was Hank Williams.

---

❖

---

CONLEY: Well, I was born and raised in the country, and my first influence in music was Hank Williams. My father was into Jimmy Martin and bluegrass music, so I guess I got so much of that in my system that it is always going to be there. And when I first started learning how to write, teaching myself and studying everybody's else's style, it was so much easier to work from the emotional side. You know, country music is based on strong emotional-type things, and it is more natural.

TURNER: A young Nashville entertainer told me that he thought country music was moving into topical-type subjects, as opposed to the emotional type of cheating and drinking song long associated with country music. What is your reaction to this theory?

CONLEY: I think that depends! I think it follows trends. It will stay geared in one position for maybe a year or so, then it will change automatically on its own because people get tired of working from the same framework all the time. I know I do, I have to have every song on my album completely different—coming from all different angles or I get bored to death with it.

TURNER: When you sit down to write, do you draw from past experiences? Where do you get ideas for a song?

CONLEY: I store up experiences every day when I am out on the road. We are all like walking computers and we store up everything we see, smell,

65

hear, taste, or whatever. I don't sit down and see one experience. Maybe one or two songs I have written came from one heavy experience period, but then I move on to another experience I might have had fifteen years ago.

TURNER: Where do you get the ability to go in depth in your songs?

CONLEY: People influence me a lot! Kris Kristofferson influenced me an awful lot, so did Tom T. Hall and some of the really heavy message songs he has written in the past. My chemical makeup or genetic makeup, or whatever it is, is just naturally intense. My father is a real intense person, very serious, so maybe this attitude or this way of life or way of thinking is so much inside of me that I naturally seek out that kind of an influence. But anyway, here is what it is to me! Now I like to have a few lighthearted songs on an album, but unless I can really feel something and get down into the very heart of something, it is almost like it's not worth doing. In other words, it takes a lot to impress me, and it takes an awful lot to get my attention, so I take it for granted that everybody is like that. Sometimes this gets me in trouble. In the past it has taken me longer to be more commercial. Perhaps because some of the things were written a little too inside, and called for a little bit too much as far as the audience was concerned. That's one reason why I cut a few outside songs per album just to make sure I have some kind of medium to bounce back and forth from.

TURNER: I find this very ironic because Johnny Lee told me that writing gives him a chance to look inside himself. Can you relate to that statement?

CONLEY: Yes. Songs come out in a lot of different disguises because usually I don't write from one particular experience. Because what you are really after is that emotional intensity. For instance, there is a song called "Crowd Around The Corner" that we made a video about. I was able to redeem myself for some of the things I didn't feel and should have felt as a kid walking the streets up there in central Ohio.

TURNER: The quality is perfect in your voice. Yet you have this intense writing facet of your life and a lot of people perceive Earl Thomas Conley as having two distinct personalities. How do you deal with this?

CONLEY: It's not easy. I have learned to love the way my music is turning out. At the same time, when it starts to become successful, you realize the responsibility you have taken upon yourself also adds pressure. So much that sometimes it seems impossible to try to be that intense in your writing and then come out on stage and not be serious at all. At times I think you lie to yourself, especially as a performer, because you can pretend for so long that everything is beautiful and what you have is fine. You've got to do that as a performer, but as a songwriter, it takes longer to make these transitions. There have been several times when I really didn't want to perform but have gone ahead, which is all right, but you can't get to the point where you have nothing inside yourself that you can identify with. That is one reason why I am anxious to get started writing again, so that I can reassociate myself with my inner self and become constructive and serious and redeem myself. It's a crazy thing that goes on inside of a songwriter, singer, or performer. He has his work to contend with all his life, but out of that pressure hopefully some of the best things in life happen, as far as music goes.

TURNER: Would you rather write a song that would last a hundred years or sell a million copies?

CONLEY: Well, that's a difficult question, because in the last year or so I have learned that you have to make a tremendous amount of money to support this group of people that you have on the road. Then you have to invest every bit of it wisely or you're going to end up with nothing. I would like to write a classic that would last forever, but if there is a possibility of having both of these, then that would be fine. Hopefully, at least three or four songs per album will have enough depth that some day, even though they are not really commercial now, maybe ten years from now they will be. If I could maintain this kind of outlook and this kind of album policy, and go ahead and do the commercial things too, then I would be pretty happy. But this is hard to do.

TURNER: Do you find that some people in Nashville are unreceptive to creativity?

CONLEY: It's frustrating; it's the most frustrating thing on earth to me. It frustrates me to think that you take the time to make sure that the melody is as original as you can possibly make it, and the lyric content is the story of this whole different picture that you have painted for the world. A gift that you are about to present to the world is so unique. All of us came here to be creative beings, whether it is to create a new way of thinking, or work in a factory. However, everything is geared for similarities. If it sounds a little bit similar, if it's a little close to something else, people don't realize that. They don't stop to think that half of the melody came from another song that some guy worked his rear end off to come up with. It's almost geared to that, almost programmed for you to sit down and do something like someone else already did. Your lasting power may be a little better if you can take the time and struggle along until things pop. You can probably last a little longer but it takes an awful lot longer to get recognized.

TURNER: Do you think the powers that be are more receptive to new ideas today than they were ten years ago?

CONLEY: Oh yes, I think so. I think country music has been able to spread out quite a bit. I don't think that that's necessarily a law just for country music alone, I hear a lot of similarities, you know, in rock and roll and all kinds of music. The person who is really into their craft loves to come up with something that is real innovative and new. Usually that's the last thing that happens.

TURNER: What bothers me is a lot of songs are built on the same tune.

CONLEY: What I would like to do is cut an album of standards of my favorite songs. But I don't want to water my albums down with a bunch of things that have already been done before. If I were going to do that I would just like to do an oldies album of all my favorite songs.

TURNER: The Country Music Association has said that they have covered the market in the U.S. and the most fertile soil to be cultivated now in country music is Europe. They would like to make it as commonplace there as it is here. Why does country music have the universal appeal that it has?

CONLEY: There is an emotional side to everybody alive, I think, and there are different levels of intensity. I think with this *Urban Cowboy* thing people found out that it's all right to get out there and put cowboy boots on and have a good time. Now I don't know if that necessarily is still in effect, but it has done an awful lot to broaden the scope of country music.

TURNER: If you could wave a magic wand, what would you want your music to do for your audience?

CONLEY: If I'm singing a sad song, I want it to bring them to tears. I definitely want them to listen and to respond to whatever effect the song is supposed to have. I want to hear a response! Some of the older crowds in country music tend to be real quiet. They're nice, but it's just that they have been raised up for a whole different program. I have been working with Hank Williams, Jr. for a while and his audiences were completely different from any audiences I have ever worked for in country music. I like the excitement of being on stage and being able to get in there and project energy and get it out of your system and feel feedback from the crowd. I have worked with others and I have loved them all and they have all been good to me. But there is a radical side of me that I have experimented with in the past year or so. It would be boring if I just had to do real soft waltzes all the time.

---

❖

## Some of the older crowds in country music tend to be real quiet.

❖

---

TURNER: If you wanted to showcase the talents of Earl Thomas Conley, what song would you do?

CONLEY: It would be a song I do every night called "You're As Low As You Can Go." It goes against everything that I was raised to believe. I can really have fun and be Earl Thomas Conley. There is a hidden guilt that I was raised up with as a Baptist, so this song redeems me. You have two different things to look at here, you are either going to kill yourself or you are going to straighten up for awhile. The thing I believe in life is that you are supposed to experience all of life without hurting anybody else. There are good sides and bad sides, and I like to express both of these, and there's a powerful message in the most intense songs I do.

TURNER: A lot of entertainers tell me that one of the greatest obstacles they have had to overcome in the entertainment business is name recognition with particular songs. Has this been an added obstacle to you?

CONLEY: Yes. I think TV has done an awful lot in the past to say, "hey, this person is an individual and he is supposed to be related to this situation—this song." When I wrote "The Smoky Mountain Memories" for Mel Street back in '74, right after I moved to Nashville, somebody said, "Did you know there is another guy here by the name of Conley?" I was just calling myself Earl Conley back then. So I went to Earl Thomas Conley and it still didn't clear things up, but the TV does an awful lot to help associate your face with your picture. It helps tremendously.

TURNER: Some of your songs may have suggestive lyrics or suggestive titles. Have you gotten any flak from the Moral Majority?

CONLEY: There was one station that wouldn't play "Somewhere Between Right And Wrong" because to them it was highly suggestive. The thing that was in the song that made it all right for me was the girl says, "but I would rather be loved or left alone than be here in the middle somewhere between right and wrong." I don't think you always have a choice when you are confronted with loneliness, and if she had her preference she would rather be loved, therefore, that redeems anything that she might do for me in the song. But, yes, you do run into that every once in awhile.

❖

I want to be really appreciated for taking the time to do this thing the best that I can possibly do it.

❖

TURNER: How do you want to be regarded?

CONLEY: I want to be really appreciated for taking the time to do this thing the best that I can possibly do it. I also want to be a star and I want to accept all the vanities that are involved in being a star, such as buying a nice home, nice cars, buses, and having all that the business has to offer and that life has to offer. But I don't want it to be the mainstay or the main topic. I want to have a lot of depth and keep maintaining my songwriting intensity, because my values come from my songwriting. For instance, just like that song "Crowd Around The Corner." I did that song because it is something good that needs to be said about old people. I want to be able to do that about many subjects throughout the rest of my life, because that makes me feel good personally. Now, if I start recording and doing the things that make everybody else happy, hell, how long am I going to stay in this business? Not for very long, because I'm not going to give it enough if I'm not going to get anything out of it myself. I like the money and I want all the success that life has to offer, but I want to maintain this intensity and this value fulfillment thing inside of me, too.

TURNER: How are videos going to revolutionize the music industry?

CONLEY: Well, people can immediately tie the face, the movement of the person, everything about that person to the music. As far as the video goes, they can put it together immediately and it is real entertaining. I think it is going to be *the* way to market music.

---

## I want to be the number-one draw in the world.

---

TURNER: The video music has a lot of creativity in it. Do you think that we are going to get the same creativity in country music as performers do in the pop field?

CONLEY: I think so, but you are going to get a different kind. I don't think that it is ever going to be as bizarre or as totally creative as it is in pop music. Some of mine will be though!

TURNER: When you first went to Nashville, were you ever told that you would never make it?

CONLEY: Yes, yes—long before that!

TURNER: Where do you want your music to take you in the future?

CONLEY: I want to be the number-one draw in the world. I want to do even bigger things than Kenny Rogers and Elvis have done. I know it's an awful lot to say, but if you don't ask for the moon, and if you don't go way, way, way out there and ask or demand big things of yourself, then you are going to end up just two or three streets down the road. You're not going to end up as anything. The more you ask of yourself, the closer you can come to getting something that is at least mediocre, so I want everything. I want to be the biggest draw, and have the longest streak of number-one records. I want to sell more albums. I want to set records. I want everything life has to offer, music-wise. I have never done this before and I have the chance to do it, so I am going to do something with it.

January 1984

*Well, writing is like genius; it is ninety percent perspiration and ten percent inspiration. It really is.*
*—Joe Diffie*

JOE DIFFIE is no "regular Joe." Diffie is "Joe extraordainaire." His magnetic personality has won him legions of fans and industry respect.

The Oklahoma native firmly established himself as one of Nashville's most sought-after demo singers before he launched his solo career in 1990 with the album. *A Thousand Winding Roads* which produced four number one hits, including the very popular "Home", and "If The Devil Danced In Empty Pockets."

"Regular Joe," Diffie's second release, showcased the consummate honky-tonker on the emotionally packed "Ships That Don't Come In," and the ever-popular "Is It Cold In Here."

With each new release, Diffie is committed to never forgetting the working man and his own early work roots in the oil fields and foundries of the west. Oftentimes he performs free for unemployed blue-collar men and women.

# Joe Diffie

TURNER: Where do you see yourself on the music spectrum?

DIFFIE: On the music spectrum? Well, I can only speak for country, I see myself as just starting to break into the upper echelon.

TURNER: I recently read a review and the reviewer said, "Diffie has a potent, powerful voice that he handles with extraordinary finesse." How much voice and how much finesse have developed while doing demo records?

DIFFIE: A lot! It helped a lot! A lot was developed and I listened to one of my best friends in Nashville, Lonnie Wilson, a session drummer. He kinda taught me the ropes in Nashville. He recently told me that he did a session and they played one of my real old demos, as a matter of fact, one of my first demos, and that my voice has changed so much and my style is different today.

TURNER: Did you ever demo a song that you just knew if you could get a shot at recording it you could take it to number one?

DIFFIE: Well, yes, there were several of them but I didn't have a record deal at the time. There was an Alabama song titled "Born Country" that went number one for them and there was a Billy Dean song called "You Don't Count The Cost" that was a great song. There have been several of them that I demoed that turned out to be big hits for other people.

TURNER: Have you ever recorded a song that you originally demoed?

DIFFIE: Most of the songs on my first albums were that way. I demoed "The Devil Danced In Empty Pockets," and the ones I wrote I demoed.

TURNER: I understand that singers learn from each other. What lessons did you learn from other entertainers while you were doing demo work?

DIFFIE: Well, I didn't get to see many other entertainers while I was doing demo work. I have learned and I still learn every day. When I get a chance I love to watch other people's shows. There is always something that you can pick up and learn from other people. For instance, I say unbashfully, unashamedly, that I got the idea of dressing my band in all black from watching Reba's show. I thought it looked real neat and it put Reba out front and in the spotlight. There are little things that you pick up from every entertainer.

TURNER: You have had great success with self-penned tunes, but, as an entertainer's life goes, you record, tour, record, tour, and record. What effect will this cycle have on your writing?

DIFFIE: It has been real detrimental to it. Everyone who is an artist, who is a songwriter, will tell you that you don't have the time that you used to have before you started touring. Actually, it is getting better now. We have done less dates this year than we did last year and hopefully next year we will do less dates than this year. The goal is to be able to balance the two and to be with my family more. Now when I get home, my wife wants me to stay home for a little bit, so I really can't run out writing every night. I am home so infequently anyway. It has affected it quite a bit, but I hope to get back into writing because it is such a great creative outlet for me.

TURNER: Do you write for the times?

DIFFIE: Yes, I kinda write for the times because that's what is happening now and I see things that I can relate to. Now when I get a chance to write, I write everything for myself, because I have such a limited amount of time in which write. If I don't get to record it, someone else does and that's great.

TURNER: How do you get your inspiration to write?

DIFFIE: Well, writing is like genius; it is ninety percent perspiration and ten percent inspiration. It really is. Basically, what you look for when you write is a hook or the idea for a song. It is the important part of a song and it helps to tell a good story.

TURNER: "Ships That Don't Come In" is a very powerful song. What appealed to you about this song that made you want to record it?

DIFFIE: To be real honest about it, I missed the meaning of the song the first time I heard it. When I first heard the songwriter's demo of it, the Desert Storm conflict was going on, and I was real hesitant to do the song because it mentioned the soldiers that died in vain. I was real hesitant to capitalize on that kind of situation. It personally bothered me that as soon as America goes to war all these people start writing these silly war songs. I felt like it was trying to capitalize on the situation. I listened to it several more times and I didn't think it was a hit until we went into the studio and did a preproduction on it. In fact we got through the first chorus and I said, "We need to record this song."

TURNER: There are a lot of people in the business who believe that songs need to be kept simple and that one should never have to dig for the meaning of the song. Did you have to convince the powers to let you record "Ships?"

---

one of the most difficult things that an artist has to do in this career is to find the image that suits him and that sells records.

---

DIFFIE: No, they convinced me. It was incredible. I didn't have to convince anybody. My producer, Brian Montgomery, was the one who found the song. The scenario that happened before, with "The Devil Danced in Empty Pockets," it was just another demo I did that day, got my money, and went home. I got a call from him saying, "Hey, we have found this great song," and I heard it and said, "I hate that song." He said, "You better learn to like it because you are going to be doing it the rest of your life." I learned a little of the song before I recorded it. The actual record version of it is so different from the demo.

TURNER: That brings up an interesting point: when you do have a successful song, you do it repeatedly over and over. Does it lose its impact and do you get tired of singing it?

DIFFIE: No, not really, it is actually the opposite tone. It is like one of your hits and people recognize them and it is fun to do them. "Ships" is such a powerful song that if you talk to me in a few years, I might have a different opinion. As of now, it gets such a great response from the people, and it means so much to people, and every night there is a new audience, so they have not heard me sing it before.

TURNER: You recently said one's image is so important in country music today. What kind of image do you want to project to your fans?

DIFFIE: That is probably one of the most difficult things that an artist has to do in his career is to find the image that suits him and that sells records. That is what you are there for, and that is what the record company signed you for. I think the regular Joe image is pretty good although it is kind of a dichotomy because it almost makes me too common in one aspect. In another aspect I feel like I can really relate to people because I was a blue-collar laborer for so long. I think that whatever image I portray will probably come around by itself.

TURNER: In your opinion, how close is the public image of Joe Diffie to the self image of Joe Diffie?

DIFFIE: Real close! It is pretty much the same.

TURNER: What has been the best advice you have ever received either professionally or personally?

DIFFIE: That is easy, my dad's advice. He said that if I was going to pursue music as a career, I needed to do something every day toward that goal. That is what I did and I was pretty fanatical about it. I would make myself do something every day that would help me reach my career goal. I was working for Gibson Guitars at the time and I would play my guitar and sing for fifteen or twenty minutes every day.

TURNER: Everyone has a story of how they got to Nashville; what is the Joe Diffie story?

DIFFIE: I was completely broke. I borrowed three hundred bucks from a friend of mine who played in the band and who owned a filling station. I was going to get one hundred dollars to get to Little Rock where my parents were living, but he gave me three hundred dollars. I loaded up everything I owned in the back of an old '76 model Olds Ninety-Eight, a big old tuna boat. I drove to Little Rock and visited with my parents for a couple of weeks, and then I went on to Nashville.

TURNER: If you were on a panel roasting Joe Diffie, what would you say?

DIFFIE: Oh, I have no idea. I'm one of those types of people . . . well, my bass player draws caricatures; he said, "I cannot draw you because you do not have any prominent features or anything" . . . I'm just a regular old guy. If I was roasting Joe Diffie, I don't know what I would say.

TURNER: How important is it to have a good sense of humor in this business?

DIFFIE: I think it is real important because there are so many things that happen—both good and bad. You just have to laugh at both of them. I think artists have a tendency to really feel important when they are not quite that important. I always get a kick out of that, I catch myself and say, "What are you doing here?" I really feel uncomfortable sometimes when people are making over me or waiting on me. It makes me feel funny but you have to be able to laugh at yourself.

TURNER: Who brings you back down to earth?

DIFFIE: I really don't get that far out there. My band is real good about keeping me in line. I go home and the kids bring me back down to earth. I've got people that I think I can trust and they will tell me if something is wrong.

TURNER: In your opinion why is country music so popular today?

DIFFIE: I think there is a whole new generation of people out there who has never heard of country music. The younger kids are discovering or rediscovering country music. Now country has sex symbols and I think that has helped a lot. In the past country was limited by having a reputation of being twanging and stuff. The younger kids have never heard the early country music so they have no idea of how it used to sound. Today country music is the accepted thing and the people like what they are hearing.

TURNER: If you were an interviewer with Joe Diffie, what would you ask him that I have not asked?

DIFFIE: That is a good question. I don't know. It is one of those weird ones. I think I would ask him where he would want to end up?

TURNER: Where do you see yourself in ten years from now?

DIFFIE: I see myself producing and producing other acts and being a publisher. I still want to be in the music industry; I love the industry so much and I think I have a knack for producing. Having done all those demos, I think I could be a producer.

October 1992

*I think probably the best thing that ever happened to me was working for years in the studio. I sang all kinds of music, all day long, every day for the first four or five years I was in Nashville.*
*—Holly Dunn*

HOLLY DUNN is a major force in country music today despite the fact that she has never had a gold record. She finds comfort in the fact that Tanya Tucker and Reba McEntire did not land gold records until they were well into their enormously successful careers.

Dunn's most successful song to date is "Daddy's Hands," a Number One record in *Billboard.* In addition to its chart success, the song won her two Grammy nominations and Top New Female Vocalist awards from the Country Music Association and the Academy of Country Music.

"Daddy's Hands" was written as a Father's Day gift to her father and was never intended to be released to the public. The song served a dual purpose for Dunn. It served as a gift to her father, and, at the same time, opened communications between father and daughter.

Dunn continues to write and record very successful songs that are adapted for the critically acclaimed Holly Dunn voice.

# Holly Dunn

TURNER: When a person hears the name Holly Dunn, what do you want them to think or say?

DUNN: The thread that I have tried to weave throughout my career has been the quality of the music—not just another girl singer up there.

TURNER: You are a prolific songwriter and entertainer. Which aspect of your career do you find the most fulfilling?

---

❖

> The thread that I have tried to weave throughout my career has been the quality of the music—not just another girl singer up there.

❖

---

DUNN: Well, you know that you get your rewards from both, but they come at different times. At a live performance, you get feedback immediately. You know when something is working—the audience tells you right away. The songwriter sometimes takes years to get the recognition back. The two are so linked that it is hard to choose which I love more—they are such a part of my personality. I have worked equally hard at each.

TURNER: Had it not been for your songwriting abilities, would you have ever considered being an entertainer?

DUNN: Oh yes, I think so. I started singing before I started writing songs. I was performing when I was just a little kid. I learned how to play the guitar when I was about seven years old. Music was really big around the Dunn household. So I do not think my writing abilities had anything to do with my entertaining abilities.

TURNER: There are those people who say to write a successful country song, the writer must have experienced hurt. What are your thoughts on this school of thinking?

DUNN: Well, there is a certain amount of credibility that you have to put into your music. I wouldn't write songs about children because I don't have children and most people know that. I believe that there needs to be a certain amount of credibility in music. That's why I don't write songs that I don't know anything about.

---

> I believe that there needs to be a certain amount of credibility in music. That's why I don't write songs that I don't know anything about.

---

TURNER: When you sit down to write a song, what do you want that song to say to an audience?

DUNN: Well, you come from different approaches. You can write a song like "Daddy's Hands," for instance, that really strikes a sentimental chord, and you are not necessarily concerned with the music part of it or the rhythm. You're not really caring if you get the audience off of their feet to go dancing. Then, on the other hand, you will write a song like "You Really Had Me Going," and it's strictly a fun song, and you want to make the audience get up and dance. Oftentimes there is really no message you're trying to convey in your music. So when you sit down to write, you must determine what the subject matter is and what you want to try and get across.

---

> Oftentimes there is really no message you're trying to convey in your music.

---

TURNER: How would you describe the Holly Dunn style or approach to a song?

DUNN: It's changing and it has changed over the years. When I first got control of my productions, which was about my third album, we went back to a very simple, almost Appalachian kind of approach to the music. There were hardly any electric instruments on the album; it was a very tight family kind of harmony. We did that so we would have some place to go musically, and from this we have built every project since then. Now the new stuff we are doing in the latest album is very hard-hitting, very aggressive, very electric, very guitar-oriented, which is almost on the opposite end of the scale from my first unit production. So to answer your question, I guess my approach sort of changes with each project.

---

❖

I think my songs have really put me on the map.

❖

---

TURNER: In almost every review that I have read, the writers are always commenting on how your voice can evoke emotions. What helped to develop the Holly Dunn style?

DUNN: I think probably the best thing that ever happened to me was working for years in the studio. I sang all kinds of music, all day long, every day for the first four or five years I was in Nashville. I sang everything from rhythm and blues to black gospel to stone country to pop records soundalikes. So really that kind of honed it all in and developed my singing style.

TURNER: Did your formal education in speech influence your pronunciation and enunciation?

DUNN: Well, I don't know, maybe a little bit. My dad is a preacher and public speaker and he always emphasized speech around our house. One of his favorite quotes was, "say what you mean, mean what you say, and make sure people understand it." I've been told people can understand my lyrics, which is good.

TURNER: Larry Gatlin once told me that once a songwriter turns into a performer, a lot of creativity is lost. How have you been able to continue writing while you are on the road?

DUNN: That is a true statement; Larry knows. We have discussed it before. The time element just gets away from you the writer. I went from full-time staff songwriter, writing sixty songs a year, to writing maybe five or six. It's a real drastic reduction in my creative output. It's real tough, it's real hard. I have seen a lot of writer/performers lose their writing ability. I think my songs have really put me on the map.

TURNER: After the success of "Daddy's Hands," did you ever wonder, "What am I going to next?"

DUNN: Well! I wondered a little bit, but luckily, Michael Martin Murphey called me and we did a duet and that really took the pressure off of me. It gave me about three months for "Daddy's Hands" to die down. The duet was so different. There was so much attention on the duet—we got a Grammy nomination and a Country Music Association nomination. It really took the heat off and it couldn't have come at a better time. Then I was thinking, "What am I going to follow the duet with?"

TURNER: After all of the applause, how do you get your head back on straight?

DUNN: I just hang out with my band. I enjoy it—it's really not an ego thing.

TURNER: Do you have a favorite line from a song, one that you can say, "This is the best line I have ever written"?

DUNN: There are several songs that I am partial to. There is "Daddy's Hands," then there is an older song called "My Anniversary From Being A Fool," that wasn't a big hit but I thought it was one of my better songs. As far as individual lines, I don't; I'm sure there are but I can't remember them.

TURNER: What has been the hardest obstacle that you have had to overcome?

DUNN: Probably self confidence. I think when you first start out in this business, there is so much competition—you can be the star on your college campus or at home, but when you go to Nashville or L.A. or New York, you find out real quick that you are just one of a zillion people in the same position. So the hardest part is to believe in yourself, to continue to be objective, and to hang in there.

TURNER: Jean Shepherd once said that it took so long for women to get from being just girl singers to being major stars. What is your reaction to this statement?

DUNN: That is very true. There is still some unevenness about it. I was talking to Reba McEntire in the dressing room the other night and she said that her first chart record was in 1976, and that she didn't get on a major tour with a male artist until 1983. Then she didn't have a gold record until like nine or ten albums deep in her career. Look at Garth Brooks! He had one hit record and sold multiple platinum and was the biggest thing since white bread. There is a real imbalance there and I think it is more of a cultural thing.

TURNER: You said on stage that "Daddy's Hands" has brought me to where I am and I hope this song will take me to where I want to go, where do you want to go?

DUNN: Well, sell more records. For some reason I have never had a gold record, and even with all of the chart success that I have had it is kind of odd. So we are working on broadening the base of fans and just getting better and better. I had three Grammy nominations early in my career and I have had a lot of other nominations.

May 1992

*I think if you are in country, you are a traditionalist whether you like it or not.*

*—Radney Foster*

R ADNEY FOSTER is emerging as a new star in the traditional country music galaxy. Foster has rapidly established himself as one of the major contenders in traditional country music after having pushed the outer parameters of country music with his former singing partner, Bill Lloyd.

Foster, born and raised in Texas, was greatly influenced by the "Bakersville Sound" that was boomed over the high-wattage illegal radio stations just over the Mexican border.

Upon graduation from high school, he enrolled at the University of the South in Suwanee, Tennessee, just a short drive from Nashville.

On weekends, he and his buddies would cram into his VW Beetle and trek to Music City. It was during this time that he made valuable contacts in the Nashville songwriting community. Convinced that his time had come, he dropped out of college and moved to Nashville. After months of bumming around Nashville, he returned to college and graduated. Armed with his diploma, he once again went calling on Nashville. Soon Nashville recognized his talents and a new singer/songwriter was born.

# Radney Foster

TURNER: Where do you see yourself on the music spectrum?

FOSTER: I think I have been on both ends of the spectrum. Certainly, Foster and Lloyd was on the very far left edge in really trying to stretch the outer envelope of country music. I think that this record is a much more traditional record and that was the intention on my part. Yet, I still think there are all kinds of funky edges on it. In one sense, I guess both ends.

TURNER: Many times people become accustomed to entertainers and certain songs and certain roles, and they are very reluctant to let them move into another area, like being by themselves after they have been with a group. Did you encounter any problems establishing a solo identity?

FOSTER: I don't know. I guess in one sense I am still establishing it. I had no trouble from the record label. Certainly, they were very happy with who I was and what I wanted to do. They pretty much gave me free reign. Yet, I think there are some people, fans of Foster and Lloyd, who are surprised by what I have done solo and how much more traditional it is. At the same time I am making new fans, and the old ones don't seem turned off by it.

TURNER: I think it was Steve Earle who once said, "The idea of country music is sort of like vaudeville; there is something for everyone there." What is you reaction to this statement?"

FOSTER: I agree with that. I think that country music, particularly now, is so healthy in that it is encompassing so many influences. I think that involved in that whole spectrum is this traditionalism that pervades the entire industry. I see that as a very good thing. I think if you are in country, you are a traditionalist whether you like it or not. You better be or the audience will know that you are trying to fool them. I think that most performers are so transparent that they don't fool audiences easily.

TURNER: Who were some of the early influences of Radney Foster?

FOSTER: When I was growing up, my parents were avid record collectors and there was always country music in the house. My grandfather was a huge fan of country music and I also heard what was on the radio at the time: Buck Owens, Merle Haggard, George Jones, Tammy Wynette, Patsy

Cline, and all those people. Also, a lot of the rock and roll that came out of the sixties, particularly the Beatles, and then later the country rock bands which were really exciting to me. What really got me started writing songs were all of the country singer/songwriters out of Austin, Texas. People like Buddy Holley, Waylon Jennings, Rodney Crowell, Guy Clark, Jerry Jeff Walker, and so on.

TURNER: That is such a tremendous group of people right there. What lessons did you learn from them?

FOSTER: I learned that you could tell stories and that was a real wonderful part of country music. I think that is the best thing that country music has to offer. It tells real stories about real people. It is very relatable stuff, and it is really an American art form that caters to a real rolling-up-your-sleeves kind of folk and beyond that. However, I think primarily it is the music of middle America.

TURNER: I recently heard you referred to as a yuppie hillbilly. How accurate is this description?

FOSTER: I don't know. I think it is because of the glasses. My daddy was a lawyer so we certainly did not grow up poor. We didn't hurt for anything. However, my mother's family raised cattle, and I worked on the farm every summer. I grew up loving country and bluegrass music. I guess that is the meeting of two worlds to be a lawyer's kid in a small town and also to chase cows. I don't like the description, but it is okay.

TURNER: Everybody has a story about how they got to Nashville: What is your story?

FOSTER: I was going to college in a place called Suwanee, Tennessee, that's just about ninety miles south of Nashville, and I met some folks in the industry that said they had heard I was really good, and they said I should give it a whirl. I couldn't resist. I was waiting for an excuse and a chance, I was trying to figure out how to make a living in what I really wanted to do: play music. At twenty years of age I called my parents and said, "Mom, Dad, I want to move to Nashville and become a songwriter." As you can imagine, that did not go over too well, but they were real understanding. I went for a year and nothing happened, so I went back and finished my last year of college and then moved back to Nashville. I guess I moved there the first time in 1980, about twelve or thirteen years ago.

TURNER: Did your dad ever say go out and get a real job?

FOSTER: No, but he sure did drop a lot of hints. They were very supportive but I think they got a little frustrated after I had been in Nashville for four or five years and nothing had really happened. I would get little brochures for law school that had little stick-on notes on them that said there is no place like home. That was his way of being subtle. I think they are really proud of my success now and they realize that this is a vision that I had to follow and something I really needed to do.

TURNER: Which accomplishment are you the proudest of?

FOSTER: I don't know if there is any one thing. On a musical level, I am really proud of writing some songs that people really love, like "Crazy Over You," and, just recently, "Just Call Me Lonesome." I am proud of being involved in the tradition of country music and in a tradition of singer/songwriters that have been around Nashville for years. I am proud of my family. I have played on the Grand Ole Opry and that is a thrill that no one will ever take away from me.

TURNER: Is the songwriter the essence of country music?

FOSTER: I think that it is one side of the coin. I think the essence of country music for me is to write a song and then get up and sing it. Getting up and singing it is the other side of the coin. The song has got to come first. If you don't have a great song that speaks to people's heart, not many people will want to listen to you. Sometimes it can be something as simple as wanting to dance their cares away for three and half minutes. I think sometimes you have got to dig deeper than that.

TURNER: John Cougar said once that as a songwriter, you get to reach inside yourself, and sometimes songwriters expose too much of themselves. Do you find that to be a true statement?

FOSTER: I tend to expose a lot of myself. I think the best songs generally come out of my own personal experiences or the personal experiences of people who are so close to me that I am involved in their sorrows, joys, or heartaches. I think part of being a good songwriter is being observant with both your life and the lives of the people you are around. Generally, if you will write about those things, then you will find something that appeals to a real broad audience, and, yet, it can be very touching at the same time.

TURNER: According to a recent poll, *love* is the most used word in country music songs, and not the usual stereotypes of cheating and drinking. Do you have a favorite word that you incorporate into your songs?

FOSTER: No. Generally I like to come up with different words that no one has used yet. Of course, you do end up using the same things, but there are only so many words in the language, and so many ways to express a feeling. I always try to think of a different twist and a different way of saying something.

TURNER: What is it about your music that has made you special in today's market?

FOSTER: I don't really know. I think the ability to find a niche and people actually wanting to go out and buy your records is an amazing thing that somebody besides me would want to listen to. I am thrilled by that fact. I think that what I have tried to do on a nuts-and-bolts level is to write good songs, sing them the best I can, produce the best records I can, and let a record company go out and market it.

TURNER: How much input do you have in the production of your records?

FOSTER: A lot. I coproduced this record with Steve Fishel, and before that, Foster and Lloyd produced their own records. We never had an outside producer. Actually, working with Steve was the first time I had ever worked with an outside producer. He was really good about giving me enough rope to let me hang myself and then reel me back in. I give him a lot of credit. He is a great person to work with. He is really great at focusing talent.

TURNER: What is the difference between the person we see on stage and the man sitting across from me?

FOSTER: Not a lot. I don't mean that flippantly either. I try to get up and be who I am. I have always been a big ham and I'll own up to it. If people view you bigger than life, that is their perception. That is how they perceive you. That and who I am could be very different. That doesn't have anything to do with me trying to get up and express myself in the songs I have written. I let the audience in for a few minutes.

TURNER: Garth Brooks said that a song is a songwriter's avenue to tell the world a message in three minutes. What message would you like to convey in three minutes?

FOSTER: They are too numerous to count. Somebody asked if this album had a theme or if it had one particular message in it. I think the message is that love requires hard work. That has been the message of this album.

TURNER: Do you try to do a theme album when you do one?

FOSTER: Not really. It just turned out that way. I try to pick the ten best songs, with the help of Tim DuBois at the record company, and with my producer Steve Fishel. Then we figure out what is the best combination of letting the audience know who I am and what I have been doing since Foster and Lloyd.

TURNER: I recently read an article that said you were one of the most promising young entertainers and songwriters. Did that put a lot of pressure on you?

FOSTER: I didn't read about it so I guess not.

TURNER: What do you think the nineties will hold for Radney Foster?

FOSTER: Work. I think my job description is to try to be a good songwriter, good singer, good entertainer, good husband, good father, good employer, and all those things. That is all work to me. It is good work and I really enjoy it. I am having a blast doing it. It is not a bad way to make a living.

TURNER: You knew you had arrived in country music when?

FOSTER: When I got to play the Grand Ole Opry. Like I told you, that was a huge thrill. It's funny, we were at this club in Nacogdoches, Texas, and this lady in her sixties was selling T-shirts and I was standing there signing autographs. She looked over at me and said, "Honey, you don't look country, but you sure sound country." I told her that my mother had grown up down the road, and that my grandmother was from Nacogdoches, and that I had worked with cattle every summer when I was growing up. Then she said, "Well, yeah, you are country." I guess those are dichotomies. People always try to figure out where they can pigeonhole you. I don't know why that is all that big of a deal to them.

TURNER: If you were an interviewer doing an interview with Radney Foster, what question would you ask him that I haven't?

FOSTER: If I were to interview Radney Foster . . . I have no idea.

February 1993

*"I'm like an old mare coming into heat. I know that about four or five times a year I'm going to sit down and whoop off some songs because I'm a songwriter.*
*—Larry Gatlin*

Larry Gatlin and his younger brothers, Steve and Rudy, have their roots in Oklahoma, where they played the gospel circuit as children. In later years, Larry also tried his hand at football and baseball while attending the University of Houston, and at law school, which he dropped after one semester.

Wishing to reenter the music field, Larry persuaded his brothers to leave Tammy Wynette, whom they backed up for a number of years, and hit the road again in a family threesome.

Discovered by Dottie West, Gatlin came into the forefront as a singer in 1977, when he had three number one songs on the country charts. His songwriting talents also grew, and his songs became popular through established stars, among them Elvis Presley. There is a Gatlin-composed song on each of Elvis's last six albums.

# Larry Gatlin

TURNER: How do you get inspired to write a song? Do you draw on past experiences?

GATLIN: I just try to keep my eyes, ears, and heart open; you know they come in so many shapes and sizes. I just try to listen to what my fellow man has to say. There are a lot of brilliant people out there in the heat of the battle of everyday living who are not songwriters, and would not know how to express themselves past the first line or little idea. But I try to listen to people, and listen to my own conscience and the things I say. That's basically where I get inspiration.

---

❖

I just try to listen to what my fellow man has to say.

❖

---

TURNER: Is self-discipline important to you?

GATLIN: No, because I'm a songwriter. That's what I do. As for me sitting down every day and disciplining myself to write, I do just the opposite. I'm like an old mare coming into heat. I know that about four or five times a year I'm going to sit down and whoop off some songs because I'm a songwriter. That's what I was born to do, write songs, and I feel it starting to come in right now and I'm starting to think. See, I have to let my brain rest for a while. I could automatically sit down everyday and write five or six tunes, but I don't want them to be that way. I want them to be heartfelt, and I want them to have some meaning.

All I'm trying to do is write ten songs a year that my brothers and I can put on a terrific album, and that's all I care about writing. And if other people cut my songs, I'm happy. That's really great. But that's kinda the gravy. My most important job is writing one really super album a year, and that's what I'm trying to do.

TURNER: If you were doing an interview with Larry Gatlin, and you could ask him one question, what would that question be?

GATLIN: Boy, that's another good one. I would probably ask him, knowing his spiritual background and his stated beliefs in God, why he (expletive) up so much. It's just that I'm a human, and sometimes people just pull me into so many different directions that I can't be anything to anybody. They want me to be something to them I can't be. Women want me to be their lover, but I can't. I got a woman in Nashville and she wouldn't think highly of it. I can't be their shrink because I'm not a shrink. I can't be all the things they want me to be, and as a result, sometimes my temper flares.

---

I wish they would let me be a human being, and come for the music and nothing else.

---

I don't want to sign their pictures. If they came to the show for me to sign something, they came for the wrong reason, because it used to be that I could sign thirty or forty from a small audience, but now we're doing shows with ten to fifteen thousand. How do I sign three thousand? They say just one, but there are five hundred right behind them. So they think that it's just a failure on my part as a human being. I really love the audience collectively, but one on one, they don't have the time and I don't have the time to be all the things they want me to be. As a result of it, I probably fail.

Sometimes I wish they would come to watch me shake my pelvis, because I don't do it. That's somebody else's trick. That's not what I would do; that's a completely different bag. I wish they would let me be a human being, and come for the music and nothing else. If they would do that, I would be the happiest man they would ever see.

TURNER: What age were you when you decided that a career in show business was for you?

GATLIN: Well, I've kinda performed all along since I was a little bitty kid. I guess since I was about ten or twelve, I knew something. I thought it was going to be in gospel music, basically, at first because that was my first love, and how we were first introduced to music, period. But I think

I've known it since I was a kid that somehow, someway, someday, I would be making music for a living.

TURNER: Do you think you have carried the gospel influence over into your current career?

GATLIN: I think so. My feelings, my religious feelings for my Master, permeate my whole being because they are very much a part of whatever or whoever I am, so I think they could not help but influence me. And I'm glad they do, because I think the things I write about—men, women, boys, and girls—are the most sacred things in the world. Love and hate, it's all religious to me.

TURNER: It is a pretty well-known fact that you write most of the material that you record.

GATLIN: I write all of it, every note, every word.

TURNER: When did you decide that you would rather perform your material rather than someone else's?

GATLIN: When we first started, it was just kinda accidental. I was going to cut some songs, and my producer said, "Why don't you make this album just all your own songs and then we'll branch out from there." Well, I kept writing songs and they kept being what we thought were good tunes and I just decided that it was a lot more meaningful for me to do those songs rather than recite someone else's words and lyrics. And where would I start? I know so many great songwriters, and there are so many other great songs. I don't think I'm the best songwriter in the world, but I think I'm the best songwriter in the world who writes songs for me and my brothers, Steve and Rudy, to sing.

TURNER: Do you take time off from your performing when you write?

GATLIN: It's all so much a part of what I do—I write on the golf course if they come to me there.

TURNER: Do you find that the people in Nashville are more receptive to creativity in songwriters and performers today than they have been in years past?

GATLIN: Less receptive, because I think the town, the system, and the publishing game, ("I'll cut your song if you'll give me half the publishing"), has driven out Kris, Willie, Roger, and Shel Silverstein, and for the most part, Newberry. They said, "Hell, I don't have to play this game." Hank Cochran lives in his yacht down in the Bahamas rather than have to put up with people saying, "Hey, I'll cut your songs if you'll give me half publishing." So I think they are less creative than they were ten years ago. I got in right on the last as those guys were starting to move out.

TURNER: So the creativity has to survive elsewhere?

GATLIN: Well, that's not to say that there's not still some creative songwriters there. I don't think it is like it was. Like I said, I moved there a year before Mickey, a year before Kris left; Willie was still there.

I don't have anything about cutting commercial records if that means cutting great records to make a living. I think that they are cutting things now that are way below the standard for what they could be cutting. I mean, I could cite examples, but there is no sense in doing that.

---

❖

> I think that they are cutting things now
> that are way below the standard for what
> they could be cutting.

❖

---

TURNER: Recently I heard a DJ say that if you're going to the Opry this summer to see the Gatlins and other new country performers, don't go, because they won't be there. Are you not still a member of the Opry?

GATLIN: Yes. I don't know what would have gotten him to say that, because we did about twenty points worth of performances there last year; I don't know where he got his information. It used to be that if you were a star of the Grand Old Opry, you were a superstar. That is not true anymore. But Don Williams and Ronnie Milsap have brought some new blood to the Opry, and we're trying to add our little part.

TURNER: How do you go about getting psyched up for shows when you really fell bad?

GATLIN: Like right now . . . I just have to pray a lot. I really do, because I get tired physically. If I am in fair voice and the throat is all right, thank God. The flowers are out there making love and they send their little pollen my way and I get a little choked up.

TURNER: What type of shows do you prefer doing: concerts, package shows, or night clubs? What makes up an ideal audience?

GATLIN: I'd rather do concerts just by myself. I only ask two or three things. I want them to be very demanding. I think for five bucks they have a right to demand that I do great. It is that simple. By the same token, I think that if they sit there and listen with their eyes, their ears, their soul and their heart—more than just their ears—I'm not going to do any fancy steps. I'm going to try to find some way to reach them if they will sit there and be quiet and listen with more than just their ears. To me that is the ideal audience. If they don't like it, they can get their money back at the door and I will make it all right with the promoter. Boy! that's a better deal than Procter and Gamble will give you.

TURNER: When you look out at an audience, what do you think?

GATLIN: So many times you can't see them because of the lights. I can sense when I walk on the stage for the first eight or ten bars whether we're gong to get to them or not.

TURNER: What do you do for relaxation when you get tired and fatigued?

GATLIN: Try to rest, play golf, take the family and just sit on the patio and listen to the birds. I do like to hunt, but I don't get to go hunting much anymore. I'm not much of a fisherman.

TURNER: What has been the high point of your career?

GATLIN: Today.

TURNER: What has been the most bizarre thing that has happened to you in your travels?

GATLIN: Oh! Geez . . . Let me think. There have been so many crazy things! That's a tough question. We have had so many. Last year at this place we had a pie-fighting contest. There is an Edward's Pie Company in Atlanta, and a boy who works there brings me pies everywhere I am because I love pie fighting. And just one thing and another. I'll be singing and the power goes off. One night I was singing in Dallas—this was back before I had the band—and I was just singing myself with the house band. Not only did we not have any people, it was opening night of the baseball season with the Texas Rangers and the stadium was about fifteen miles from where I was working. I made some comedies about the Rangers' opening night drawing all my crowd away. There were only about twelve or fifteen people there—ah, there were quite a few more than that, maybe two hundred. I was talking about the Rangers and bugging them and all of a sudden over the loud speaker we picked up the radio frequency, and to add insult to injury, the ballgame started coming through this bass man's speaker. I said, "I can't get away from the Texas Rangers; they're driving me crazy." You know things like that just happen as a matter of course.

TURNER: I have heard some rumors that you might be considering doing a TV show. Is there any truth in this statement?

---

I believe I am here for a purpose. God gave me whatever talents and abilities I have for a reason.

---

GATLIN: Well, you know, TV is the instant starmaker even if it flops. If you have a summer replacement show, you can afford for them to cancel you and never be on TV again, yet you're still a TV star. TV has a way to make a career. So from that standpoint, we had hoped it would have come about, and still do, I guess, but it hasn't. We were thinking we might have had a summer replacement. It hasn't happened, and I have to think it's for the good, because I have placed everything in my life in much bigger hands than my own. I believe I am here for a purpose. God gave me whatever talents and abilities I have for a reason. I have seen TV wipe out so many people. You know, you can just look at them. It has taken and made stars out of them and then we don't hear from them for five or six years. Some of them managed to make their way back. Tom Jones and Glen Campbell are good examples of those that TV made starts out of and didn't ruin. So it's for my own good. I don't question it; I just realize that one of these days we're going to have a bunch of hit records and they're going to want us to do a TV show. Then at that point in time, I'm going to say, "Oh! Guys, I'll do six specials a year. Don't take me and make me do thirty shows and burn me out and burn my music out and burn my audience up. Don't kill me before my time. So with that in mind, we would have liked to have had it because it is just instant success.

TURNER: What do you think the immediate future holds for Larry Gatlin?

GATLIN: We're going to Dothan in the morning. That is about as far ahead as I think. We have a new album coming out. I think it is the best thing we have ever done, or at least the best since the "Pilgrim." We're really looking forward to that. We've got a bunch of really good gigs for the rest of this year. The bank and I are starting to know each other after a year—we're really picking good. I quit smoking last April and the throat is in good shape. It takes that long for it to quit screwing up. We've got the whole world ahead of us.

Musically, I hope some of the records start getting into the pop market, not just for the money or to make me a star, but I believe there are a lot of people out that don't listen to country radio that would like our music if they heard it. We are slowly but surely making progress in that direction—just making music.

May 1978

*I don't want to be known as a Jerry Lee Lewis. I don't want to be known because I play piano. . . . I love to do things on a spontaneous-type basis where I can get out with the audience and do things with them.*

*—Mickey Gilley*

SINCE MICKEY GILLEY first gained national recognition in 1974, he has had eight number-one records. In the summer of 1980, he broke chart records again when he had two songs simultaneously in the top five.

Even before the movie *Urban Cowboy* brought Gilley into the limelight, the singer and his Houston, Texas club, Gilley's, were thriving.

Prior to opening his club, Gilley spent ten years working the Texas honky-tonk circuit. He must have known stardom was somewhere in his future. Fame runs in his family; his cousins are Jerry Lee Lewis ("The Killer"), and the Reverend Jimmy Swaggart, the well-known radio and television evangelist.

# Mickey Gilley

TURNER: Country music/cowboy music is enjoying prominent success at this time. How would you differentiate between cowboy music and country music?

---❖---

> I've been doing the same type music since Moby Dick was a minnow.

---❖---

GILLEY: I don't think there's really any difference as far as the cowboy scene is concerned. I think it's just a situation where there's so many films reflecting the image of the cowboy, like *Honeysuckle Rose* and *Bronco Billy* and Loretta's film, which is not really trying to show what the cowboy life is all about. There's been cowboys almost since Columbus discovered America. The music hasn't really changed that much. I've been doing the same type music since Moby Dick was a minnow. I started in the music business in 1958 and I've been doing basically the same style music, which at the time I considered rock and roll. Then all of a sudden everything went hard rock, and all the stations started splitting. The DJs who had been working stations that were top-forty went to hard rock. The next thing I knew, they were programming what they call the country stations. If the music scene hadn't changed a tiny bit, it would not open the doors for people like Milsap, Mickey Gilley, Crystal Gayle, Charlie Rich, Jerry Lee Lewis—you name it. It's the majority of the people—Conway Twitty, Waylon Jennings, Willie Nelson, all those people who are in the same category, are doing the same style of music that they've been doing for many, many years. Willie Nelson's been singing the same kind of music since 1961. And I've been a fan of his. He changed his dress code and put on his bandana, his tennis shoes, blue jeans, and T-shirt and walked out with a guitar and said, "Hey, I'm Willie Nelson," with his beer and the whole bit, and took off that little string tie and suit. He continued to play the same kind of music and everybody in the world went crazy. So, I really don't think the music has changed that much.

TURNER: Do you think that your style has changed that much since '58?

GILLEY: I think some of the things that I've done have changed a tiny bit. For instance, the song "Stand By Me" was arranged by a guy by the name of Jim Ed Norman, who produces Anne Murray, and I look forward to the change in Mickey Gilley because I like to do things that are a little bit different. Everybody compared me to my cousin, Jerry Lee Lewis, for years and years and years, and I love to play the boogie-style piano a little bit, but I love to do, more or less, the type of music that I'm doing now, that Jim Ed is helping me create. In other words, he has given me a thing that I can reach back and say, "Hey, this is more or less the style of music that I love and enjoy, and I'm having a good time with it." I mean, "Stand By Me" is not a typical Mickey Gilley type of sound, but he's the one who created that thing for me, like in the film *Urban Cowboy,* and "True Love Ways" is not a basic Gilley's sound, although it's closer than "Stand By Me." I'm really looking forward to doing some more things with him because I think the guy is a genius when it comes to music. I don't really want to be known as a musician. I'd rather be a singer than a piano player. My cousin, Jerry Lee Lewis, is a super piano player and singer, too, but I don't really care about doing that type of thing all my life.

TURNER: That brings up another question. For a long time it appeared that you were locked into this category, somewhat, from the fact that you did a lot of performing from the piano, and, as of late, it seems like you are graduating from it and doing more material standing up. Has this been awkward at all—adjusting to a new approach to an audience?

GILLEY: I enjoy getting up and doing things away from the piano. I'm looking forward to having a bigger band behind me and I would like very much to do a thing with maybe even a bigger orchestra. I'm looking forward to a chance to go on out to Lake Tahoe and doing a thing in the main room of one of the casinos with an orchestra behind us and a production-type thing in the background. I know that there are certain things we can do that will create excitement for the audience. I'm a spontaneous performer and I love to perform, and with the right people working with me. Just like having writers, if they can write the things out for me, I can go out there and accomplish it if I feel comfortable with it. I don't want to be known as a Jerry Lee Lewis. I don't want to be known because I play piano. I enjoy the piano and I enjoy doing a certain amount of things and I do not intend to take it completely out of my act, but I love to do things on a spontaneous-type basis where I can get out with the audience and do things with them.

TURNER: I read somewhere that you have had pop success and crossover success and yet you haven't sacrificed the Mickey Gilley principles. Do you find that it's easier for your type of music to cross over to the cowboy element and be accepted than hard country?

---

## Country music is about everyday life.

---

GILLEY: I think as long as anybody does any type of song that you can relate to, and if it's recorded well, they can be accepted by any type of person. To give you an example, a song that Johnny Lee had out, "Looking For Love," is a perfect example of what a song can do if it is written well and performed right. This song has crossed over the barrier of country music and is basically a country song. Just think how many times you see people get out of town or they get away from their wives and start looking for another woman. A lot of people, they want to call it something else, but they are looking for companionship. The song is written, "Looking for love in all the wrong places . . . looking for traces . . . ," this type thing. The lines in the song are things that people can relate to. I recorded a song "Don't The Girls Always Get Prettier At Closing Time." Have you ever been in a saloon at night, and watch the people as they come in? The girl won't have anything to do with the guy at the first part of the show, but maybe at the end of the show she's leaving with him. The girl might look bad or the guy might look bad; who knows? But it's a typical situation. Country music is about everyday life. Go back to the late and great Hank Williams. He wrote some songs that are classics. If you take the song "You Win Again," the first couple of lines to the song tell you the whole story. "The news is out all over town that you've been seen running around." You see, it tells you what it's going to be about. So that's what the type of music we do is all about. About things you can relate to.

TURNER: When a song is sent to you and you're looking at material for future recording, what feels comfortable for Mickey Gilley?

GILLEY: Well, usually when a song is sent to me, if I like it I pass it on to the guy who's gonna do the production of the session: the producer.

TURNER: How much artistic control do you have now?

GILLEY: Well, I went around and around with the record company because of a couple of things that didn't please me. Like the photo sessions. But I think I've got their attention now and I think that the things that we're gonna see in the future on Mickey Gilley is gonna be topnotch quality, well done, and I know the music is going to be well done because I'm gonna pay the money to make sure that it's done right, and if we do something that's not right we're gonna can it and do it until we get it right. Actually, that's what a recording is all about, because when you take a recording home with you and you put it on your stereo, you can listen to it over and over. If I make a mistake on the bandstand up there, you're gonna hear the mistake and it's gonna be gone, but if it's on that record, you're gonna say, "I wonder why they didn't fix that." So this is one of the things that I want to eliminate from my career. I want to have good records and if I release an album, I want ten good songs on it. I don't want two hits on it and eight dogs. That's the reason why I say I don't care who writes 'em or where they come from. I want the best ten songs that I can find to go on that album when it goes out.

TURNER: Without a doubt, you're gonna go down as one of the major forces in helping return country music to the masses. What influence would you like to be remembered for having left on this type of music?

GILLEY: Well, I'm very excited about the fact that Gilley's has become a driving force in the country scene. We've promoted country music out at Gilley's since 1971, and I'm awfully proud to be part of a musical scene that is really catching on bigger and bigger. It's really one of the highlights in my career to do the film with John Travolta. I've made this statement many times, that if John Travolta could do just a fraction for country music what he did for disco, it would really give us a boost in our movement. And he made people stand up and say, "Hey, this music is good." I think the more people that are involved in what we're doing are beginning to realize that we're not hillbillies. We didn't come out of the sticks. The country music scene is the American culture. This is what our lifestyle is all about. Like I said before, there have been cowboys since Columbus discovered America. I played cowboys and Indians when I was a kid, and it's just a spinoff of everything that's happening. Everything's got modernized. The music has also grown. It's not like "Back In The Saddle Again." The music has progressed to a point that we have good songs. I'm not a good writer, but there are people writing music in the country music scene—take

"Lucille" for instance. Kenny Rogers was a rock act for the First Edition. He comes out with "Lucille" and it's a country market, a pop market, the middle-of-the-road market; it went everywhere. It made Kenny Rogers a much bigger star than he had ever been in his entire life, so I think any time you can take a song that people can relate to, it's gonna make you a much bigger act. The song "Looking For Love" put Johnny almost up to the same status as Mickey Gilley in just one song. I haven't had the type of pop success that Johnny's had with "Looking For Love." His record went to number five in the pop charts and number one in the country charts. I've had nine number-one country singles, to give you an idea.

---

❖

## The country music scene is the American culture.

❖

---

TURNER: Some historians believe that country music/cowboy music is closely related to the economy, faith in our government, things like this, and they contend that one of the reasons that we're so popular today is the fact that we have uncertainties in the world today and that we can find strength in the fortitude of the cowboys and our forefathers. Can you buy this theory?

GILLEY: I think that a lot of the songs are written about the everyday life. To give you an example, Merle Haggard wrote a song "We Don't Smoke Marijuana In Muscogee" when we were having all the trouble of the sign-carrying people from Vietnam and all this kind of thing, and Charlie Daniels came out with "If You Don't Like America" kind of stuff. I believe that this is the greatest country in the world. I know we have our problems, but I am an American. I don't believe in certain things we do every now and then, but this is my country and I'm one of the first guys that will stand up and fight for it if I thought it was a good cause. I didn't believe in the Vietnam War because there were several things I didn't believe in that I thought was a waste. I think it's a waste any time anybody goes out and loses their life on a cause that there's no way to win it. If the United States is gonna get involved in a conflict, I want to win it. If I gotta give my life up I want to make sure we're gonna win it. I don't want to go over there and see one of my kids killed or one of my friends killed over nothing. To me, that's a waste. Then ended up with nothing in the first place. If we're gonna go over there to fight and take it like we did in World War II, yeah, count me in, 'cause it's the greatest country in the world and I've been to Europe. I don't care anything about going overseas. I know that I'm living in the greatest country in the world. I don't have to go over there and see what their lifestyle is like.

TURNER: There are certain elements in Nashville and in the industry who are afraid that the popularity of cowboy/country music is at a fad stage and the fad will fade out eventually. How do you feel about this?

GILLEY: I can't believe that anybody could say that country music will ever fade out because it's been with us ever since Stephen Foster wrote "I Dream of Jeannie With The Light Brown Hair." I cannot believe that anybody would say that. The country music scene has never been as popular as it is right now. I think that we have grown steadily. One of the things that really caught on was when Elvis Presley took country and rhythm and blues and combined it. That's the reason why I say that Presley opened the door for everybody and this is one of the driving forces of creating what the music scene is all about. I think that the movement right now with the cowboy scene or the country music scene has probably increased close to where it was when Presley opened the door. The only thing that's happened to the music today is that there are so many disc jockeys who are playing top-forty, and when the hard rock came in they didn't understand it. I didn't understand it. I still don't understand it. My son once came to me and said, "Daddy, if you want to become a real big star, you have to play music like this." He took me back and he put an Elton John record on. I said, "There ain't no point in playing it for me; I don't understand it." I don't. I mean, it's over my head. I don't even have a Fleetwood Mac album. Now, there's gotta be something wrong with me because here they are selling twenty million LPs and I can't even sell a hundred thousand, but that's not my cup of tea. I don't understand that kind of music.

TURNER: Do you think anybody really understands it?

GILLEY: I don't know. I don't know if the kids are buying it or what, but somebody loves it. I wish the kids would buy the type of music that we're doing. They're buying Fleetwood Mac and Paul McCartney and other people like that. But I will never get out of doing what I am doing right now because it's the only thing I understand—it's the only thing I love. I think any time you can take songs you can relate to, it's good music. Somewhere down the line it's got to catch, and I think it's grown steadily.

TURNER: I was talking to Don Williams, and he said that Texas is full of great talent and music that has never been tapped. Do you think the fusion of national sound and Texas sound can revolutionize the music industry?

GILLEY: I think the closest thing that came to the Texas-sounding music was probably Waylon and Willie. I have always done a particular style of music and I don't really consider myself a Texas-style sound, although Texas is my home. I was raised in Louisiana, and I was around the type of music that I've always been around, and it was more or less the boogie-woogie blues-type sound.

TURNER: What has been the greatest influence on your career?

GILLEY: Well, if I had anybody to relate to as far as the musical thing is concerned, it would have to be my cousin, Jerry Lee Lewis. If it hadn't been for him, I'd have probably never thrown my hat in the ring and said, "Hey, I want to play country music." But I saw him doing so well with what he was doing, and I always loved music, but I never really understood it that much in the public life. But when I threw my hat in the ring, I got to the point where I really enjoyed it and I started playing night clubs and I had such a good time playing music and meeting people—you know, the public relations-type thing, trying to get them to come back to the club—and it got to be fun. It was like I had a good time; I had the best of every kind of life I wanted because I was getting to perform and play the kind of music I wanted to. I was getting to meet the people. I loved aviation; I was flying an airplane on weekends, I was playing golf during the week, rehearsing a couple days a week. I had the bull by the horns. Then all of the sudden, when I got relaxed—I'd been recording for seventeen years—and I walked into the studio one day and cut "She Called Me Baby All Night Long" and "Room Full Of Roses," the son of a bitch hit, and I'm saying, "What, after all this money I spent on records, I go in and do a little screwball session in Houston and it hits!" Why? Then as I look back, I know why. Because I didn't give a damn anymore. I sat there and I did this song for two hundred juke boxes, not caring who's gonna hear it, and I was very relaxed. I sounded like I did in the club, and that's what people want. Like my producer said, music is magic; it passes by one time and if you don't have it on tape, forget it.

TURNER: If you could wave a magic wand, what would you want your music to do to your audience?

GILLEY: Well, if I could wave a magic wand, and say, "Hey, look, this is what it's gonna be," I'd like to have number-one records right across the board, like Kenny Rogers did for "Lucille." That's asking for a lot. You gotta find the right song, you gotta have the right recording, there's gotta be all kinds of chemistry work, and it's gotta have enough promotion on it. The people have got to accept it. Like, you may as well ask God to speak to you.

TURNER: You were a successful businessman in the nightclub area. What aspect did you learn from success in the nightclub that helped your success as an entertainer?

GILLEY: The only thing that I can say helped me be a success in the nightclub was the fact that when I went in to do the music in the club, I did songs people could listen to, and I did songs they could dance to. I tried to keep it within the understanding of everybody coming to the club. I didn't try to play songs that were far out and nobody knew what the hell I was trying to do. And as long as you play good dance music, where they could dance to it every once in a while, they would block their ears off to the world. But the beat was there so they could dance.

TURNER: You are one of the few entertainers who appears not to have changed with success. How have you been able to keep everything in perspective and maintain a level of normalcy?

GILLEY: I was raised in a very poor family. We never had anything when I was growing up. I learned to appreciate everything my mother and father could accomplish for me as a kid growing up. I mean, I had to wait on the bicycle; I had to wait on the motor bike; I had to wait on the piano; I had to wait on the guitar when I asked for it. Everything was, "Wait 'til Christmas and Santa Claus will bring it to you," this type thing. When I got it, I was very appreciative for things that happened to me. The same thing happened in my musical career. I thought when I first walked into a recording studio, all I had to do was cut a record and I was gonna be another Elvis Presley. It didn't happen. Eighteen years later I'm almost starving to death. When I had a hit record, I appreciated it, so I'll never change. I realize that people are the ones who make you a star; you don't make yourself a star. If the people don't buy your records and people don't come to your concerts, you can hang it on a wall and forget it. I read on a restroom wall the other day, "Will Rogers never met Larry Gatlin." I didn't say that, now.

TURNER: If you were a reporter doing an interview with Mickey Gilley, what question would you ask him that I haven't asked you?

GILLEY: Oh, that's difficult. I don't know; you've just about covered everything. You ask me one thing and I get off into nine other things, so it's kind of hard to really say. The only thing I can think of if I was gonna ask somebody something: I would probably ask 'em if they had something they would like to do other than what they were doing—what would they choose as a profession? If you asked me that particular question, and if I believe in reincarnation, which I'm not saying I do, but if reincarnation was possible, and I could come back, I'd like to come back as a professional golfer if I could be good. Like Arnold Palmer or Jack Nicklaus, or somebody of that status, because that's one of the things I've always enjoyed. I used to think it was such a silly game 'til I went out and played it and found out how difficult it was to play, and then I got real excited about it. I got my game down in the eighties, but I'm a terrible golfer and I'd give anything in the world if I could shoot in the seventies.

TURNER: There are some people in the industry who are saying that concerts are going down because of the economic crunch and all this. What direction do you see the music industry taking?

GILLEY: Well, that's very difficult for me to answer because I don't have any control over the economy, and, as the economy drops, I'm sure the concerts will drop. It worried me when gasoline and diesel fuel kept going up, up, up, and I thought they were going to ration diesel fuel. I was wondering if we were going to be able to travel to do shows. If we were able to do shows, were the people going to be able to get there? We do have a problem. I don't know which way the economy is going to go; I don't know what the answers are. That's something that depends on our government.

September 1980

RYAN AND TATUM O'NEAL may have played the father-and-daughter routine on the big screen, but fans know that in the country music world, Jeannie and Royce Kendall are the reigning father-and-daughter act.

The Kendalls started out in St. Louis, Missouri, where Royce worked as a barber. But after they were talked into cutting their first record, they never left the music world again.

The Kendalls were thrust into national prominence with their risqué hit "Heaven's Just A Sin Away," and are still going strong.

*The thing about a partnership or a group is one person can do one thing and another person can do another thing. And I think that is what you have to have to have a good group.*
*—Jeannie Kendall*

# The Kendalls

TURNER: What mistake do writers make about you?

ROYCE: Well, you want to know what most of them ask us most of the time—and think they are asking something different? They will ask us what are we doing singing sinning and cheating songs seeing we're a father and daughter act.

---

I think anybody that is related, close relatives anyway, usually have a little something in their voices that makes the harmony a little better.

---

JEANNIE: Cheating songs.

ROYCE: That's what most of them ask, first thing. They think, they're asking you something different, but that's what most of them ask.

TURNER: What qualities about your father do you admire the most?

JEANNIE: A lot of things, that's hard to say.

ROYCE: She can't think of anything.

JEANNIE: He's so nice.

ROYCE: You just said that because I'm here.

JEANNIE: I think he's got a lot of determination. Let's put it this way: I probably wouldn't be sitting here if it wasn't for him. I don't have that much determination and drive—that you probably need in this business. The thing about a partnership or a group is one person can do one thing and another person can do another thing. And I think that is what you have to have to have a good group.

TURNER: Do you think that by being family that your voices have better quality and more harmonizing qualities?

ROYCE:  I find this to be true, I think anybody that is related, close relatives anyway, usually have a little something in their voices that makes the harmony a little better. You take a lot of different brothers and sisters, and they always have better harmony.

TURNER:  Up to this point, what has been the high point of your career?

ROYCE:  We've had several. I guess each week when "Heaven's Just A Sin Away" kept staying number one, that was the big thing. That was the first big thing. Then I guess the next big high was when we won the Grammy, which was early after "Heaven's Just A Sin Away." And then the CMA and *Music City News* Awards.

TURNER:  How did the father-and-daughter idea come about, and did you practice as Jeannie was growing up?

ROYCE:  No, we didn't really, not while she was real young. Till she was about fifteen, we never even thought about singing together. One day we just started singing around the house, then in about a year, our friends and neighbors would say, "Well, you two sing good together; why don't you go to Nashville and cut a record?" We lived in St. Louis at this time. So we did. We went down and paid for our own session a couple of times, then we cut a thing called "Leaving On A Jet Plane" that ended up in the top twenty for us. After that, we moved to Nashville and we have been in the music business ever since. We've lived in Nashville about ten years now.

TURNER:  "Leaving On a Jet Plane" was primarily a folk song, wasn't it?

ROYCE:  Right.

JEANNIE:  Yes, we kinda redid it into a little bit more of a country style.

ROYCE:  Peter, Paul, and Mary had had it out.

TURNER:  Had you really planned for it to fall into the country music category?

JEANNIE:  Yes, definitely. That was really back before songs crossed over from field to field.

ROYCE:  Even though if they were kind of country they wouldn't even cross over if they were pop.

JEANNIE:  Another artist had to do it usually before it would cross over.

TURNER: That's interesting. When you go out on the stage and the audience acceptance is great for your music, how can you account for the tremendous popularity in duo singing or harmony singing?

ROYCE: I've always loved harmony, that's what I've always done. My brothers and I used to sing together years ago. People have always really liked it. I think what has really made country music grow and become so big is the availability of records. You can buy them in any market now—country records are really selling more now. In the past, record companies didn't think that a group could ever make it big; I don't know why, because I think people have always liked harmony—really!

JEANNIE: I agree with you. I think the reason group singing was not as successful and not as many of them is due to the lack of faith of most of the record labels.

ROYCE: Well, and I think also economic parts of it probably made a difference in it. You take four in a group; there's four families and country music didn't get much money up until the last few years, so that also made a big difference.

TURNER: When did you do "Leaving On a Jet Plane"?

JEANNIE: About 1969.

TURNER: There weren't that many people singing duos back then. And now there are several duo acts. Weren't you pioneers in this area to a great extent?

ROYCE: Quite a bit, yes.

TURNER: When you go to look for a song for you two, what do you look for in a song?

ROYCE: We look for something that's got good harmony and a song that says something. We look for one that has good lyrics; we try to find a good melody, good harmony, and something easy to remember. It's hard to find everything you really like. It's so hard to find when you're trying to cut an album. We always like to put all good songs on an album, not just put a couple of good ones and the rest of them out of somebody's publishing company, playing politics. When we go into the studio, we try to treat every song we cut as if it could be a single release. They don't all turn out that good, but at least you end up with a good song.

TURNER: That's a good idea. How would you describe the Kendall style to someone who has never heard you sing before?

ROYCE: It's hard to describe, I guess, because some people like pop or something, and they'll like us. And the real country like us, so we're somewhere in between. I think we've found something in between—I don't know what it is, really. Maybe our music is a little up-class from the real country, but basically we sing country. Jeannie was a little more into the folk thing; that's what she really grew up on and really liked. And I was George Jones-type country, and so maybe that gives us a little different sound.

---

Maybe our music is a little up-class from the real country, but basically we sing country.

---

JEANNIE: A combination of two different types.

ROYCE: I'm kind of the Louvin Brothers-type harmony.

TURNER: The fact that you were into folk music brings in the songs that tell a story, and I guess that's what relates so much to your music.

ROYCE: That's right.

TURNER: And that has been your influence?

JEANNIE: I guess, I don't know. Materialwise, we generally agree on most material.

ROYCE: Yes, we do. That is one thing we really do agree on, most of the time, and we make the decisions together, you know. I get out and find the material. We cut what we want, not our producer. We cut what we want to.

JEANNIE: That way if it doesn't do good, it is our own fault.

ROYCE: I had rather do it that way then if it's bad, you had nothing to do with it.

TURNER: Do you do a lot of writing?

ROYCE: Jeanie writes quite a bit.

JEANNIE: I do some.

ROYCE: She wrote "Sweet Desire," which is a number-one record. I really think it is a great song.

TURNER: Do you have a timetable: I would like to be at this point of my career by this time next year, or things like this?

ROYCE: No.

JEANNIE: No, we'd like to sort of let it flow a little bit more.

ROYCE: We just hope to keep getting hit records and wherever it takes us.

TURNER: Of all the awards you have won, which one means the most to you?

JEANNIE: That's hard to say; I don't know. Every one of them means different things. The *Music City News* Award is really a good award because it's voted for by the public.

ROYCE: The people vote it.

JEANNIE: But the CMA is voted for by your peers, which you appreciate, too.

ROYCE: And the Grammy is voted on by all musicians. So every one of them means a lot.

TURNER: What has been the biggest influence on your career?

ROYCE: I guess Brian Fisher, our producer. We do it together which makes it work, I think. He's not really like a producer; he's more like a friend. We do our suggestions, and he does his suggestions, and we let the pickers get in there and work, and it seems to turn out good for us.

TURNER: Hasn't he been with you for a long time?

ROYCE: No, we had known him a while, maybe a couple of years. I have known his brother for a lot longer; he lived in Chicago. Then Brian moved down to Chicago and we just got to talking; we were dissatisfied with our situation. We had been on Dot for about three or four years and we had been on UA for a year or so, but nothing was happening, so we just left there, and we didn't do nothing for about six months. We said if we couldn't do what we wanted to, in songs, we just wasn't ever gonna cut again, because if you can't do something you like, as Jeannie says, if you don't do something you like, how are people gonna like it? 'Cause you can't get into it if you don't really like it. Then Brian got the deal for us to do an album and do whatever we wanted to on Ovation. "Heaven's Just A Sin Away" was the first song we cut on the album. But we didn't recognize we did it on the B side to start with.

## we're a whole lot better singers than we were when we first started.

TURNER: What do you want for yourself in the future?

ROYCE: Oh, we always like to upgrade our show, naturally. We want to make our show better and we want to go on to play bigger and better places, you know.

JEANNIE: We'll probably do some more TV shows.

TURNER: Do you feel that your style has really changed that much since you initially started back in St. Louis?

ROYCE: No, not that drastic of a change.

JEANNIE: I don't know that it has changed so much. I think maybe we were just sorta searching for a particular groove.

ROYCE: We were a little green, maybe. And I'm sure we have materialized a little better, don't you?

JEANNIE: Yes, we're a whole lot better singers than we were when we first started. I listen to some of the old things and I kind of cringe.

ROYCE: You were a little more proper, I'd say, living in St. Louis.

JEANNIE: Yes, but see, for several years we've been wanting to try some things with another harmony over the other harmonies.

TURNER: Are you going to come back and dub over your harmonies?

JEANNIE: Yes, and so that's basically the change we made in our sound. Doing the material that we want to do was the basic change that we made.

When we were on other labels, we couldn't do that. They wanted us to have background voices and all that.

TURNER: I guess that puts the depth in there, doesn't it?

ROYCE: It kind of fills it up; you don't really hear it much, but it is there.

JEANNIE: It's not on all our records, but it is on some.

ROYCE: One where it fits good, I do it. If it don't, why do it?

October 1979

*I would . . . like to call the promoter and say, "We are doing a show for you and all we want is expenses and you take the rest and give it to all the little kids around who don't have any place to sleep, nothing to eat, or who are being abused, and things like that."*
*—Sammy Kershaw*

$S$AMMY KERSHAW grew up in Kaplan, Louisiana and says he can't remember when music was not a part of his life: "My mama used to rock me when I was a baby and sing Hank Williams songs." As the years passed, Kershaw's love of music grew. By the time he was five years old, he could deliver a haunting rendition of George Jones's "Things Have Gone to Pieces."

At age eleven Kershaw's love of music intensified when his grandfather gave him a Western Auto Tel-Star electric guitar. Shortly thereafter, Kershaw joined local musician J. B Pere's band as gofer and singer. After about eight years, Kershaw bid Pere farewell, joined a group called Blackwater, and toured with them throughout Wyoming and New Mexico.

Suffering from burnout, Kershaw decided to pursue a career as a carpenter, and was hired by the Wal-Mart Corporation as a remodeling supervisor.

Kershaw's love of music was resurrected after he was asked to send a tape and an eight-by-ten photo to Harold Shedd and Buddy Cannon of Mercury Records.

Recently the young Cajun singer sat down and reflected on his rollercoaster life.

# Sammy Kershaw

TURNER: Where do you see yourself on the music spectrum?

KERSHAW: We are building a lot of ground right now. This is the first year we have laid a lot of ground, went a lot of miles, seen a lot of people. So really I guess we have got another year to go before there will be a position for us. Right now we are still working hard—of course we will always be working hard. That's one thing I promised the guys: we won't take three or four months off at a time; there's no way I could do that. It would drive me crazy. Maybe next year, if you ask me that question, I might be able to give you a little straighter answer.

TURNER: A lot of people are referring to you as a young George Jones. In your opinion, are they comparing your style, your approach to a song, or the way you execute the song?

KERSHAW: Well I think that George Strait, Joe Diffie, and I are young guys who have a certain tone in our voices and there is no way we can get away from it. I think that's where they are coming up with the comparison, and plus, you know, George Jones has been my hero all my life. I think if you take one of my albums and one of George's albums and play it side by side you can tell the difference. But there are a lot of people that are comparing us, and that really doesn't bother me, because as for as I am concerned, Ole George is the King of Country Soul. It is just like if I were a baseball player it would not make me mad if they compared me to Johnny Bench or Yogi Berra. I take it as a compliment.

TURNER: Does this comparison with George Jones put added pressure on your career?

KERSHAW: No. I don't worry about anybody or anything. You know I'm Sammy Kershaw. I don't have time to worry about everybody in this business. I need to worry about what we are doing. We have to make sure we take care of our business. We have fun with the fans. We just try to do everything right; we don't want anybody to be able to write anything bad about us. I guess to answer your question, no, there is no pressure on me at all. I think people put pressure on themselves. I am not going to let that happen to me. Like I said, I need to worry about myself.

TURNER: Jean Shepherd once said there are a lot of people out there hoping to be singers and those who do make it have a special something. What do you think that special something is that Sammy Kershaw possesses?

---

❖

## If I have not lived the song, I can't put my heart into it.

❖

---

KERSHAW: Well, I think when I sing a song it comes from the heart. See, if I haven't lived the song I won't cut it. I don't care how big a hit it's probably going to be. If I haven't lived it, it is going to be a hit for someone else; it is not going to be a hit for me. I think the people and the fans can detect when you're singing from the heart and mean what you're singing or if you're faking it—I don't want to be fake about anything. What you see is what you get! What you hear is what you get! If I have not lived the song, I can't put my heart into it. If I haven't lived it, how am I supposed to get into it without faking it.

TURNER: There are those people in power that contend that a young entertainer can not convincingly deliver a song that deals with hurt unless he has suffered hurt himself. Do you believe this theory?

KERSHAW: Well, yes, I do. There you go back into the faking part. I have already been through two divorces. A couple times I lost everything I had in life. I have almost died a few times. I have had a lot of different jobs in my life to keep this dream alive. I've done a lot of living, you know. My dad died when I was eleven years old, so I had to grow up real quick. I was the oldest of four kids and I started playing music in night clubs in south Louisiana when I was twelve years old. I played five nights a week and went to school during the day and worked at a gas station in the afternoon. I've been through a lot for a guy that is just thirty-four years old.

TURNER: Everybody has a story about how they got to Nashville. What is Sammy Kershaw's story?

KERSHAW: Well, you know, I got out of music for a while about three years ago—I had to get myself together. I just kind of forgot why I got into this business to start with. I got into this business to have a little fun.

It was fun! I always said if I ever stopped having fun I would go to the house. Well, that's what I did. I was not having fun anymore, so I went and got a job with Wal-Mart as a remodeling supervisor. I traveled around the country and remodeled Wal-Mart stores. I made good money, and all that stuff. I stayed there for about a year and a half to two years. While I was working in Arlington, Texas, I got a phone call from this guy that had heard me eleven years earlier in Lafayette, Louisiana, in a place called Cowboys. He remembered who I was. He told me that there was this guy in Nashville by the name of Jim Dowl who was looking for new artists. So I sent a tape and picture to Jim Dowl and he took it to Buddy Cannon and Harold Shedd at Mercury Records. He played my tape for them and they arranged for me to fly to Nashville and do a showcase for them. The next morning, we were in Harold Shedd's office talking about a record deal. I just got lucky.

---

## I got into this business to have a little fun.

---

TURNER:  What percent does luck play in an entertainer's career?

KERSHAW:  I think it plays a lot. Well, on my part anyway. Me and the boys have really been lucky this past year. There are a lot of people in this business who are not working. We've been working steady—maybe a day or two off a month. We've been working hard since last October. We have put a lot of miles on this bus; we have seen a lot of people. We have really been lucky, and the good Lord has taken care of us. He is driving the bus; that's all I can say.

TURNER:  Do you come from a musical family?

KERSHAW:  No, I don't. I am the only one in the family that plays. Well, my grandpa played accordion and harmonica. He was one of those old Cajuns that liked to have a lot fun. We never did play together. He passed away a few years ago and we never got to play together.

TURNER:  How are you related to Doug Kershaw?

KERSHAW:  We are third cousins.

TURNER:  Have you ever done a show with him?

KERSHAW: About thirteen years ago we did a show together. He was doing a show at this club and I happened to be there that night. He found out I was in the audience and he asked if I would come up and sing some harmony with him. So I got up on stage and sang with him and that was the last time I have seen him. However, I talked to him on the phone about a year ago and we finally found out how close or how far away we are kin to each other.

TURNER: In your opinion, what are the ingredients that go into making a hit record?

KERSHAW: Well, number one has to be the song; the songwriter has to be able to sit down and write a song that I have lived: something that I can put my heart into. I guess that is why there are producers, they can hear what the musicians should be doing and where they should be playing. I just have to have lived the song and be able to feel it before I can cut it.

TURNER: If you really want to showcase the talents of Sammy Kershaw, what song would you select?

KERSHAW: Probably "Anywhere But Here," the brand new single. It is my favorite song on the album. I don't know why. Maybe, it's because the song is about breaking up, but it is a funny song if you think about it. There are not too many funny songs you hear about breaking up. I think that's why it has got to be my favorite song on the album. It's a lot of fun. I love to do that song on stage.

TURNER: Every time I see you on stage or at a show, you act like you are having a blast up there. Are you really having that much fun?

KERSHAW: Yes!

TURNER: Isn't it wonderful to be able to do something one likes that much?

KERSHAW: Yes sir! and play golf during the day. Today my bass player, Skip, and I were out playing golf and as we made a dogleg right, I looked up and saw these guys building a house right on the golf course. I could not help but think to myself I could easily be one of those guys up there building that house rather than out here playing golf had it not been for the blessings of the good Lord. All I can say is that I have really been lucky these last couple of years.

TURNER: You have gotten some wonderful reviews; which one are you the most proud of?

KERSHAW: I don't know if I have seen many of them.

TURNER: You have gotten some wonderful reviews. You had a great review in *People* magazine.

KERSHAW: Well, I guess that's my favorite one.

TURNER: We are all aware of the emphasis being placed on images of entertainers today. What kind of image do you want to project to the fans?

KERSHAW: I want to be a nice guy. I want everybody to look at me and say, "Man, that's a nice guy, and every time you see him he's the same. He'll talk to you and he don't walk away from you thinking he's better than you are," because I am not. I'm just glad the people let me have a chance to do what I love to do.

TURNER: How important is it to be yourself when you are fist establishing an image?

KERSHAW: Well, I think it's very important. You only have one chance to make a good first impression. Why not just go ahead and make a good impression the first time instead of spending five or ten years time trying to make it right with the person that you hurt their feelings. There is no need for that.

TURNER: What do you want for yourself in the future?

KERSHAW: Well, five years from now I would love to be able to drive up to any venue in the country and sell it out to the rafters. I would also like to call the promoter and say, "We are doing a show for you and all we want is expenses and you take the rest and give it to all the little kids around who don't have any place to sleep, nothing to eat, or who are being abused, and things like that." If we can do something for the kids in five years, that is all I want to do this for.

TURNER: Would you retell the story about being scared for the first time in your life?

KERSHAW: Well, it was like I said. When I was twelve years old, if anyone asked me to get upon stage and sing, I would do it in a heartbeat. I was not old enough to be scared of the stage because I think you are taught fear. The only time I have been scared since I started twenty-two and one half years ago was probably four months ago. That was when I did the Grand Ole Opry. I have never been so scared of going on stage. I did not know why until I stood in the circle that was cut from the floor of the old Ryman Auditorium and put into the new Opry House. To me, when I got in that circle, it was like all the ghosts of the former Opry stars were standing in that circle with me. It was like they were saying, "Okay, this is our house and here is your chance. What are you going to do with it?" It was really an eerie feeling.

---

❖

I think the one thing that helped me get started so early in the business was the fact that I got to open a lot of shows for a lot of the great artists: George Jones, Conway Twitty, and Cal Smith.

❖

---

TURNER: George Jones once had a song, "Who's Going To Fill Their Shoes." Whose shoes do you see Sammy Kershaw filling?

KERSHAW: That's another good one! I would like to be one of those ghosts in that circle. I have not yet been asked to become a member of the Opry. Hopefully, someday I will. It would be nice. It is a life long dream.

TURNER: The other night I covered the Hall of Fame show and I thought about all the great entertainers and the wealth of information that these people possess and how the young artist should be out here soaking it in like a sponge. What is your reaction to this observation?

KERSHAW: I think the one thing that helped me to get started so early in the business was the fact that I got to open a lot of shows for a lot of great artists: George Jones, Conway Twitty, and Cal Smith. I guess I was lucky because at twelve years old I was getting to see what some of these artists were doing and what they were not doing and what I should and should not do. I think there was a lesson to be learned from being around all these guys. I paid attention to them.

TURNER: What was the best lesson you learned from these great artists?

KERSHAW: The best lesson I ever learned was, when something happens on the road it needs to stay there. It needs to stay out on the road because your job is not at home. It just makes things rough for everybody. Another thing is, when you are done with the show, you need to go to bed and get some rest, because there is going to be another show tomorrow. If you get out there with no rest, eventually it is going to run you down. I learned that really quick. The first four or five months that we were on the road, it was tough for me. I went home one day in three months. The boys would drop me off at an airport somewhere and I would do an in-store promotion at a Cadillac dealership or a Wal-mart while the boys drove to the next town where they would pick me up at the airport and we would do a show. I was so run-down—until then I had not had a cold in five years. Then last year I had the flu twice but I just had to keep on going. I hit the stage two nights with a fever of 104 degrees and one night I don't even remember walking out of this bus and on to the stage. Another lesson I learned is that alcohol and drugs do not work in this business. I quit both of them about nine years ago. I don't allow them in the bus. We have a case of beer on the bus, but the contract says no one drinks before the show or during show. With thirteen people on the bus, each one can have a couple of beers and nobody will get drunk. Everyone gets drug tested, including myself, to make sure everyone stays clean. If fans come around the bus talking drugs and cocaine, I will get rude and throw you out of here. I *will* throw you out of here!

TURNER: Do you feel that entertainers are promiscuous?

KERSHAW: It has changed a lot in the last five or six years.

TURNER: If you were doing an interview with Sammy Kershaw, what question would you ask him that I have not asked you?

KERSHAW: That is a great question. I have never heard that one before. That's a good one . . . maybe, what does it take to make it in the music industry?

TURNER: What does it take?

KERSHAW: Well, I will tell you what it takes. I think about this all the time. I know where I have come from, and I know where I have been. If I can remember those two things, I can always know where I am going. I see a lot of this, and if getting to the top means stepping on somebody's toes, I won't make it. I will fall short—way short.

October 1992

**B**ORN IN TEXAS CITY and raised on a dairy farm in the East Texas town of Alta Loma, Johnny Lee grew up listening to rock and roll. But when he was hired as a singer by Mickey Gilley, Lee found his niche in country music.

Lee was catapulted into stardom by the movie *Urban Cowboy*, and finally enjoyed the fruits of his longtime musical apprenticeship as the veteran featured vocalist at Gilley's Club.

In addition to his music, Lee is also known for his much-publicized marriage to *Dallas* star Charlene Tilton.

*The really good feeling that comes to me is when I do the concerts and I see little kids, from five years old to eighty-five, singing the words with me to my song. That's the big thrill for me. The rest of it is a business.*
*—Johnny Lee*

# Johnny Lee

TURNER: In your opinion, what has brought about the tremendous success cowboy music is enjoying today?

LEE: Well, I think a lot of the exposure came from the movie *Urban Cowboy.* I think not only *Urban Cowboy,* but just a lot of new exposure to so-called "country music" to a lot of new fans who really didn't realize what they liked was called "country music." The same way with country music fans. They really didn't realize what would be classified rock and roll—not

---

Country music has always been alive and it'll never die, but it has expanded so much, and so many different people have been exposed to it

---

a heavy type rock. Right now I think it's a in stage of just good music. I'm not saying that country music of a long time ago is bad; that was just what was happening at the time. It's a trend. Every ten years or so, I think, something different goes and something new comes up. Country music has always been alive and it'll never die, but it has expanded so much, and so many different people have been exposed to it who say, "Hey, man, that's a good song." They might have heard an old Hank Williams or Jimmy Rogers song that was a good song, where a long time ago they might have said, "Here's a country song for you," and they might have said, "No, I don't like country music" before they gave themselves a chance to listen to it. Now it's getting the exposure that is so well deserved, and a lot of people realize it and say, "Hey, that's a good song." I think it's just a matter of people coming together with good music. I like old country music myself, and I like the new country music. I think it's contributed to the exposure that the music's getting.

TURNER: There are a certain few in Nashville I have heard who are afraid that cowboy music, or country music, is at a bad stage like disco was a couple of years ago. They are afraid that it might go out.

LEE: Well, you know everybody's gotta believe in something. If they think it's a fad, well, more power to 'em. Like I say, country music's been around since Moby Dick was a minnow and it'll always be around.

TURNER: How would you describe your particular type?

LEE: The type of music I do I would classify as "feelgood" music: Songs that I can relate to, songs that I like to deliver to the audience. I might sing a fast song that the story might not be something that really touches my heart, but it's really an ass-kicking song. People clap their hands and stomp their feet—they feel good. I like to play music that people can either get into or get off to.

TURNER: How has it felt to have such overnight stardom? I know you've been working at it a long time, but it seems like the success came overnight.

LEE: Well, it didn't come overnight. I started when I was fourteen. I always wondered how I would feel to get to do television, to do radio, to do the press, all this stuff. I always wondered how it would feel to do that. Then, within two or three weeks, I found out. It took me so many years, sixteen or seventeen years, to get to do that. Let's see, I started when I was fourteen, I was in service for almost four years, and then I got out and got back into music. So really, to be honest with you, I have been so busy, so involved with what's going on right now, I really haven't had a chance to sit back and say, 'How does this feel?' I may have a few free moments at an airport or between tapings or something, and I'll sit back and say, "Hey, man, you got the number-one record in the country!" And I'd stop and think about it. The really good feeling that comes to me is when I do the concerts and I see little kids, from five years old to eight-five, singing the words with me to my song. That's the big thrill for me. The rest of it is a business. When I do TV shows I'm really honored to get to do them. I just do the best I can do. It's a lot of work; it really is. I'm working harder right now then I've ever worked in my whole life. I love it and I'm not complaining. I'm grateful.

TURNER: Once you have a big hit, is it better to go into another type of song, or should you try to follow up with a similar song?

LEE: Well, I'm not trying to lay me any pattern. I want the people to know Johnny Lee, they'll know what I do. I'm not trying to get a song that's almost the same progression. I just try to record good songs. We take it from there. I'm not trying to set any type pattern.

TURNER: You said you had been in this business several years. Have you ever stood there and played for somebody else, or sat there and said, "Hey, man, I'm as good as they are—will it ever come my way?"

LEE: No, I never did. It was always in my head and I knew that I'd worked all my life to try to get to this certain point. I never said, "Hey, I'm as good as this guy or that guy," because everybody has their own identity. I'm not trying to be like Merle Haggard, David Allen Coe, Johnny Paycheck, or Willie Nelson. I'm trying to be me because I'm the person who has to live my life. I'm just trying to be successful; I love playing music and I love people that get off on what I do, so I'm just trying to do stuff that keeps me out in front of the public, to make them feel good, and in return they make me feel good.

TURNER: Do you find that there is a difference between cowboy music and country music?

LEE: No, there ain't no difference.

TURNER: How did you ever go about getting to record "Looking For Love?"

LEE: Two school teachers from Gulfport, Mississippi wrote the song. They sent it to Combine Music, Bob Morrison doctored the song up a little bit, and I did the song the way I felt like doing it. It was presented to Irving Azoff for the movie *The Urban Cowboy*. He listened to it and he thought I could sing the song, so they put it in a big cardboard box of tapes that were submitted for the movie. I went over to a hotel one night and listened to thirty or forty songs, pulled out "Looking For Love", and they asked me to rate 'em all on a scale of one to ten. I gave it a ten. I went to L.A. and recorded it, and the rest is history.

TURNER: Have you encountered any problems you couldn't handle, or you felt very uncomfortable with?

LEE: The only thing I feel really uncomfortable with is getting up after about two and a half hours, or an hour and a half after I've gone to bed. People are really nice in this business and it's really great, the caliber of

people that I'm working with. I did a *Merv Griffin/Mike Douglas Show,*
*Midnight Special, Dionne Warwick Special, Dick Clark,* the award shows.
All these people are beautiful people and they treat us all really nice and
it's just like family. I'm very fortunate, like I said.

TURNER: Did you have any idea that you could be this successful?

LEE: Nobody ever has any idea. No, I always wished for it and one of my
wishes came true.

TURNER: When people send you tapes to listen to, what do you look for?

LEE: Hits.

TURNER: What would include a hit?

LEE: Whatever I can feel, or if I feel like I could have written the song.

TURNER: Do you go a lot by gut feeling?

LEE: Gut feeling, that's the only way to go.

TURNER: Do you do a lot of writing yourself?

LEE: I try to. I used to 'til I got so busy. I write every chance I get.

TURNER: What has been the biggest influence on you or your career?

LEE: I think just the whole thing about the music business—the entertainment field has always intrigued me. Naturally, when I was a kid, I grew
up on different types of music. Even to this day I still get influenced by
different types of music. I've got different ideas about different kinds of
music. I guess the man who's taught me the most about this whole thing
is the guy that I love just like my brother, Mickey Gilley. We've been together since 1968. Our word and the handshake has always been good,
and when you've got friends like that it's kind of hard to get influenced by
anything else. He's always been behind me and supported me. My success
to this point is not as high as I want to go. I have other plans—movies,
recordings—but I would have to think that Mickey Gilley taught me the
most. The most about people, about business, about music, about crowds,
about the concerts and nightclubs. Those are a few things I thought I
knew, but can't take away from somebody, what they call "'experience."
Mickey has always made me aware. I was aware anyway, but he stresses to
me how important it is to be friendly with all your fans. There are people
who come to see us; they're the people who keep us going. When they

show up for a concert, applaud for us, stand up, that's just a thrilling, personal experience.

TURNER: Could you single it out to one most important point he's made to your career?

---❖---

> Live every day like it's your last, 'cause one
> of these days you're gonna be right.

---❖---

LEE: Live every day like it's your last, 'cause one of these days you're gonna be right.

September 1980

*. . . if I write a song, I write . . . about how people are living. . . . This way, I know it's going to touch people. It's got to touch people, because I'm just like they are, and if it touches me, it has to touch them, too"*

*—Loretta Lynn*

For Loretta Lynn, the hard knocks and rough times of the coal fields of Southern Appalachia were the stuff of which dreams were to be made. In an entertainment industry that prides itself on the rags-to-riches sagas of many of its brightest stars, hers is the story that still stands out.

Loretta might be the first to admit that a movie script for the story of how a young girl from near the coal mines of Kentucky found fame and fortune atop the country music world would just about strain the Horatio Alger mold to its limits.

Born in a shack in the hills of the Bluegrass State, Loretta has made her way to the top. Her mother, worked until the end of her life, even though her daughters were superstars. Loretta carries on the down-to-earth philosophy of her family.

And yet, despite the success she has achieved, there is one great tragedy in Loretta's life. Her father, a poor coal miner, never lived to see his beloved daughter reach the heights of stardom.

# Loretta Lynn

TURNER: One question has always been on my mind. Several years ago, I think you made a quote on the Wilburn Brothers Show that really touched me. I remember you saying, "One of the great regrets I have is that Daddy never got to hear me sing professionally." Does this still stand out in your mind?

---

Daddy never had nothing nice, and I would have liked for Daddy to have lived long enough for me to have bought him something nice.

---

LYNN: Yes. He never heard me sing! Except like sitting in the swing hollering and rocking the babies to sleep. He would never have guessed all this. It would have been the farthest thing from his dreams, that I would ever sing. I guess he always knew I could sing, you know, by listening to me. But he never dreamed that anything like this would ever happen to me. That is the one thing that I hate most of all about becoming a country music singer. Daddy never had nothing nice, and I would have liked for Daddy to have lived long enough for me to have bought him something nice.

One day it's not been long ago . . . you know back in the days when I was growing up, bologna was known as coal miner's steak. If you got bologna, man, you were really doing something, you know? And I just said, "If Daddy could see the price of bologna today, wouldn't that be something?" It's like steak was back in them days, really.

TURNER: Looking back, do you see anything you wish you had or had not done in your career?

LYNN: I wish that I could have been home more with my kids. There was a period three or four years ago that I really, really got depressed, be-

131

cause when I first started singing, we figured that I would be home with the kids when they needed me more. I had four kids in school when I started singing. I was about three years older than Crystal Gayle is right now when I was a grandmother. And I look back now and I think, "Oh gee, look how young she looks, and I was a grandmother when I was not much older than her." But back when I was thinking of grandmothers, grandmothers were usually forty years old or more, right? Here I became a grandmother at twenty-nine. That's pretty hard to swallow, it really is.

TURNER: Some of your songs have touched on controversial issues. Did you do this on purpose because maybe your fans need this type of information?

LYNN: Not really. When I hear a song, or if I write a song, I write the song about how people are living, and how I would be living, or how I am living. This way, I know it's going to touch people. It's got to touch people, because I'm just like they are, and if it touches me, it has to touch them, too. So then I will release a song I know is going to be a hit with the people, your everyday working people; that's where I want to be. I don't want to be any higher than that right there, and I never will be, in my mind or in any way, any better or live any higher than my fans.

TURNER: These are the best people.

LYNN: These are the best people, and these are the people that I want to sing to. And these are the people who will go out and buy your records. I guess like "You Ain't Woman Enough To Take My Man." How many women can sit around and watch some woman flirting with her husband and not jump up and say, "Hey, you're not woman enough to take my man." I would say this is right down to the ordinary people, maybe not a president's wife, or a bigwig's wife, because maybe they're doing it behind the curtain. Ordinary people, like us, we like to get out and have a good time and if we want to smile at somebody, we're going to do it in front of everybody, right? These are the people I want to identify with and perform for.

TURNER: Without a doubt, you will be remembered as the first woman who really made it big in the world on country music. What kind of influence would you like to be remembered for having left on country music, something you can tell your grandkids about?

LYNN: Well, I think probably what I would like to say is always be yourself with the people that made you in country music. Don't ever feel that you're any better than they are, because you're not. I would say that would probably be the best thing to leave anybody.

TURNER: It's very good that you can still relate to those people who helped you make it so big in country music.

LYNN: I guess it was so long, you know. I can feel for people. As I look out in the audience and I see somebody that I know probably spent their last penny, that's got a big family, and the will to come see the show, I'm like you, it depresses me, it hurts me. I will do my best to speak to them after the show and go to the kids and talk to them. And a lot of time if I know someone that's hard up, and they come through the line with a piece of paper, I'll give them a picture.

TURNER: By your definition, are you a success?

LYNN: I would say so, maybe. I don't really know. What do you think?

TURNER: I definitely think so.

LYNN: Well, I guess I probably am—in country music.

TURNER: Something I've always wanted to ask you is, you're daily associating with people who are college-educated, business executives, people who are college-trained. How have you been able to maintain your particular speech pattern and not let others affect you—like a lot of times we have southerners who go northern and within two days they have a northern accent—how have you been able to do this?

LYNN: Well, it's never affected my speech. I've traveled all over the world, and really, it hasn't changed my speech one bit. I think sometimes some people have a hard time understanding me, maybe. But I have a hard time understanding them, so it's vice versa.

TURNER: You know, today's music is getting softer, a lot less steel. And a lot of entertainers say they would not put a steel guitar in any of their music. Can this music last?

LYNN: Yeah, in the pop field, not with country music, and they are fixing to hurt it, real bad.

TURNER: Do you think that maybe a lot of people are fans of a particular song at a time, rather than a particular performer in this "middle-of-the road" business?

LYNN: Well, I'll tell you what—take a really, really big song like "D-I-V-O-R-C-E," and songs like that. They had steel in it, and it was country. Well, it got played in the pop field, just like "One's On The Way." But it was country, right? Well, today they're taking the steel out, like you said, out of everything that makes a song sound country.

---

## I love my fans and I think they love me.

---

TURNER: Is the traditional country gone?

LYNN: Yes. If the disc jockeys don't stop—if they would just start refusing to play the ones that's too far out. My own opinion is like this: The record companies shell out money to the trade magazine, and the disc jockeys see them in the charts, and then they start playing them. They say, "Well, if they're in the charts, why not play them?" It says it in this country chart. They're the ones that's doing it. It's the disc jockeys and the artists. They're doing it themselves, so when I hear the disc jockeys complain about the pop songs, if they are playing them, it's their problem.

TURNER: They are shortchanging the true country music fans because we don't get what we really want.

LYNN: That's right. Some of the stations right now are going back to playing nothing but true country. Some of them are doing it now, but the ones that have went way out in the pop field are not going to have the country fans. So they better make it in the pop field big.

TURNER: Because once you get a country fan, it seems like he's with you for the rest of his days.

LYNN: Now, this is how my fans do me.

TURNER: You can't find any more devoted fans than Loretta Lynn fans.

LYNN: Well, I don't know about that, but I love my fans and I think they love me. When I get a record out and it's not up to par, not as good a song as the last one, they'll still go out and buy it.

TURNER: Have you ever worried about this bit: "Will I be as good the next year?"

LYNN: No, I haven't worried about that because I think you're as good as your songs. I don't care how long you're in the business. Just like Larry Gatlin. He told me the other day that he had been singing for over twenty yeas. Well! That's longer than I've been singing. Larry said that lots of people would come up to him and say, "Well, Larry, you were an overnight success," and he would say, "Yeah, so was so and so, and so and so." They'd only been in the business fifteen to twenty years, and they were an overnight success one day. But this is how it happens. The major people don't know that you've been in the business that long 'til you get a big record. And I have been really lucky. I have really searched for songs and I have wrote most of my songs. For a long time I wouldn't sleep 'til I would get the next hit wrote. And I would know immediately when I'd wrote the next hit.

TURNER: Could you visualize it before you put it on tape or anything?

LYNN: When I started writing it, I knew it was a hit. Now, I wrote three or four songs a day, but I would only write one good one in twenty or thirty songs. But I would know when I wrote the hit.

TURNER: What is the biggest mistake that writers make about you? What would you like to clarify?

LYNN: Writers make about me? Well, I read a lot of writeups and I don't know if they really make any mistakes or not. A lot of times some of them make little mistakes. I don't know if they want to lie about something—I don't believe that they really do. I think maybe they just misunderstand a lot of things and they will kind of put their own touches to things and say, "Well, maybe it'll sell better this way." They are doing their job, like I have to do mine. I don't really get that tore up about it anymore. Used to when I first started getting writeups, some of them would be a little off-color or a little bad—it really hurt me. But it doesn't bother me that much because I understand their problems, too.

TURNER: The fact that you have won a lot of awards, does this take away from the meaningfulness of these awards?

LYNN: No, it doesn't. Every award I treasure. I guess it tickles me just as much to see somebody else get one, because I know how they are feeling. If I'm one of the five nominees for a girl singer award and I get the award, well it thrills me to death; it still thrills me to death. But if one of the other girls gets it, it thrills me just as much, 'cause I'm sitting there saying to myself, "Well, I know how she feels." I've been there and I know. Like me and my sister, when we're up for the singers, I vote for her on all my votes. I have to, you know, because I can't vote for myself and she's my sister and she hasn't won that many. During the awards I really put on a show and didn't even know I was doing it. I told her, "Fix you hair pretty, now." I had her make these big rolls, and I was really telling her how to dress, because I said, "You're gonna get the award." I just knew she was going to get it. So, I went out in front. I was supposed to stand backstage to make sure I was back there if they called me on. But I knew she was going to get it so I went out in front to see her take her award. I was out there just jumping up and down and hollering, "That's my little sister; that's my little sister." I guess they got a lot of pictures of my jumping straight up and down. It embarassed me after everything was over with.

---

## Well, I always say if you don't like to be hurt yourself, then don't hurt nobody.

---

TURNER: Of all the awards you've gotten, which one are you most proud of?

LYNN: Entertainer of the Year.

TURNER: You were the first female to win the coveted award. What aspect of your career do you find most fulfilling?

LYNN: When I'm on stage singing and after the show is over with and I'm signing autographs.

TURNER: Do you have a motto that closely describes your philosophy to life, like "live and let live," or something like this, something you try to live by?

LYNN: Well, I always say if you don't like to be hurt yourself, then don't hurt nobody. I feel this way: I don't want to hurt him because I know how I'd feel if he hurt me. So I'd say if you don't want to be hurt then don't hurt anybody.

TURNER: Are you very critical of yourself?

LYNN: Very.

TURNER: I do appreciate you giving me this interview and taking this time.

LYNN: Thank you.

September 1979

*I'm country only because that*
*comes out of me no matter what*
*piece of material I'm doing. . . .*
*I think I'm a country performer*
*who can perform any type of*
*music.*
*—Barbara Mandrell*

BORN ON CHRISTMAS DAY in Houston, Texas, Barbara Mandrell was raised on music, and knew it would be her career someday. In the late 1970s, Barbara took the country music industry by storm, both through her number-one hit songs and her television show, where she was joined on stage by her sisters, Irlene and Louise.

Mandrell sings country, rhythm and blues, rock, and ballads, but in addition to her musical versatility, she is also a skilled businessperson and is involved in music publishing. Mandrell also manages to be a devoted wife and mother, and is raising a son and daughter in addition to managing her career.

# Barbara Mandrell

TURNER: We hear a lot and read a lot about the description of your music. Where do you see yourself in the music spectrum?

MANDRELL: I think I have my own style. I mean, I think there is a Barbara Mandrell way of approaching a piece of material. I'm country only because that comes out of me no matter what piece of material I'm doing, as I have done many times with old R & B songs or something. It still transcends that country flavor, I suppose, because that's a big part of me. I think I'm a country performer who can perform any type of music.

❖

> I like to try all things and hopefully there is a style that's my own and that's unique just to me.

❖

TURNER: You perform it well.

MANDRELL: Well, thank you. I don't know about that, but I like to try all things and hopefully there is a style that's my own and that's unique just to me.

TURNER: You are now reaping the rewards of success. How has all this success changed your self image?

MANDRELL: My life has not changed all that much, this year or last year. Other than one area, and that one area is a tough one because I can't fight it and I can't find a solution and that is *time*. A real bad enemy—it's frustrating, it's tiring. There never seems to be enough time to accomplish everything: family, career and me. Actually, people commend me often for being able to shuffle it around, but it's not me. I'm lucky. I'm surrounded with really good, capable people and that helps me a great deal. But if I'm feeling good about my career and pouring myself into my career, if I'm not careful I tend to have feelings of guilt about my family. Then if I'm with the family and neglecting my career, then I have a twinge of guilt that way.

139

And it seems like it never ends up something just for Barbara—just me. Fortunately for me, I enjoy my career enough and my family enough that that gives me enough satisfaction. Now sometimes I do things just for me.

TURNER: When you were a little girl, did you want to be a singer?

MANDRELL: No. When I was a little girl, and people would say, "What do you want to do when you grow up?" I would say "I want to be a jet pilot." I've always had this tremendous fascination with aviation. I just think it's terrific.

TURNER: A lot of press has been built up about your being a sex symbol. From what I read and understand, you are a homebody-type person. How comfortable do you feel with this type of image?

MANDRELL: Well, I'm flattered by it and that's an honest answer. I'm a woman who's been married several years, I have two children. Any woman who has been married for a long time and has children, I would think, would be flattered to be called a sex symbol. And if she tells you differently, she's probably not telling you the truth. All my life, including now, I've been very much a tomboy. I grew up very competitive with the boys in track and ball games. I was always rather petite. I was never the tallest in the class. I was mostly referred to as "cute." So it's nice as long as it has a wholesome sexy connotation.

TURNER: Who taught you showmanship, your father or your mother?

MANDRELL: Showmanship was really taught to me more by my father. You are talking about my career, aren't you?

TURNER: Right.

MANDRELL: Yes, more by my father and by the people I performed with as a child, some of the really greats in this business. I started right off the bat working with people like Gordon Cherry, Little Jimmy Dickens, Joe Maphis, the legendary country guitar player, and Tex Ritter. By the time I was thirteen I was touring with the Johnny Cash show. My father was the real ham and the real showman. He has been in the business either performing or behind the scenes all his life. My mother, on the other hand, has the book knowledge. Had my mother had the credentials, she could have taught certain college courses such as chord structure and music theory. She is a very knowledgeable woman. She was self-taught. She was a music teacher and she taught me to read music when I was five years old. The showmanship came from my father.

TURNER: The fact that you are so proficient in so many areas, does this intimidate the studio musicians?

MANDRELL: No, you'd be amazed at how many Nashville players really do read. More and more all the time. When we do television shows, they hire an orchestra to come in and they have twenty-some-odd pieces. Half of those are studio musicians who do the country session. They are reading

---

❖

## I like to think that I know how to entertain and put on a show,

❖

---

and they are playing what's written for them. You're better off doing a session to go with a head arrangement because it usually is in the groove more. Once that's laid in there, then the arranger comes in and writes the string parts and the string players come in and play what's written. But the guy that's playing the drums, the bass, the steel, the piano, and the steel guitar, he is laying it in there out of his head. I will work on head arrangements sometimes prior to a session; I do a little advance preparation. But a lot of things happen and are created right then and there. I don't think any of them are intimidated at all by me. They shouldn't be and they aren't. I think my band appreciates it because they know I can appreciate what they are doing. They are all exceptional. They know when they're really on and I know when they're really on.

TURNER: With your instrumental ability, has it opened doors that might have been closed to you as an entertainer?

MANDRELL: I'm sure it has, though now it really takes a back seat because of the hit records. I am not as proficient as I used to be. I used to play four hours a night, every night as a side man. My bread and butter now is the singing. But I think in terms of performing, entertaining people. That value of it, I think, is immeasurable.

TURNER: Tonight was one of the most well-received acts.

MANDRELL: I like to think that I know how to entertain and put on a show, and what I basically go for, and I have to do this as a whole, I mean the whole spectrum. Now, during the year I'll change a few things, but I play places about once a year. Obviously we can't go back to all the same places, but those that we do, we want the people to see something different and better than they saw last year. So we spend a great, great amount of time and effort revising the show and working out the new stuff. I try very hard to come on strong, hold that momentum as much as possible with a lot of variety within this period of time. Towards the last twenty minutes of the show, I'll just climb upward. I'm talking emotional. To me I feel that is the right kind of performance.

TURNER: Do you feel that maybe your approach to songs and your approach to an audience changes along with the show?

MANDRELL: I don't think I understand the question.

TURNER: Growing as an entertainer, do you think that you will change the arrangement?

MANDRELL: Well now, the records I maintain as close to what's on the record as possible. I may phrase a little different because I'm interpreting the song different. I try to maintain as close to that sound as possible because people expect that. I know I do; when I hear artists perform, that's the arrangement I want to hear. I think over a period of time, my experience hopefully does change my show, hopefully for the better. I may be innovative, more creative. I demand more of myself all the time.

TURNER: I have watched you on award shows and read magazine articles and I get the impression that you are not afraid to let your real emotions show.

MANDRELL: That's what living is all about. I'm also very happy when my family and other people do well for themselves. I remember one time R. C. won an award and I got real excited. I didn't know I was on television until I got home and saw the tape and I looked like Jack-In-The-Box. I was jumping up and down, up and down. I try to tell people constantly that I am human too. I'll pick out somebody I really admire, a celebrity or whatever, and I want them to be what I want them to be, but they are people—just people, just like I am. What's the old saying? We all put on our pants one leg at a time. A little plug there for women's lib. In most of the things I read about myself I'm depicted as just so sweet and wonderful. But you know, I get mad, too. I lose my temper, too, a lot, also I cry and I yell and I scream. My husband and I fight just like anybody else. I am just a person.

TURNER: How has this image helped in your rapport with your fans and with your audience?

MANDRELL: Well, I put my best foot forward when I hit the stage. I can't lie about that. Otherwise, I'd got out in my jeans or my housecoat.

---

## I put my best foot forward when I hit the stage. I can't lie about that.

---

My job is to do the best I can do, and I demand that of my men, which they freely give. Whether you're ill, tired, hungry, whatever, you give your all and nothing second-rate. So that, to a certain degree, could be interpreted to mean that there's a bit of phoniness about a performer. I'm very much the same person off stage as you see on stage. Basically, I'm a very bubbly, happy person. Obviously, I get more turned on when I'm on stage because I love what I'm doing at the time. I get just as excited at a ballgame or whatever I'm pouring myself into at the moment. I think what my fans see of me is really that real me.

TURNER: In doing television, do you have to be selective about what you will do?

MANDRELL: Yes, Fortunately there's a lot of good television. You'll hear many people say that's wrong. Usually though, I'm like Erma Bombeck: if I like it, it'll be off in three weeks. But there's a lot of good television, a lot of good tools to use on television. In recent times, I have been offered another weekly series on several occasions, which I politely declined. I'm not interested. I may do some specials in the future. That's a different story doing something like that. Films I'm very interested in. So far all it's been in seeing scripts and saying, "No, thank you." It is there again, that we very carefully constructed a product—me—for my fans, and they expect certain things from me. No matter what direction I go, it will be with them in mind. What they want to see me do.

April 1980

*I do believe, William, that in the beginning every performer or musician needs to find someone he can really look up to, whether it is a guitar player who plays like Chet Atkins or a singer who sings like Loretta Lynn. There is always somebody you pattern your life after until you find yourself.*
*—Ronnie Milsap*

WHEN RONNIE MILSAP was a student at Young Harris College, one of his professors was overheard saying, "Ronnie Milsap might make something of himself if he would leave that old music alone."

But Ronnie Milsap couldn't turn loose the thing in life he had come to love the most—music. He had aimed for a career as a lawyer, and while at Young Harris had received a scholarship to Emory University. But Ronnie never used the scholarship funds. The North Carolina native who had been born blind was to go instead to make music that was to light up the country music world and earn for him the industry's highest honors.

After a few years on the small club circuit, Milsap got his first big break in Nashville in 1973, when he joined the Charlie Pride road show. It wasn't long before his first hit, "I Hate You," was the number-one song in country music. The very next year he was named Male Vocalist of the Year by the CMA and won a Grammy as the leading male singer in country music.

However, contrary to his professor's prediction, "that old music" has earned Milsap country music's most coveted awards along with fame and fortune.

# Ronnie Milsap

TURNER: Early in your career you had the Ray Charles sound. Who had the nerve to stand up to you and say, "Hey, there is a Ray Charles—we need a Ronnie Milsap"?

MILSAP: Ray Charles himself. I met him in 1965 for the first time and then on subsequent occasions he heard some of my records. The guys told him this Milsap guy sounds just like Ray Charles. He said, in so many words, "Ronnie, find yourself, and in all due respect sing like Ronnie Milsap and not like Ray Charles." I do believe, William, that in the beginning every performer or musician needs to find someone he can really look up to, whether it is a guitar player who plays like Chet Atkins or a singer who sings like Loretta Lynn. There is always somebody you pattern your life after until you find yourself. I was going through that when I met Ray Charles.

TURNER: In reading your bio sheet, it said, "Ronnie decided to move from Memphis to Nashville, so he called Mr. Jack Johnson." Was it all that easy for you?

MILSAP: Well, William, it was a combination of things! I had known Charlie Pride for two or three years and Jack was managing Charlie. And I decided to move to Nashville so I got a job there working at the King of the Road Hotel. Then I called Jack and talked with him and Tom Collins, who has been with me all the way, co-producing my records. We put together a team of people—you know it takes hundreds of people to make it happen. Jack was very important in those early years in Nashville because he was a very good manager and he gave me a lot of very good directions.

TURNER: Was it hard to bridge the gap from blind institution to a sighted world?

MILSAP: It was! It sure was, because for thirteen years, kindergarten through high school, I went to a school for the blind. I went to Young Harris College and for the first time everything was visual. All the teaching programs at the school for the blind were geared around the braille system and geared around taking notes with either the tape recorder or with braille. At Young Harris it was all different; everything was written on a blackboard. I didn't know what was going on.

TURNER: How did music help you bridge this gap?

---

❖

it does take special drive, ambition, initiative, and courage to make doors open, because they don't open by themselves.

❖

---

MILSAP: Well, a couple of the guys I was rooming with, as well as everybody else at Young Harris, were very sensitive. They had never been around a blind person before or gone to school or had any exposure to anybody who was blind. I remember one day they went over to the next dormitory to do their laundry. I went with them and stopped off at the little parlor which had a piano in it. One of the guys said, "Oh, you play the piano," and I said, "Yes." So they went on to do their wash and when they came back I had the room full of people and they were all asking for requests. I was playing all of their favorite songs. All of a sudden, because of my music, and I'm thankful for it, I was popular in a sighted world. So all of a sudden I became one of the group because they were no longer afraid of me. I think probably without my music that bridge would have been a lot harder for me to cross. I also spent one summer in Gainesville with Fred and Inez Lotheridge and I got a job at the Elks Club. It gave me a chance to live in a "normal" world. I really had a good time hanging out and doing a lot of nothing.

TURNER: Where would you like to see your music take you in the future?

MILSAP: I would like to do key television things! We have talked about specials. It sounds real crazy, but I would really like to do a lot more of what I have been doing: recording records, playing personal appearances, turning out hit records, and trying to do hit shows. I bought a building in Nashville and it has its own recording studio. It was the first forty-track studio in the east. I look forward to spending more time at being more creative. The records are going to be a lot better. There is so much I could do. I am just sorting out possibilities. Publishers are wanting a book—I'm not so sure that I want to write a book at this point. Because, William, you know how it feels when you write a book: people think you have peaked or it is the end. Maybe there's a lot of interest in my life because it does take special drive, ambition, initiative, and courage to make doors open, because they don't open by themselves. There are all kinds of opportunities available to do all kinds of new things. But basically I would like to use the same focus I have always used on record and concerts.

TURNER: You mentioned your building in Nashville—how does this make you feel when you call your organization and the receptionist answers, "Ronnie Milsap Enterprises"?

MILSAP: It makes me *very, very* proud. Years ago, I had heard about "James Brown Enterprises," "Ray Charles Enterprises," and I thought, Boy *that sounds big.*" You know it really does. I got to Nashville and things started happening so fast. I have had a lot of help, William, and a lot of people are responsible for making it happen. It is a team effort and I am very proud of it. We have a good office staff. We have people who are in charge of different parts of my career. They all do a good job. A whole bunch of folks do a good job.

TURNER: You have worked so hard in achieving success. Have you had time to enjoy it?

MILSAP: Not enough! I think this happens to a lot of entertainers. I have known Stevie Wonder since he was fifteen. I remember watching Stevie every single day, and it seemed that he was always writing or recording a song or working a concert. And I wondered the same thing: when does he ever have a chance to enjoy all this? But, strange enough, you enjoy doing this so much that just having a chance to work and produce brings the fulfillment that you want. I'm not so sure I know any other way to enjoy life. If I stopped playing and tried to do something else, I would be scrambling back to music again. Just by participating and doing what I do every day gives me all the enjoyment I'd ever need.

September 1978

A SELF-DESCRIBED "third generation rodeo brat," Oklahoma-born and bred Reba McEntire's musical roots run deep. When she was younger, she accompanied her parents on the rodeo circuit, and would often sing with her family from the back of their pickup truck.

After a decade of professional barrel racing, McEntire turned to a musical career. While singing the National Anthem in Oklahoma City, she was heard by Red Steagall who offered to produce a demo for her.

McEntire took him up on his offer and landed her first recording contract in 1975. She now has many hit records to her credit.

*I want to stay in country because I'm country. I don't think I could walk into a pop audience and say I'm rock and roll. I talk country enough to where I don't think I would be very convincing.*
*—Reba McEntire*

# Reba McEntire

TURNER: How would you describe your music to someone who had never heard it before?

McENTIRE: I would describe my records as kind of like a smorgasbord. There's lots of variety. We do fast, slow, deep, hardcore country, a little bit of rock and roll: a great variety. We try to have a lot of fun on our show and our music displays that.

TURNER: In your opinion, what makes a great country music entertainer?

---

People in the music industry who have had longevity are those personalities that can and do relate to an audience.

---

McENTIRE: Someone who can relate to the people, and can sing a song that everybody can relate to. The personality, I think, really makes it. The song may make it for a year-long career, but the personality, the warmness, that friendly down-to-earth type of person will probably last for more than five, ten, or fifteen years. People in the music industry who have had longevity are those personalities that can and do relate to an audience. I don't think it has so much to do with talent or being a great singer. I think it has to do with relating to the public and giving the public exactly what they want.

TURNER: What do you look for when you are selecting a hit record?

McENTIRE: Something that everybody can relate to. Here lately I have been trying to figure out what the kids would be singing, and memorizing. When "Swinging" came out, all the little kids knew it by heart immediately. I'm trying to get something that the kids can relate to and that the older people will relate to also. It's tough. If anyone knows the solution, I want to meet them.

TURNER: It is a well known fact that you are a third generation rodeo-type family. Is family tradition and heritage important to you?

MCENTIRE: Very much so. Last night we played the Grand Ole Opry, I wore my western skirts with the fringe and rhinestones, and my western cowboy boots. Of course, I wear my belt buckle at all times. This portrays the cowboy image. I sing the national anthem at the National Finals Rodeo in Oklahoma City each and every year.

TURNER: Still?

MCENTIRE: Yes, I started in 1974. Gary Gist gave me this buckle along with John Smith, and so I wear this as the cowboy part of my show. Even though I've got the flash and all this stuff, I always wear my belt.

TURNER: How did the training on the rodeo circuit help prepare you for a career in the music industry? Has it opened doors for you that might not have otherwise been opened?

MCENTIRE: Well, a lot of the people in the rodeo business hired us to do shows, but mainly more than anything I am used to traveling. I know how to read a road map and I know how to sleep very well on the bus. I was always sleeping in a pickup or a car going down the road and I adjust very well to times. If you've got to get up early this morning, you can sleep late the next morning. You go to bed late; you go to bed early. I'm getting to where I can adjust real well. It is tough. It's a hard life to travel and then go home and everybody at the house is going to bed at 10:30 and you're used to staying up to 1:00 in the morning and sleeping till noon. So you have to adjust. I've learned to do that by rodeoing, and then also in singing. It's kinda similar.

TURNER: One thing that I noticed in an article I read was the fact that you said you really liked traveling. Most of the people say that traveling is the bad part about the entertainment business, and I found it interesting that you would enjoy it.

MCENTIRE: Most of the times. The worst part to me is nothing to do in a town where you have to stay in a motel room. If it is a boring part of the country, I can always catch up on my sleep.

TURNER: What does the love of animals and rodeos tell us about Reba McEntire?

MCENTIRE: Oh, I really don't know the answer to that question. I like nature, that's why we still live out in the country. I have always lived in the country, and we have lots of cattle and horses and dogs and cats. I love nature.

TURNER: If I were to stop someone in the street in Chochie and say Reba McEntire, how would they respond to that?

McENTIRE: She grew up there. A little mean, red-headed, freckled face kid. Always pulling pranks and running her horse too fast, that kind of thing.

TURNER: Is it still a rural area?

McENTIRE: Yes. It is right on a major highway, and is down to four or five families now. It is just a little town. There was never over thirty people there in the time I lived there. Before I lived there, there was a rock crusher, a bank, a filling station, and all that kind of stuff. The rock crusher pulled out; so did the railroad station and the bank and all the other things. There's just a small community there now.

TURNER: You were once quoted as having said, "The best way I know to show off my singing voice is by singing a Patsy Cline song". What did you mean by this?

McENTIRE: Patsy Cline was always the best singer in the world to me. Emotion, volume, and talent in portraying the song. If I get close to her style, I feel like I have showed off my voice the best. Because she was the best and she picked the best and hardest songs to sing.

TURNER: Who has been the greatest influence on your music?

McENTIRE: Mama and Patsy Cline. Mama because she was always teaching us kids to sing and started us out; Patsy Cline because I schooled myself listening to her and heard something there that I was always striving to achieve: the control, emotion and such. Mother was always there to correct me and Pete and Suzy, my brother and sister, when we were singing three-part harmony. And we would always get into fights about who was on whose part. Mama was always in there helping us out. She was always the referee, encouraging us and taking us when we had to go sing. She still is very much the critic. She was the one who brought me down to Nashville to do the demonstration tape when Red Steagall first discovered me. So I would say Mama is the biggest part of my musical career.

TURNER: You credit Red Steagall as having discovered you?

McENTIRE: Yes.

TURNER: How did that come about?

McENTIRE: I sang the national anthem at the National Finals Rodeo in Oklahoma City in 1974, just to help out with the expenses because I was always up there watching the barrel racing at the finals. I met Red Steagall and he later told someone that he knew that anybody who could sing the national anthem and who was red-headed couldn't be all bad. So mama asked him if he could help me and Pete and Suzy get into the music business, but he thought that three at one time would be pretty tough. Pete was rodeoing and had a bunch of cattle at the time, and Suzy was still in high school. So he took me to Nashville and cut a demonstration tape and that's where it all got started.

TURNER: That was back in what, 1974?

McENTIRE: We cut the demonstration tape back in March of 1975. That summer I went back home and tried to forget it. He told me to have lots of patience and don't call him, he'd call me. Then he called me and said, "Let's go back down; I think we've got somebody that is interested," and it was Mercury. Glen Keener was the producer there, and he listened to the tape and we signed up November of 1975, eleven months after I had met Red.

TURNER: I read that you worked checking government leases on oil rights. Is that right?

McENTIRE: Yes, that was after I got married. That was November of 1975 when we signed up, and then, of course, I went back and sang at the finals, and I was still running barrels too. I got into the GRA, which is the professional end of the Women's Barrel Racing Association. It was Girls' Rodeo Association at the time. Now it's WRPA, Women's Professional Rodeo Association. I got into that and was running barrels on Pete's horse. I was winning pretty well. I filled my two permits real quickly. At the first two rodeos I went to, I also met Charlie Battles. He and Pete were real good friends and rodeoed together. Well, me and Charlie fell in love and we got married in June, 1976. About that time I started checking records for an oil lease company. I was singing whenever I could and I was having one job every two or three months. It finally started picking up and I got a little bit better. Five years ago I got a band together.

TURNER: The entire world has really opened up to country music. What impact has this had on your career?

MCENTIRE: The urban cowboy movement really did help because everybody started wearing cowboy outfits which I had been wearing all the time.

TURNER: You weren't out of style anyway, were you?

MCENTIRE: No. So I changed just to be different, because I didn't want to be dressed like everyone else. It really did help country and western music. It got us into markets where we weren't even accepted before: New York and northeast mainly, California and places where they didn't have county music before. It has just opened a lot of doors. It helped me at a time when I was just breaking in. I had my very first top-ten single at the time. It just kind of prolonged and boosted the country music field. It helped all of us.

TURNER: Getting back to your job before you went into the business. At what point did you say you had made it now and could leave your job back in Oklahoma?

MCENTIRE: Well, I think the reason that I quit the job back in Oklahoma was that singing jobs were getting better and I wasn't going to be able to stay there and work. You had to work every day or just be laid off, and I didn't want to keep them on the string. I wanted to say, "I'll either work for you or I'll go sing." So I thought I had better go sing and do them right.

TURNER: Some say the popularity of country music is due in part to the fact that it has a beginning, a middle and an end, like a novel. What are your feelings about that?

MCENTIRE: That's true. For instance, we have a song that's going to be on the new album that Bill and Sharon Rice wrote. I heard "Demo Tape" and fell in love with it, but it didn't have an ending. What happens: do they get married, do they break up, does he send her back or what? Jerry Kennedy took the song back to them and they wrote another whole verse and gave it back to us. It was okay and they all lived happily ever after. Yes, I agree with you one hundred percent, I want to hear an ending.

TURNER: When you have experienced success in one area, is it better to move into another area or to remain true to the tested market?

MCENTIRE: Everyone has their own opinion of that, of course. I want to stay in country because I'm country. I don't think I could walk into a pop audience and say I'm rock and roll. I talk country enough to where I don't think I would be very convincing.

TURNER: There are few quality female acts existing in country music today. Do you think it is harder for a female act to break in than it is a male act?

McENTIRE: No, I think if they're good it's not. Everybody keeps telling me that, but I don't feel like I've had that much trouble. I just feel that there are certain things that you have got to have for the public to accept you. They always say that clubs are harder for a woman to play than for a man because the women in the audience get jealous if the men are watching the woman. That may be true, but I sure wouldn't discourage any woman trying to get into the business. I hope they do. The more the merrier.

TURNER: This is a quote that I read: "You can be as nice as you want to be, wild witch of the west, but until you prove yourself, you will be a nobody." How do you prove yourself?

McENTIRE: By working hard, and paying your dues. If feel like I have finally paid my dues because I've been just as homesick as thunder and cried on the phone to Charlie saying, "I want to come home." But he'd say, "You've got two or three more days out there and you've got to do them." I'd say, "I don't want to do them; I want to come home to see my mama." Charlie would say, "No, you have got to stay out there. I'll fly out there if you want me to." If I had got my first number-one record in 1977, it wouldn't have meant half as much to me as it does now. At the Grand Ole Opry, people like Bill Anderson and Billy Walker come up to me and say congratulations, it's good to see that someone like you finally got a number one record. That means more to me than one hundred and ten number-one records, because I admire those people. They're people who have fought and worked hard and have made it, and just to be on the same stage with them means a lot to me.

TURNER: Where would you like for your career to take you?

McENTIRE: To bigger and better things. What they are I don't know. I want a better stage show, more television, that recognition I don't have yet: people just walking up on the street and knowing who I am. The visual contact isn't there. I was in Maryville, Indiana and someone said, "I thought you had long, black hair." No, I've got short red hair and freckles. There's just that visual aspect. They don't really know who I am yet.

TURNER:  What keeps you going?

McENTIRE:  The good Lord up above and only Him.

June 1983

THE OAK RIDGE BOYS have evolved over the years from a gospel group to a best selling country band, which has successfully bridged the gap into contemporary pop.

The band now includes members Bill Golden, who has been an Oak Ridge Boy for almost twenty years, Duane Allen, Joe Bonsall, and Richard Sterban.

Although the switch to rocking country songs such as "Elvira" and "Bobbie Sue" has alienated some of their gospel fans, the songs have also introduced the Boys to new audiences throughout the world. (William Lee Golden has left the Oaks and is currently pursuing a solo career.)

*. . . I feel like I grow from being around so many people, so many different things, so many different sources. Musically, I grow from those who are close in the circle of the twelve that we travel with.*
*—Bill Golden*

# William Lee Golden

TURNER: Where did the name The Oak Ridge Boys come from?

GOLDEN: It came from Oak Ridge, Tennessee. It all started at the atomic energy plant during the Second World War. There was a group of country singers and musicians that had a four-part singing group, and they were allowed inside the atomic energy plant and compounds to sing for the engineers and scientists and the people who were under the project and development of the atomic bomb. They would sing to these people on Sundays and special occasions, and were very popular there. So then they took on the name the Oak Ridge Quartet. They traveled mainly through the Southeast for several years, and kept branching out further and further until they got up to touring all over the United States and several other foreign countries. They were touring from 100 to 250 days a year, every year.

TURNER: Are any of the original members still with the group?

GOLDEN: No, we were all fans of the group. I know it affected me that way. I was in a group in south Alabama and I heard their albums on Warner Brothers, this was in 1962, and I was attracted to them. I like rock and roll, country, gospel; I like all music. But there was something about their albums that really turned me on. It made me want to be a part of that organization and to try to get the singing part that I now do. I saw them around and heard their records and thought that they should be on net-work TV. So it took a long time and a lot of hard work and believing in each other.

There were changes over the years, guys would drop out and others would join the group. I came here nineteen years ago and there have been several changes since then. Our lead singer, Duane Allen—he's from Paris, Texas, or rather Taylortown, Texas, which is right outside of Paris—he's been with us seventeen years, and Joe Bonsall, the guy who sings the tenor—he's from Philadelphia, Pennsylvania—he's been here about nine years, and Richard Sterban, the bass singer, is from Camden, New Jersey. He's been here about eleven years. He worked with Elvis for two years before he joined us. That was in the late sixties.

TURNER: At what point in time did you decide, I'm going to change, I'm going to sing country rather than gospel?

GOLDEN: It was kind of a tradition. The Oak Ridge Boys were primarily gospel when I went with the group. That's what we did, we toured the big concerts and put on performances, concerts and shows all over the country. We won four Grammy awards in gospel music. It was like we had had such a great team together, we were at the top of one field and there was nowhere to go to expand. It's either move ahead and reach bigger goals and greater goals or either go down. So we decided to expand on our talents and see what all we could do with what talent we had as a team and as a group. This group has that special spirit and now we've finally got here, so it was kind of a high-risk situation. A few years ago, we decided to start venturing in the country direction, so we went to Jim Halsey's agency out of Tulsa, and it has worked out for a fantastic future because he's super; he's in the right business. He was an honest guy, and that is what I appreciate about him. He never built us up for some situation and then it never come through. Any time that he even said that there was a possibility that something could happen, it seems like it always happened. We signed with him and things have come along since then. Then we moved to ABC and sparked off the *Y'all Come Back Saloon* album, which was the perfect thing to break the stigma that most of the American public and most of the people around the country had of the name Oak Ridge Boys. They had that gospel stigma, that kind of helped break it away because of the controversy and talk.

TURNER: Was this the point in time that you decided you would like to be called the Oaks rather than the Oak Ridge Boys?

GOLDEN: Well, I think that was the developing time. It's a thing that a lot of our friends and fans were tagging on us. It will probably develop into a situation. There was an attempt made at it one time when we first went with Columbia Records, but there was never enough volume to kind of pull it off.

TURNER: In changing from gospel to country, did you encounter any difficulties or any adverse reactions?

GOLDEN: Yes, because you had to put together a new show weekly and start hunting for original material. We had to spice it up gradually, and there was a point there that we were doing half country and half gospel. As the new albums would come out, they would build our records up more to today's music and today's albums that we are recording. Our manager put us in the hands of some of the most qualified people in the music business to find us materials. They found the materials and musicians and arranged all of that for us. Almost everything is from other writers who are young or people who they have respect for.

TURNER: Do you do any writing yourself?

GOLDEN: No sir, I don't write; I am a very poor writer. In fact, my secretary majored in journalism. So I really feel awkward writing. I can't seem to get down on paper what I mean.

TURNER: How about the influence of gospel in today's music. Can you detect any influence that gospel might have had on today's sound?

GOLDEN: Yes sir. I think it had a strong effect. Gospel music is a music of the release and expression of emotions. So I think that is a thing that you acquire and develop by getting into a lot of those high-energy situations. You get filled with the music and the music gives you a feeling of wanting to sing, wanting to move. I think it's a carryover of harmonies and singing with feeling rather than just singing technically. Some of our guys have had technical training. It seems like when they get to the point, they sing with feelings and expressions, and when we get into it, the people get into it. It's kind of contagious.

TURNER: When you made this changeover, were you ever told that you would not make it as a country act, or were you encouraged to make the changeover?

GOLDEN: There was a lot of skepticism, mainly in the gospel music industry. There were certain people who would say little things, but they were the type of people who were always talking about everything and everybody else. I never worried that much about them. We were doing what we felt was right, because it's a business. We are professional singers; that is how we get our income. I never joined the church, so I never told anyone that I was there for any reason other than the enjoyment of singing. So that is what it was to me, a great feeling, and I enjoy the feeling of singing.

TURNER: Do you think any other quartets will join suit, now that they can see that you have been so successful?

GOLDEN: They already are.

TURNER: Do you think the time will come in country music where there is a tremendous demand for quartet singing?

GOLDEN: I think that the timing for harmonies could not be any more perfect. It hasn't been in pop music since way back in the forties. I grew up in the country on a twelve hundred-acre farm. I was raised on plowing tractors, working around people, picking cotton, the blacks the whites out in the field working together. I was one of the slow pickers, too interested in playing and having a good time.

---

❖

> I grew up in the country on a twelve hundred-acre farm. I was raised on plowing tractors, working around people, picking cotton, the blacks the whites out in the field working together.

❖

---

TURNER: What would you say has been the biggest influence on your career?

GOLDEN: I think it's a combination of things. There are certain highs that you reach, certain plateaus, certain levels, stature that you're working in certain prestigious situations. You have to obtain a certain amount of stature in order to have the opportunity to be there because those things are great highs to me. To experience and be there, I feel like I grow from being around so many people, so many different things, so many different sources. Musically, I grow from those who are close in the circle of the twelve that we travel with.

TURNER: Is there an event that stands out as a high point of your career?

GOLDEN: There are a lot of events. I think that one of the things that had a greater impact on most of our lives was a trip to the Soviet Union. You actually go behind a restricted area to go there and perform for those people who really don't understand English. You have to create some kind of a communication by giving them yourself and your feeling that you are there to represent the good, not the bad. You are there in peace and friendship. We wanted to play our music and sing our harmony. We do it all together as one because we have worked together and played together and have shared together. To go there and experience and see their culture and the point of development that their country is at today is just incredible. The freedom that America has of allowing people to come from one step of society and excel and become great in another step of society. The freedom of stimulating people to succeed and giving them opportunities to succeed is marvelous. I am more impressed with our country.

---

## I don't regret anything that I have ever done.

---

TURNER: Do you have any immediate plans to go back?

GOLDEN: No, we have turned down tours because of financial situations. There was a lot of money involved—we would have had to turn down a lot of money here to have gone. At that point, it was necessary to stay here and make some right steps. Every day we have either been recording or doing television in some way. We very seldom have days even when we are off.

TURNER: Is there anything that you wish you had done, but you have not done?

GOLDEN: I don't regret anything that I have ever done. If I did everything over, I would do it basically the same. I have no regrets. I have a lot of great memories, some of the highest. I feel more fortunate than anybody I know. I really don't have any regrets.

TURNER: Do you think that you are in direct competition with the Statler Brothers?

GOLDEN: No, not at all. They paved the way in one respect, in country music. They showed country music long ago that four part harmony could be commercial. I think that they're good singers. They're great guys and very good friends of ours. We worked a television show with them and we spent more time talking to them in their dressing room and cutting up than we did anybody's.

TURNER: Who determines we will record this or we will not record this?

GOLDEN: Rod Chancey, our producer. He does a lot of independent work and does a lot of work for ABC, too. We select songs. We go in sometimes for three hours for a listening session. We listen to maybe forty or fifty songs and we might get four or five possibilities. Then we'll come back another time and listen to them a little more and get a few more possibilities, and sometimes you have listened to about two hundred songs to finally get the tune that you want. You can go through and say, "Well, I don't like that."

TURNER: When you start to pick a song, do you think commercialism when you start to record?

GOLDEN: Yes, I think so. When you think being commercial—things that other people can sing along, they're good feeling songs and you feel like they're kind of unique.

TURNER: What type of song do you like to sing best, ballads or tempo?

GOLDEN: Probably ballads with me, because I probably sing a little more country than some of the other members.

TURNER: What type of show do you prefer doing?

GOLDEN: I like concerts in stadiums or coliseums. We're new at some of these things so we're liking them right now. We are seeing a tremendous growth in attendance, sales and everything. A light and sound company that we hired goes on the road with us and they work the dates that we work. In most situations, we're doing a big light show. We're getting more into the production thing. It takes a lot of work. Sometimes the hardest crowds to sing to are Nevada crowds in Vegas. They're sitting there eating or they have just finished eating—they're hard to sing to.

TURNER: What makes up an ideal audience in your opinion?

GOLDEN: When you've got the representation of most types of people. I like it from the kids to the old people and everybody in between. Especially to be exciting for teenagers and young married couples and those type people: people who are out to have a good time, people who work and have responsibilities. They're out to forget about their jobs and their hassles—they're out to stomp their feet, clap their hands, sing along and get involved with the music. Our kind of music is a mixture of pop, country, and gospel. I don't know what it is; I don't know what they're going to wind up calling us.

TURNER: Do you have a label that you tag your music?

GOLDEN: Mainly progressive country.

TURNER: Do you feel like a country entertainer?

GOLDEN: Well, I am and Duane is, but Joe and Richard, they're big-city boys. They're northern boys and we're southern boys. So we are completely halved up.

TURNER: How do you get psyched up for a show when you feel horrible?

GOLDEN: A lot of times we listen to music on the bus. We have one of these videocassettes; we get to watch videos of other entertainers and have a good time. We enjoy each other; we all like each other. We get along well. There are never any major problems, any major fusses or fights. We're like a bunch of loud and rowdy kids sometimes. Everybody has to let off steam, whether they're young, old, or whatever. It's kind of like major league sports. We're major league entertainment. We go out there and give the people something exciting, get into it and do a good enough job and get enough energy going to get the people up out of their seats two or three times. I might jump out of my seat two or three times during a major league game, but Joe and Richard, they're up and down like yoyos all the night. They're great fans. They grew up around Philadelphia and would go to see the 76ers and the Phillies. Those teams are having good years and they're just cheering every day and it's entertaining to be on the road and involved with those fans.

TURNER: Everyone gets down and out and depressed at times. How do you cope with this, when you get down and depressed?

GOLDEN: I think everyone copes with their own expressions, feelings, emotions and depressions. We kind of help each other. If we see one of the other guys getting down, we do things to cheer him up. It works both ways. If the guy is bothered with something, we allow him to be by himself. There are never any real serious problems other than normal daily depressions that any twelve people you put together in one confined area would have. You've got all those different personalities working closely together and living closely, and everybody is bouncing off of each other. That's kind of how we grow—off of each other.

TURNER: What is the wildest thing that has ever happened to you in your travel?

GOLDEN: I don't know. There have been so many wild things that have happened. It would be hard to sit here and tell you the wildest.

TURNER: Probably the most exciting would have been your trip behind the Iron Curtain, wouldn't it?

GOLDEN: Yes, as far as myself. I didn't study as well in school as I should have, so it was interesting to go and see and feel and grasp.

TURNER: When you were growing up on a farm in Alabama, did you want to become an entertainer at an early age?

GOLDEN: I think so because I've played and sung ever since I was a small kid. My sister used to play. She played the mandolin and I played the guitar. We played and sang together. I started in grammar school playing the guitar, and as I got older and got into high school, I played and sang, but my interest got more on outside things, the girls and things. I was not developing as fast on the guitar as I thought I should and I got lazy with it, so I just kind of got away from it. But I kept up the singing, I enjoyed singing.

TURNER: What does the group want for itself in the future?

GOLDEN: To grow and go on. To provide a good situation to do something good and to be around good people. We're here to make at least comfortable salaries to support whatever our needs are. We have a big recording studio in Nashville. We own two office buildings there. We want to explore some other things in television and other things in concert productions. We're getting involved with a lot of creative people around us who have a lot of great ideas that we would never have dreamed of. They can see what characters and talents and things that we might have that they can play on. Hopefully, we can develop in a lot of areas, to keep going forward and try to put out quality work. Our whole team works hard. If you don't work hard, that's when we get most depressed. If you do a bad show and you can't quite get into it, then the crowd can't get into it. There isn't that hot, hot communication there. We feel like we get more depressed at those times, when it seems like we're having problems getting a crowd aroused.

TURNER: Is there anything in an interview that you have not been asked that you would have liked for them to have asked after they left?

GOLDEN: No. There aren't any other projects other than our careers and our business and people involved in it, where it can go and what it can do.

Hopefully, it can help a lot of people as well as help us. Our organization includes about twenty-five people with or around us, plus our management company. Everybody is growing and it feels good.

June 1979

*I'm not much on writing about political things of the day or the social things. . . . I usually go for the things that are the basic strands of the human emotions . . . the hurt times, the good times, the blue moods, and the good moods.*

*—Eddie Rabbitt*

W HEN EDDIE RABBITT, the New Jersey-born son of Irish immigrants, stepped off a Greyhound bus onto the streets of Nashville in 1967, he walked into a life of exploitation at the hands of music promoters. He saw others reap glory and fortune with his songs, and there was little he could do about it.

Most people don't remember Rabbitt for the first great song he wrote. That was because a Nashville producer arranged for Elvis Presley to hear "Kentucky Rain" before Rabbitt recorded it. Elvis wanted the song, and he usually got what he wanted.

But by 1972, Rabbitt was singing his own songs and the country music world was on the verge of "Rabbitt Fever." He has now written over three hundred and fifty songs for his own publishing firm, including numerous number-one hits.

# Eddie Rabbitt

TURNER: You were in Nashville for a few years with mediocre success. You had some good times and some bad times, I am sure. How did this affect your music in general?

RABBITT: When I got off to myself or with my writing partner Evan Stevens to write, there are no good or bad times. It's just a good thing happening right there. I don't know if it has affected it or not. Everything has happened so quickly. I've always felt about the music the way I do. I love to do it and there's nothing to stop me from doing it. I've just got a drive to make music.

TURNER: Do you think your early days helped to set the mood for today's type of music?

---

## I've just got a drive to make music.

---

RABBITT: They could have, they really could have. That's interesting. I've never thought about it from that angle before. See, I come from up around New Jersey and grew up with a lot of different influences—country, rock and roll—and I think that's sorta of what I write in my songs. It's kind of a mixture of all those things.

TURNER: Do you feel you draw on your past experiences for ideas?

RABBITT: Oh yeah, sure, imaginary and real. I'm sure they are all mixed in together.

TURNER: When you set out to write a song, can you visualize what it is going to sound like before you put anything on the tape recorder?

RABBITT: Yeah, I usually can almost see it, if I know it's going to be a ballad or up-tempo. I can almost see or hear it in my head how a song will sound when it is finished. I strive to get it like that record I hear in my head. That's the hardest thing, getting the hit you hear in your head.

167

TURNER: In your music, can you go back and recreate a song or do you have to move forward?

RABBITT: I'm not sure I understand the question.

TURNER: Let's take "Kentucky Rain," a big hit for both you and Elvis. Could you go back and duplicate that type of song or have the ideas of the music world and nation changed?

RABBITT: I don't know—that story is not too stuck into a time period as far as that goes. It's about a guy who travels the back roads of Kentucky looking for a girl who got up and left him in the middle of the night. I suppose you could write about that today or fifty years ago or fifty years from now. I'm not much on writing about political things of the day or the social things of a particular period of time. I usually go for the things that are the basic strands of the human emotions, that have always been and probably always will be: the hurt times, the good times, the blue moods, and the good moods.

TURNER: Do you feel that Nashville is more receptive to creativity now as opposed to the time when you first went there?

RABBITT: They may be more acceptable to a wider range of music and ideas than when I first went there. When I first went to Nashville, it was pretty much a country mecca for country music. Someone coming to Nashville with songs that were, say, folk songs or more rock, might not have found many outlets as there are today. There has been an influx of people in the last few years; since I have been there, people from all parts of the country have been coming in and slowly adding to Nashville and changing a little bit of what used to be country music. Most of the people ten to twenty years ago came from the south, southeast, or southwest and gravitated to Nashville. Now you've got people coming from everywhere to Nashville and they bring a little bit of where they came from with them, and naturally that's going to change the feel of things and the songs that are produced and the type of things that come out.

TURNER: One of your songs that I liked a lot is the "Song Of Ireland." What prompted you to write that particular song?

RABBITT: My dad and my mom came from Ireland. I have a great feeling for that heritage, even though I've never been to Ireland. I grew up with letters from relatives over there and that whole history is really a part of me. When I wrote "Song of Ireland," my thoughts were that there are probably a lot of people like me out there who have roots sorta in where they were born, but have roots again maybe in a heritage of their people. I've never been to Ireland, even though I feel that if my parents had never come here, I'd have been an Irishman in the true sense of the word. I would probably be sitting in a pub somewhere talking about "me day's work." So these are some of the same songs my dad played on the violin when I was growing up. There is one song in particular that I liked. It's the one that's on the record. I left a little space at the beginning and end of the record for this tune which I love called "Mist in the Meadow." I had my dad come in and play it on the record. He was tickled pink; he was very proud.

---

❖

## I write music, I don't write country music or rock music; I write music.

❖

---

TURNER: Burt Bacharach once said, "I find it more challenging to create a song and more fulfilling than to perform it. I feel that anyone can recreate it after the writer has created it." How do you feel about this statement?

RABBITT: I like both aspects of it real well. The writing part, I really love. But I also like getting out there and performing with my band for the people, and having the people like what you have created back there in your head. And here you are out there making something manifest, something that was just a thought and then getting maybe five thousand people to react to it. To me that's quite a thing too.

TURNER: Why is your music not labeled?

RABBITT: Well, they are labeling me pretty good here lately with some of the new records. I tell a lot of people, who are hardcore country and don't think some of my songs are country, that I write music, I don't write country music or rock music; I write music. I like all kinds of music. There are classical pieces that I like. There are rock and country pieces that I like. I learned a lot of chords when I was a kid. I learned minor chords and diminishing chords; to leave them out of a song just because I'm afraid that in a particular type of music it won't be played—to me that's a crime. If I hear a melody in my head going to that minor chord or to that diminishing chord, I go there. Maybe the idea is not about drinking or broken marriage or something like that; that doesn't necessarily mean that I'm not going to write it. I write about what I feel and see out there. I don't go around all day, when I am writing a song thinking country song, country song. I love country music and it is really a basic part of me. I grew up with a lot of country music, but even more than that, I grew up with music. I think to write only one kind of music would be a little closed minded. To me, for people to get stuck in this kind of thing where if it's not country then I don't like it is kinda closed minded. I kinda like each individual thing as it appears to me, and if it doesn't sound good then I don't like it. If it sounds good, then I like it. There are things the Bee Gees have done, that probably a lot of country music fans hate, but I think they are wonderful pieces of music. I think to not like something just because it is rock and roll is not right.

---

❖

> I grew up with a lot of country music, but even more than that, I grew up with music.

❖

---

TURNER: Your appeal is very diverse. You have a universal following.

RABBITT: If people have listened to me from the first album I ever did, I have had things that were more than just country. They've just been a little bit more. Now that we're getting a little bit of success and recognition, they jump on our latest album or record and say, "Hey what's this?" All they need to do is to go back to the very first album I put out. I had songs on the first couple of albums which were not any particular classification of music. They were just entertainment.

TURNER: I hear your name come up often as being the heir apparent for the position Kenny Rogers has occupied in the music world for so long. Are you taking precautions to make sure that you ascend into this position?

RABBITT: That's the first time I have heard this statement. I guess what they are saying is that in the big middle of the road there in the sky, that there's a pretty good place for me. Well! I hope they are right, because I would rather have ten thousand at a concert than to have two thousand. Because you are getting to more people and can have a bigger show, and you're making more money—it is just better all the way around. To be honest with you, and it may sound a little corny, but everything has happened so fast, I'm still kind of amazed at what's happening. I really don't try to think about it a whole lot because I am afraid it will go away.

TURNER: I was reading in some of your press material that some of your friends, when you first went to Nashville, reached popularity with the masses of people earlier than you did, but their careers seemed to have peaked. There are indications that yours will last longer. How much planning goes into your career?

RABBITT: Yeah, they were there before I ever got to Nashville. You never know, things may turn around and I might be out looking for a job next year. My career is pretty much well thought-out. I have some really fine managers out in L.A. and we really talk quite a bit about what we're going to do. We make plans six months to a year ahead of time about things we will do. I agree with you; I think we're going to be traveling down the road for quite a long time. I think our music—not to say someone else's won't—will last quite a while. I think ten years from now I will probably be doing a show out there on the road. At least I hope so.

TURNER: When you write a song would you rather write one which has long-lasting ability or one that would sell a million copies overnight?

RABBITT: I like to write both of those kinds. A song I wrote called "Suspicions" was literally written in less than ten minutes. That may sound like a P.R. story to you, but it's true. We were in the studio recording an album. The musicians took a break, and "Suspicions" was written in less than ten minutes. While the guys were gone, David, myself and a piano player sat down and got to doodling around with the piano. We wasn't even trying to write, we were just kinda up and full of music. After about a minute of playing around with the melody and these lyrics, I told Pete, our engineer, to turn on the tape so at least we could save what we had gotten and maybe we would get back to it later and write it. Well, the moment he turned on that tape the drummer walked in and the piano player, who was there, was playing and I was singing. The three of us did just kinda like a little take on this tune just to save it. Well, the drums, the piano, and the lyrics that you hear on the record were what happened at that moment. We only changed two words in the lyrics from that take that we took after we spent thirty seconds kinda doodling around. Two words we changed in the whole lyrics. That is amazing to me—I had never done that before. The piano and drums on there were taken just like that. In fact, I told our engineer, Pete,—I thought for sure he had put it on a two-track just to save it—"Gee Pete, I wish we had that on a twenty-four-track because the piano, drums, and the lyrics on that sounded just great." He said, "It's on a twenty-four," and I said, "All right." So the guys came back from supper and they put their part on. The song is about four minutes and twenty seconds, I think, and we only spent a minute before from the time it was born: from the time the first couple of notes were hit. It was such a good-feeling song all the way through the session and everything, that when it came down to it we just put it out as a single. It was kind of a magic song from the beginning. It was really a great feeling.

TURNER:  In your opinion, who influenced your style the most?

RABBITT:  Well, as long as I can remember, my dad played music around the house, so I'm sure there's a little of that Irish in me. I listened to various artists growing up. I was never hooked on anyone in particular. I guess you might say a few people like Jim Reeves, Hank Williams, Johnny Cash, Roy Orbison, Buddy Holly, and Elvis, those artists during that period influenced me quite a bit because I was listening to them. I never had a real strong hero or one individual person. I like individual works, whatever turned me on at the time.

TURNER:  You once said that country music is like a soap opera. It's stories that relate to the people right on the street. How are you going to continue to relate to these people on the street and get their stories now that you are a superstar?

RABBITT:  I guess you just have to watch yourself and not fall into that trap. Just a few days ago we spent $15–20 for something, I can't remember what it was, and it seemed like an outrageous price. I was talking to my road manager about it and I said, "Hey, I've still got street pockets, man. That's a lot of money." I still know what a dollar is. I think I'm the kind of guy who remembers how the hard times were with my family. All you can do is just hope that you don't get so big up there in the penthouse section that you don't see what's happening down below anymore. I don't think I'm like that, I enjoy life pretty much. I'm still interested in looking and watching people. I'm a great one at studying human nature. So let's just hope that doesn't happen.

TURNER:  If you were an interviewer doing an interview with Eddie Rabbitt, what question would ask him?

RABBITT:  That's a good question . . . what would I ask myself? I really
don't know. What I do in my spare time, maybe? Drive my motorcycle up
and down the mountains around where I live. I've got a trail bike and when
I get all wound up and back from the road, I like to take this CT90 Honda
that I have and tear up and down the Tennessee mountainside. There are
some good trails out there. That's a good question; I'm sorry I haven't got
a better answer.

June 1980

*When you get thousands of people out there screaming and yelling and chanting your name, or striking lighters, or whatever, that is the greatest possible feeling you can get in your career. There's nothing, no award, no acclamation that can match that.*

*—Collin Raye*

THERE IS NO QUESTION that Collin Raye has arrived in country music. He made his thunderous entrance with the smash hit "Love Me," which stayed at number one on the *Billboard* country chart for three weeks, a first for a debut artist.

Raye began entering talent shows at the age of seven and spent his teen years playing honky-tonks in his native Arkansas. Immediately upon graduation from high school, he and his brother Scott worked their way west by playing clubs from Oregon to Nevada. After the brother act broke up, Raye decided to pursue a solo career and met with immediate success as a solo artist on the club circuit in Reno. It was during this time that Raye developed his articulate, muscular voice and his showmanship skills.

Today, Raye enlists these valuable traits as he entertains audiences throughout the United States with his hits or songs from his more than four-thousand-song repertoire.

# Collin Raye

TURNER: Where do you see yourself on the music spectrum?

RAYE: I think I'm definitely a country singer. In fact that's where my roots have always been. No matter what I try to sing, and I like to think of myself as being pretty versatile, I still sound like a country boy singing. With the records we put out I like to think that we don't really classify ourselves. We haven't really set any boundaries. On this new album we really tried to do that; we really tried to make sure that we made ourselves more appealing to everybody. You know you can't please everybody all the time, but if you're in live performance you can do a lot of different things—why not record them that way and see what happens?

TURNER: Did you find music or did music find you?

RAYE: I think the latter. I think music found me, in that I was always surrounded by it. I don't remember when music wasn't a big factor in my life. The only other thing I ever cared about or thought I might want to do was to play ball. Like every other nine- and ten-year-old, I dreamed of playing professional ball, but that idea didn't last long. My mom was a singer and my dad played music (he loved country music) and my older brother was playing guitar when he was six years old. I also had an uncle who was a professional picker. I was always surrounded by music. I don't remember it ever being new to me. When I was four and five years old I remember going to George Jones and Merle Haggard concerts. If they were in a one hundred fifty- to two hundred-mile radius, we were there. For me music was a part of life—like breathing and eating.

TURNER: Who has been your biggest encourager?

RAYE: I've had a lot! I'm going to go back a few years because once you're pretty good at something and you're having any semblance of success, even if it's on a club level, people are quick to encourage you. So I'm going to go back to my teens. Which I think is the most formidable time for any-body. Right there is when you develop confidence or you don't. During those real impressionable years, my biggest encourager was my mom. She was always very, very supportive and made me believe I was good. She also taught me invaluable lessons about the business, such as how to relate to

175

an audience and how to make an audience feel comfortable. At the time it didn't register with me that she was showing me these things. Many singers, entertainers, and actors have to fight the stigma in their homes of "when are you going to get a real job"—"it's not going to pay." I never had to fight that; it was always full steam ahead. My mom was always real proud of everything, I did and she's going to be proud and justified now that I've done what I've done. An amazing ingredient for anyone in any walk of life is just getting confidence in what they do, and I think that starts in the home. I don't get to see her very often nor talk with her a lot these days.

---

❖

> My mom was always real proud of everything I did and she's going to be proud and justified now that I've done what I've done.

❖

---

TURNER: How did playing clubs in the Reno area help groom you for where you are today?

RAYE: I think a great deal! Again, so much of it goes unnoticed at the time, but then as I look back on it I realized what all I learned. When I started out I was kind of shy on stage. I was never scared of getting onstage, but just shy about opening up too much to an audience. I was confident that I could sing and I felt I had a pretty good knowledge of the music, but I was real shy. If you want to keep working in Nevada and find a home for yourself, you have to open up to the audience. In Nevada, I became so comfortable talking to the people because you cannot depend on just your music. The sound system is never on your side. The management doesn't want you to be heard, let alone be loud. Mark O'Conner, the greatest musician in the world, would not impress people in Reno because they could not hear him. You have to let the audience see something or otherwise they'll get up and walk across the street to another casino or go back to the pit and gamble. If you want to make a name for yourself, you really have to work at establishing a rapport with the audience, and if you work at it long enough it becomes instinct. That is what I call learned instinct.

TURNER: Did you ever feel like a commodity rather than a performer while working in Reno?

RAYE: Yeah, and it was always real tough there because you don't know exactly what your role is. Like now I know what my role is. I realize that people have paid hard ticket money to see me perform or me and whoever else is on the bill. It's very simple; my job is to entertain them and make sure they walk away saying, "Well, he really gave us our money's worth— I didn't expect him to be that good." That's my duty, so to speak. It's very simple—hopefully we do that. I can remember when we would be up on stage and I'd think, "We're really doing good tonight," then about that time the pit boss would come over and start screaming at the sound man because people would be leaving the pit to watch our show. You must remember they didn't like that. I constantly had to wrestle with this split philosophy in the clubs. Oftentimes I would ask myself, "Why are we here? Are we an ornament or what?" I guess you do feel like a commodity—not a real vital commodity at that. Then I'd think, "I'm lucky I'm here making this paycheck because if I don't like it then there is someone else who can come in here and stand here and do this." After a while you start to develop a little following and a little clout and they do give you a little more rope, 'cause they do realize that you are bringing people in the door to come see you.

TURNER: Do you think "Love Me" is a career song?

RAYE: Without a doubt! I hope it's not my only career song. I hope I have more, but if I don't—well, even if I do—I think "Love Me" will always be the one that people will identify me with first. For instance take Glen Campbell—how many great hits did he average, but "Gentle On My Mind" always comes to my mind first. Everybody has that one song that's sort of their signature. I close my show with "Love Me" now. I'm sure I probably always will. Not only because it was my first big, big hit, but it's a great closer. We have a real high energy, full-speed-ahead type of show. We lead up to this big finale of excitement and then close with something poignant like "Love Me." Nowadays, I like to do it with just a piano. Singing it with just the piano is real powerful yet so subtle. It almost like "less is more," and it is a perfect way to end the show. Almost every show we do we get a standing ovation for "Love Me." I'm not saying that in a bragging way; I say it as a tribute to the song. People feel so good about the way we lead up to it and then do it. It always brings the audience to their feet. The standing ovation allows you to come back and do an encore. That song always gets the job done. In the past I never closed my show with a ballad.

TURNER: It was so popular, it set chart records, etc. What was it that appealed to you—what made you want to record that song?

RAYE: To be honest with you, a lot of it surprised me. I thought it was a hit song because the book was so emotional and so well written—you know about the letter. When I first heard the demo, I thought, "What a great song." I thought it was a hit! I cut it because I thought it would be a hit. It didn't have any real personal impact on me simply because I was always distant from my grandparents. I loved them when I saw them, but I didn't see them very often. Our relationship was never like in the song where the kid is very close to his grandparents. I believe that you can feel their closeness in the song. I thought people who loved their grandparents and vice versa are going to love this song. People taught me real quick after it came out and started flying up the charts that the message in that song is far bigger than the story. Lots of people told me they had "Love Me" played at their weddings. Once, during an autograph session in California, a young lady told me that her husband was in New York and that they were separated for months at a time and that they drew their strength from their song—"Love Me." I thought about her comments and I guess I can see where the message could be worked around to say, "Forget the actual story about the letter on the tree and everything—it's just the sentiment that counts." People even have it played at funerals. One person had the chorus line carved on a gravestone. When I hear things like that it makes me realize this song is much, much bigger than I envisioned at first glance. In the past few months this song has had a great impact on the fans, so naturally its success gives me a great feeling. I sing it with more enthusiasm than I did when I recorded it because I realize now that it means so much to so many people. I could go on all day talking about stories that would break your heart. "Love Me" has a happy ending. The song didn't make the fans feel bad—it made them feel good about a really bad situation. What a compliment! I may have bigger hits, but I don't think I'll ever have a song that will have such an impact on the fans. It makes me feel good. It reminds me of why I started doing this in the first place. I never dreamed I would be so lucky as to get a song like "Love Me," especially so early in my career. It makes me feel like I'm doing something worthwhile.

TURNER: How do you go about choosing the next project after such a monumental record?

RAYE: Well, it's tough. The one thing I was quick to jump on was the fact that I didn't want to look for another "Love Me." Because there ain't going to be another one. I think people who duplicate are insecure about their future. I could have said, "Let's put out another grandma/grandpa death song or whatever." I thought, *"no way!"* That song was special. It always bothers me when people come back with a carbon copy of their last record. Believe me, I've been pitched hundreds of "Love Me" clones, and every time I turn away from them because I don't want people to think that I'm trying to cash in on their feelings and, in a lot of cases, their hardship. I feel I got lucky with "Love Me." It is a great song! I'm going to sing it in earnest for the rest of my career. I will continue to look for good songs. On the second album, we went through a whole bunch of songs. We got pitched a better group of songs and a better class of songs than we did on the first album because I was a proven hitmaker. So that made the job a little easier than it was the first time, but again, I don't want to be known as just a ballad singer. I sing everything! I love doing ballads but I also love doing the rowdier stuff which we do in our live shows. We're going to try to put more of the live show energy into our next project. On the next record we may still go a little further. On the second record we got a lot closer to the live show energy than we did on the first album.

TURNER: Kenny Rogers once said, "A career is built on change." Do you agree with this statement?

RAYE: Absolutely! I think that's how you last. Kenny started out with "Something Burning" back in '68 or '69. Then he went away for a while, then he came back hotter than ever. It is very true that people's taste changes. They get tired of hearing the same thing. You'll always draw a few hundred people to a show to hear you do the oldies. But for the most part, people want to see who's hot at the moment. It's like "what have you done for me lately" type of thing.

TURNER: You said that you have many different styles. What is the real Collin Raye style?

RAYE: I guess I can lock it down to two styles. They are two very distinct styles and I don't think one is like the other at all. I like songs that are a little bit rowdy. "I Want You Bad And That Ain't Good" is a good example of a rowdy or rock and roll-edged type of song. To me the beat and energy of a song like that is begging for that type of lyric. It's a little big edgy. I really look for those types of songs. I'm really critical when I look for ballads. They have to be really strong. They have to say something that I haven't heard before. There are so many ballads that sound like a scrabble game: they just reshuffle the letters and throw them out there again. Ballads have to really come from the heart—I can feel this in a writer's demo. I can tell if a writer meant what he wrote or if he is just sitting there coming up with something he thinks the girls will like. I think "Love Me" and "In

> There are so many ballads that sound like a scrabble game: they just reshuffle the letters and throw them out there again.

This Life" are good examples of songs written from the heart. Hopefully all the ballads I do will fall into that category. I like to think of this as the Collin Raye ballad style. I won't ever cut a song that's not like that. If I can't find a ballad like that, I won't do one. The two styles are very diverse. Again, I think the real successful artist must cover a wide spectrum, or throw a wide loop, so to speak. I think this is true in any kind of music. The guys who are able to do this are the ones who really rise to the top. There is always a place for people who specialize in one thing or another. However, if you can do it all, then why not do it? I feel like you cheat yourself if you don't. Do everything you can do as well as you can and you will be all right.

TURNER: If you really want to showcase the talents of Collin Raye, what one song would you select?

RAYE: That's a tough one. Well, I might go back to a cover, the songs I recorded on my own. They fall into one of the two categories I just described. There are very few songs that show a little bit of both. So, just thinking off the top of my head, I would select an old ballad that Bob Seger wrote and recorded a few years ago called "We've Got Tonight." I always thought I did a real nice job on it. It's very melodic and pretty. I did it with a lot of energy and edge to it. It is hard to get a ballad that has both. I always thought that song did both. From what people have told me, that is one I can show off a little bit on and stretch a little bit on, combining both things. In fact I quit doing the song, but I was doing it in my show up until about three months ago.

TURNER: Most female entertainers respond with a Patsy Cline song.

RAYE: That's true! Because you look at all of your heroes. If I really wanted to show how well I sing country, I'll do a Merle Haggard song. But if I want to show off how I can stretch, I'd do "Hot Legs" by Rod Stewart. It's one way or another. It's hard to think of one tune or one type of tune that combines all elements into one song.

---

> If I really want to show how well I sing country, I'd do a Merle Haggard song.

---

TURNER: You put so much emotion into your songs, and they are so power packed. What do you get back in return?

RAYE: A lot! Because, people come up to me after a show and they say you are good, the show was good, and what I always tell them is, "The audience was good because we basically do the same thing every night." To what degree we make the show is up to the audience. If I get an audience that is fired up and ready to go, they are going to get a great show. They're going to get knocked out. But if they're kinda quiet, sitting on their hands, I'm still going to do the best I can but there's things we can't do. We really will do them but we're not going to do them with the same energy 'cause you do what you think you can get away with, so to speak. When an audience is giving it back to me, that's the greatest. It's not for money; it's not for gold records on the wall, the platinum records on the wall, or awards. That's all gravy. The reason you start doing this is because it's something you feel like you can do. When you are young, if you can get five people to really like you, you feel like, "I'm going to do this now." When you get thousands of people out there screaming and yelling and chanting your name, or striking lighters, or whatever, that is the greatest possible feeling you can get in your career. There's nothing, no award, no acclamation that can match that. The beauty of it is that we get it on a regular basis. It makes me feel like a very lucky guy. There's not that many people in life who get to have a lot of the experiences I've had, let alone have people on the edge of excitement. You realize you've made a difference in their day when they go home and talk for weeks about how much fun they had at a Collin Raye show. That's great. I'd do this for nothing. To me you should get paid for the traveling. You shouldn't get paid for what I do on stage.

TURNER: For someone who has never been to a Collin Raye Show, what should someone expect from a Collin Raye Show?

RAYE: I'm still new enough that a lot of people out there haven't seen me. The comment I hear a lot is that "I didn't expect that." They kind of expect me to sit on a stool and play "Love Me" and play ballads like that. That's not what they get. They get a variety of songs. I like to think that even when we do the ballads we present them in a very big way. There's no energy drop—it just slows down. We do a lot of hard-driving songs. I like to create a big party atmosphere. I do things like that on stage. They go "Wow, I can't believe he did that." Therefore, they feel like they can cut loose a little bit themselves. Music, movies, TV, and books are all escapes from reality. No matter what your job is there's times you want to get away from it. Most people live their lives by rules and boundaries—always limitations. You can do A and B but don't do C and D and E or you're going to get fired. When they pay money to be entertained, I don't want to just sing for them—they can play my tapes to hear that. I want them to say, "WOW that was fun! Let's do it again." So when I come back around the next time they'll be ready for it, be excited! I'll try to top that. I won't do the same thing in the same town twice. I'm a little bit extroverted when I get on stage, and I think I use this to my advantage. Even the most subdued laid-back introverted person really wants to let their hair down occasionally. I think we all need to do this. We try to create this type of atmosphere for an hour and a half or whatever I've got. They walk away feeling tired— they've worked up a sweat.

TURNER: There are entertainers who come along to take the places of older performers. Whose place do you see yourself taking?

RAYE: I can't really answer that question because the people that I admire a lot, I would never say that I could take their place. I really believe that my heroes are bigger than life. There's no way I could fill their shoes. I can't really think of an artist who has come before me that I could take their place vocally, because I'm a tenor in country music. There have not been that many tenors in country music—just about a handful. As for as an overall performer, I don't think there's anybody that's approached it the way I have. Hopefully I can carve a little spot for myself.

Maybe someday I'll inspire some kid to come out and try to do better than I did. Do it my way but do it a little better. The people I idolize did not really influence my style because our styles are so different. I don't know why, but I learned from them. I use them as a barometer to determine what's good and what's not. I just find myself doing things that I've never seen anybody do before. I'm sure if I went back far enough I could find that everything I do on stage or in the studio is taken a little bit from this guy and a little bit from that guy. We all copy even though we don't mean to. It's a form of flattery. I don't think I have tried to emulate anybody, knowingly or unknowingly. Waylon Jennings is one of my big heroes. And I've always loved Kristofferson, Glen Campbell, Johnny Cash, and Elvis. The list goes on and on and on. There's no way I'm going to fill any of those guys' shoes. I don't even want to try. I'd rather just honor them when I can. Every once in a while I do songs made popular by these guys. I recorded "Big River," which is an old Johnny Cash classic that I thought had not gotten enough runs at it. I think Roseanne Cash did it as an album cut a few years ago but nobody really heard it so I wanted to do it again. That's a form of a tribute to him, but I definitely did it my way. I wouldn't even think of doing it like him. It would be disrespectful.

TURNER: When it all boils down, what is it that Collin Raye is after in show business?

RAYE: I don't really have specific goals as far as when I reach certain points. For example, if I were a football player, the Super Bowl ring would be the reward for winning the Super Bowl, or if I were a boxer, the heavyweight title would be the reward for winning the match. There's not that one specific thing you can use as a barometer in the music business. It's a crapshoot. You have to get out there and make as much noise as you can— do it your way and do it from the heart. In other words, take it as far as you can, not just to make more money. What ever you do, do it the American way: take it to the limit. For me that includes acting. I had my first taste of that about a month ago. I really enjoyed it. I was told I did a pretty good job, so we'll see. But I'd like to use that to pursue other things in that area because I love it. I think acting is a great way of expression. It is a whole other dimension to being a performer. To me it's all the same— people specialize but it's all entertainment. Sure I'd like to have a platinum record or a triple platinum record, but if I don't get one I won't feel like a failure. I'll just say my music didn't quite reach that many people. It if reaches ten million, I'll say my music reached ten million people. That's a great achievement. As far as awards and things, I take all that in stride because I know the business. I know it's a political thing. Things happen because it's your turn or it's not—you have to wait your turn. If the powers that be choose to look down on you with favor then you'll get a shot. To me the one award that would be really nice to win would be the ACM or CMA Entertainer of the Year award because of what it says. To win that once would be real gratifying. It says you've touched all bases in the music business. You really hit a home run and you affected a lot of people. It says an awful lot about the individual. I would take any award with great pride. The Entertainer of the Year award would be the pinnacle. It would be a nice experience. But again, a lot of my heroes never won any awards, but they're still the best to me. As far as I'm concerned, I'm just going to keep going as hard, as fast and as aggressively as I can. This includes making friends, good music, and affecting as many people as I can. That's really what it's all about.

TURNER: If you were an interviewer doing an interview with Collin Raye, what question would you ask him that I haven't asked you?

RAYE: That's a good question. I've never been asked that question before. I've been interviewed so many times, and I thought I had been asked everything. I don't really have an answer for that question. I can't think of anything that I've always wished somebody would ask me. It's funny because certain questions make you feel more at ease than others. However, I don't think fans quite realize how difficult it is to do what we do on a daily basis, such as getting from point A to point B and making everybody happy. That bothers me because I've always been a person who likes to please everybody, especially if they are paying money to come see me. I guess the one thing I wish would be brought to the attention of the public is how our lives are controlled by schedules. You're constantly in a rush. It's really tough, and the bigger you get, and the more popular you get, the more is expected of you. I feel like there are a few people out there who feel that Collin Raye is a jerk because he didn't stay long enough at a venue. I hate having anybody think that about me. If I have one regret over the past year, that is it. I also get misquoted in the media sometimes. *Cosmopolitan* magazine misquoted me in that they didn't print the question they asked me and they only printed one sentence of my answer. The way in which they presented it made me look like a real prima donna, and that broke my heart. And as a matter of fact I lost one of my biggest fans—one of my top five fans—over the article. After the article ran she wrote me a letter and read me the riot act. And I thought, "Well I lost a fan because of the misquote, and I wonder how many more I lost who didn't bother to write." There's times I wish I would get a chance to lay things bare and explain some things. A television format would be good. I've heard Clint Black say the same thing. I don't know anybody in the business who doesn't like their fans—everybody loves them. We're really thankful to be here.

August 1992

*I know you hear a lot of people say, "Well, I want to do this and I want to feel this way." I just want to have a good time. I don't want to get heavy.*

*—Jerry Reed*

ASK JERRY REED what his brand of country music is all about and you'll get the kind of reply you would expect from a guy whose greatest ambition is to "fold it all up and go fishin' the rest of my life." He just wants to have a good time.

Atlanta-born Reed is the man who made "Amos Moses" the most famous of the Louisiana Cajuns, and has added hit upon hit to his musical resumé. But his ambition is not limited to music alone. He is now a full-fledged movie star.

Reed has gone from playing the "good ole boy" sidekick in movies like *Smokey and the Bandit* to central roles opposite heavyweight actors such as Walter Matthau.

But whether he's making a movie or making music, Reed always makes sure he's having a good time.

# Jerry Reed

TURNER: What was the greatest influence on your career? Was it a person or an event, one that really changed your course of life?

REED: William, I always knew what I wanted to do. I had a lot of inspirations. A lot of different sources. Excuse me, I just stepped on my drummer's ingrown toenail—I'm sorry. Chet Atkins, I would say, had the biggest influence. He and Merle Travis on the guitar. Of course, Hank Williams made a big impression on me. When I was growing up there was a lot of great talents. I had a lot of people to aspire to.

TURNER: What about the motion picture industry?

REED: I've always been interested in movies.

TURNER: Do you find that you enjoy this type of work now that you have made motion pictures?

REED: Oh yeah, it is a lot of fun and I enjoy it very much. It's kinda like the army, hurry up and wait.

TURNER: How do you account for the success of *Smokey and the Bandit, Gator,* and all these fast-moving action movies that are being produced today?

REED: Well, you know, they are so earthy and so real—I think people identify with these movies, William. *Smokey and the Bandit,* you see that going on every day. All you gotta do is get in your car and turn on the CB radio and drive up the road and everybody is into it. *Smokey and the Bandit* was a funny, funny movie. Burt and Hal Needham know how to make entertaining movies—maybe regional movies. Burt is really into southern movies.

TURNER: Had you ever had any acting experience before you met Burt?

REED: No. *W. W. and The Dixie Dance Kings* was the first picture I was ever in.

TURNER: You haven't been spending that much time on the road doing concerts, have you?

REED: No, I have a lot of things going at home, consequently I travel primarily on weekends.

TURNER: What type of show do you prefer doing? Would you rather do a package deal, night clubs, or concerts?

REED: They are all fun, William. They really are if you have got a good house and a good crowd.

---

I enjoy dramatic television. I hate variety shows. Variety shows are really the turn-off of the world.

---

TURNER: How about TV? Do you enjoy it?

REED: No! I hate it.

TURNER: You would not like a TV series?

REED: I enjoy dramatic television. I hate variety shows. Variety shows are really the turn-off of the world.

TURNER: Do you think you would like to be a dramatic-type actor?

REED: I like to dabble around in it. I would not get very serious about it.

TURNER: What could be done to improve the image of country music on variety shows?

REED: Well! That's a good question. I don't really know because I'm not really into variety. I don't even watch it anymore. It bores me so bad. Every show is the same, just a different face.

TURNER: You are labeled as a superstar: you are a success on the guitar, you are a success at writing, you are a success at acting, and you are a successful singer. How do you account for all this success?

REED: Hard work—hard work, a lot of hard work. Yes sir, I mean hard, hard work. It has not come easy for me anyway.

TURNER: When you are at home relaxing, do you ever listen to music?

REED: No, I go fishing. The first person who makes any music in my house I whip 'em good.

TURNER: How often do you get a chance to go fishing?

---
❖
---

## Mother bought me my first guitar for seven dollars and I played it with nickels, dimes, and quarters.

---
❖
---

REED: Well, it comes in spurts. Like I fish every night some weeks.

TURNER: Who are your fishing buddies?

REED: Ah, you wouldn't know 'em. Well, I fish with Porter Wagoner sometimes. He's really good at fishing. Of course, we've all got radios in our boats and we all get out on the lake and shoot the breeze and enjoy one another.

TURNER: Do you remember holding your first guitar?

REED: Yeah. I was eight years old. Mother bought me my first guitar for seven dollars and I played it with nickels, dimes, and quarters. I didn't have any picks. The strings were about an inch and a half off the neck—I thought it was beautiful. I played the first day and I remember the second day I couldn't even touch it because my fingers were so sore. My mother showed me three chords and I just sat and played those three chords for about fifteen hours. Then the next day I couldn't play because my fingers were like raisins.

TURNER: Was your mother musically inclined?

REED: Yeah, and my daddy was, too.

TURNER: Were they in show business?

REED: No. They played dances and things.

TURNER: Do you play any instrument other than the guitar?

REED: Not very well. I tinker around with some. I like to play bass. I like bass better than I do anything.

TURNER: Do you get a chance to play bass often?

REED: Yeah, I've played it on my records. I don't normally, but I go in and overdub it when someone screws up on the recording.

TURNER: Do you jam with other musicians?

---

❖

## I'm not a jammer. I can't play off the top of my head.

❖

---

REED: I don't! I'm not a jammer. I can't play off the top of my head. I have to sit and think about what I'm going to play. I never could jam—I never was into that.

TURNER: Do you read music?

REED: Not enough to hurt my playing. No, I never got into reading. I always just wanted to play what I heard and what I felt.

TURNER: When was your first professional job?

REED: It was in Decatur, Alabama. I made fifty dollars.

TURNER: Do you have any favorite artist you like to listen to or associate with their music?

REED: Oh, gosh! There are a lot of them I enjoy, William—I could name 'em all night. But I really don't listen to music because I have a tendency to copy. So I stay away from listening because I will really get into a rut. You know, taking other people's stuff. If I like it I might put it on one of my records, and I don't want that.

TURNER: If you were starting over, is there anything you would do differently?

REED: I don't think so. If I was the same person, I would probably do it the same way. I started so young. I had to grow up in the business. That's really a good way to do it.

TURNER: How old were you when you started in the business?

REED: Sixteen.

TURNER: Where are you originally from?

REED: Atlanta. I was born at Grady Memorial Hospital. My mother still lives in Atlanta.

TURNER: Is Jerry Reed really your name?

REED: Yeah. It is my first and middle name. Hubbard is my last name.

TURNER: From what I understand, your daughter has performing ambitions. Did you give her your blessings or did you try to discourage it when she told you she would like to give show business a chance?

REED: Well, at first I didn't want her in the business. But it became apparent that she was going to be in the business, and once she committed herself, I backed her one hundred percent. I told her it was hard and to get ready. She's ready, so I'm going to help her all I can. You know it's a very hard business.

TURNER: If someone were to come to you tomorrow and tell you that you had to pick one of the facets you have done in your career and do it for the rest of your life, what aspect would you pick?

REED: Whoo—that's a good question. If I could do it well, I would write, because you could enjoy the business and meet a lot of great people. You could be behind the scenes. The only nerve-wracking part of the business is the people; when you are tired they don't understand that. Rightly so, because they pay their hard-earned money to come see you work. You really don't have the privilege of being tired. And in show business, you lose your privacy. I am a very private person. I wish you could make pictures, do television, and make records and then put on a different face.

TURNER: What draws you and Burt Reynolds to the south so much?

REED: I think that's where he found his success, and you always have good feelings for where you are successful. Our roots have always been in the south—the south is Burt's region.

TURNER: Is there one event or moment that stands out in your career?

REED: There have been a million memorable events that were just great. Not just me, because any time anything good happens to me it's a thrill in this business. A thrill that I don't think you get in any other business, because you are so in the center of everything and when it happens, it is so enlightening, so uplifting—Gosh! There have been so many great things that have happened to me.

TURNER: Are there any plans on the drawing board to do another movie?

REED: Maybe—I'm not sure yet. We have been talking with Hal, the gentleman who wrote and directed *Smokey.* We're going to meet with him.

---

> I'm not smart enough to figure music out or figure people out. I just try to make the best records I can make.

---

TURNER: From what I understand, Hal was Burt's stuntman, am I correct?

REED: Right, and a very dear and close friend. He was Burt's stuntman for about twenty years.

TURNER: What are you really after in your music?

REED: I don't know—haven't gotten the foggiest notion, if you want to know the truth. I'm not smart enough to figure music out or figure people out. I just try to make the best records I can make. I know you hear a lot of people say, "Well, I want to do this and I want to feel this way." I just want to have a good time. I don't want to get heavy. Because there ain't nothing heavy about me—at a hundred and fifty pounds I can't get heavy.

TURNER: What is your biggest ambition?

REED: I would like to be able just to fold it all up and go fishing for the rest of my life, and I really mean that.

TURNER: Could you really be happy doing that?

REED: Yes sir! Yes sir, I would love to be able to. But of course you can't quit in this business. I want to get my own business so that when it gets on my nerves I could just say, "To hell with it; I'm going fishing boys, you can find me in the back of Mine Lick on Center Hill Lake and that's where I will be until I get sick of that."

TURNER: You do a tremendous show, and you put everything into it. You are a visual entertainer and one enjoys your work ten times more by seeing you on stage than from your albums.

REED: Yeah, yeah it is pretty hard to put all that, the licks, into albums. I can't jump up and down on them.

TURNER: Why did you record "Alabama Wild Man" twice? I know it was successful both times.

REED: We just wanted another shot at it. That's why we did it twice.

June 1978

MARTY ROBBINS, the balladeer of Old West gunfights who put El Paso on the map in music, died in 1982, but he left behind a wealth of music for the fans who loved him dearly. With over five hundred tunes to his writing credit, Robbins managed to place his songs in the top ten of country music charts in every year but one since 1959.

Robbins began his life in Texas and ended it as one of the most prolific singer songwriters the music business has ever known.

*People call what I do country, and that's all right. I don't care what they call it, as long we they like it well enough to call it something.*
*—Marty Robbins*

# Marty Robbins

TURNER: Today's music is getting away from the traditional country, it has steel and it is getting to be a softer type of music. Can this last?

ROBBINS: Everything has to change; you name it. From the type of clothes, type of hats, type of coffee. I don't care what it is; it cannot remain the same. Nothing stays the same; if it did it would die. Country music might eventually come back around to what they call "country music:" Acuff style, Ernest Tubb style. There are so many different styles of country music, because Ernest Tubb had what you call Texas Jukebox style. He's honky-tonk country. Roy Acuff is mountain country, Bill Monroe is bluegrass country. There are so many different types of music in country and what we call "country and western," and what I do is definitely not something Roy Acuff would do. I recorded twenty years ago in New York City with Mitch Miller and Ray Conniff with a big orchestra and a big chorus, along with some other top-ten songs. But still they were country songs. People call what I do country, and that's all right. I don't care what they call it, as long as they like it well enough to call it something. I used to work in Las Vegas and I have had many people come to me and say, "I really like your singing, Marty, but I don't like country & western." Well, I can't say anything about that because I've had hit songs that were not country and western, and I've had people come to me and say, "Marty, you're my favorite country & western singer," maybe two minutes later, so all I say is thanks. I have to let people decide.

TURNER: You have such a knack for making people feel at ease. Have you always had a knack for making people laugh?

ROBBINS: Well, I don't know if it's making people laugh, or if it's just everybody has a good time, you know. I never really started even having a good time on stage myself until about ten or twelve years ago, because I always thought that you had to be somebody that you're not. And then all of a sudden, I just started feeling . . . well you know, I believe the people would like to see just what the person is like in real life, so on the stage I'm just me. If I didn't have to dress for it, like I'm wearing jeans right now, I'd be the same twenty-four hours a day.

195

TURNER: So on stage you're the same as you are off stage?

ROBBINS: Sure, I'm so happy that people are here to see the show. And the problem I have is not being able to sleep after a show. I think it's because I get so excited and I think about the show for a long time after it's over. And that keeps me awake. But, I just love the business so much; I'm glad I love it, and I'm glad people come to see Marty Robbins, because I will never do anything that offends the people. I don't think I use any kind of offensive language—I don't use foul language—which is all right if people use it, you know. I get mad; I've got a bad temper same as anybody else. Boy, I just cuss like a sailor. I know that it's not right in front of ladies and little children—I just try to be me and have a good time and that's it.

TURNER: You are a novelist, songwriter, performer, actor. Which area do you find most fulfilling?

ROBBINS: Being on stage. I have more fun being on stage. I can be me. If I did something else I'd have to be somebody else.

TURNER: When you walk out on that stage and the audience is very receptive, and it is evident that they are receptive, how does it make you feel?

ROBBINS: I want to grab all of them and hug them. All of them at once. I keep looking at them and thinking, "They're keeping me from working for a living. They are keeping me off the streets."

TURNER: At this point in your career, do you find yourself with any aspect of it that you would trade off?

ROBBINS: No, I don't want anything to change, and I don't plan anything. I just let it go. The only thing that is planned are the show days, they are planned. I don't think of a show day next week.

TURNER: What kind of shows do you prefer doing: concerts, package shows, night clubs?

ROBBINS: I prefer doing selected concerts where you don't have to get dressed; you can be yourself. But I do enjoy the nightclub work, where you can dress—the people are dressed in evening gowns, it might be furs or whatever. I enjoy that; it's a different audience, but it's not as close. I still relate to them just the same because it's still a Marty Robbins fan, and the audiences in nightclubs are small because most of the clubs we play seat about six hundred people. At the dinner clubs, they charge a big price, so the person who pays a big price to see Marty Robbins has got to be a Marty Robbins fan. So, it just happens to be that they are dressed differently in the nightclub than they would be dressed in the park. In the park they wear shorts; in the nightclubs they wear evening gowns.

TURNER: Marty Robbins still has that fan who can't afford that high price, true?

ROBBINS: Absolutely. There are about ninety to one hundred large clubs to be booked. The club operators bring in all these big acts, Las Vegas acts, and they make a lot more money than I do. The owners bring them in and they are very happy to bring Marty Robbins in because they'll make money off Marty Robbins. I'll make a living and they'll make a living. It's real bad to have to charge so much, but when you go to a club like this you can expect to get dinner and see a show for the price they charge. So, it's kind of a Las Vegas-type thing.

TURNER: Do you find that there is a trend of entertainers going back to the small houses? For better rapport with audiences, maybe?

ROBBINS: I don't know. I don't play a lot of package shows. Most of the shows I do are by myself. I enjoy that a lot more than playing package shows. If I play a package show, it's usually with Merle Haggard, and we're a good package. We're absolutely two different audiences. I don't think Merle and I have ever played to under ten thousand people, unless it was in a house that didn't hold ten thousand people.

TURNER: When people speak of country music, usually they refer to it as country and western music. Where is the western part of the music today?

ROBBINS: I don't know who ever started country and western music, because western music is cowboy music. Cowboy music is not being done, so they call it everything. But to me western music is like American folk music, from the western part of the United States. That is cowboy music which is from that particular part of the United States. And we have Dixieland jazz down in New Orleans; that is also American folk music. We have bluegrass music down in Kentucky and that part of the country; that is also folk music. We have three of four different types of folk music in the country; it's a big country, a lot of people. We have different types of music that can be called folk music. But cowboy music is not country and western. What we're referring to right now should be called just country. At one time there was Bob Wills, who played western swing. That was not cowboy, but it was western because he was west of the Mississippi. If it had been east of the Mississippi they would have called it eastern swing.

TURNER: You have been able to have a top-ten record for how many years, twenty?

ROBBINS: Since 1959 I've had a top ten every year except 1975. Then in 1976 I had two number ones.

❖

I write when I'm inspired to write, and usually it's a very decent song.

❖

TURNER: So that made up for it. How do you account for this success? What do you look for when you look for a song for Marty Robbins?

ROBBINS: Something that I like. It's the only way I can go by. I have to do what I like. When I can sell me on a song then I have a better chance to sell it to Marty Robbins fans.

TURNER: Do you have to be talked into recording a particular song or do you know immediately what is right for you?

ROBBINS: I know what is right for me. But I listen to what they bring me, because I don't know it all, and I don't think anybody else knows it all either. So I listen to what they bring me and if I like it and the producer likes it, then I think we have a winning combination. Billy Sherrill and I work very well together. I have a lot of respect for him and what he can do, and I think he had a lot of respect for me and what I can do. Together we make a pretty decent team. If he can't sell a song to me, then he knows that I can't sell it to the public. If he can sell it to me, then I can sell it, because I am sold on the song. It's a nice combination.

TURNER: What would you say is the motto that closest describes your philosophy of life?

ROBBINS: Live and let live.

TURNER: Are you going to continue to race or do you still own your racing car?

ROBBINS: I still have a car, but, I don't get to race too much.

TURNER: How are you inspired to write songs?

ROBBINS: Usually it's really by being inspired by something I've seen or heard or done. I used to write all the time, but I don't do that much writing any more. I write when I'm inspired to write, and usually it's a very decent song. It may not be complete, but it's a very well written song.

TURNER: Was "El Paso" your biggest selling song?

ROBBINS: That's the best seller, yes. And then "White Sport Coat."

TURNER: Who wrote "White Sport Coat"?

ROBBINS: I wrote "White Sport Coat" in El Paso. I've had eighteen number ones, and I think thirteen of them are ones that I wrote myself.

TURNER: Thirteen out of eighteen.

ROBBINS: Some of the best sellers were songs that I wrote. But I think in life you reach a piont where, as a writer, you just about run out of ideas. Then you have to be really inspired to write, and then when you're inspired to write, boy, it comes quick.

TURNER: At any point did you ever worry about your creative well drying up?

ROBBINS: No, I'm not even worried about it now, because I know now that I may not write seventy songs a year—I may only write three songs. But the three songs that I write will be better than the seventy songs I would have written. I don't care about how many I write; what I care about is how good are the songs.

TURNER: What do you want for yourself in the future?

ROBBINS: I don't know, I just enjoy life. I couldn't ask for anything more than just the way life has treated me.

TURNER: If you were doing an interview with Marty Robbins, what question would you ask him?

ROBBINS: I guess I'd have to ask everything. I might not have an answer for everything, but I've been asked everything, I'm sure.

June 1981

NOT MANY country music singers start their careers by getting drunk and stealing a goat, but that's exactly what Johnny Rodriguez did.

While sitting in jail on goat theft charges, a Texas ranger who had heard Rodriguez sing persuaded the sheriff to let hi out of jail long enough to audition for a job at the Alamo Village. He was hired, and his singing career was launched, with the assistance of Tom T. Hall, who caught his act one night.

After several years, Rodriguez established himself with "Pass Me By," a single that exploded onto the country charts and still commands numerous requests.

*One day I just said, "Hell, I'm just going to go to Nashville and see what I can do for myself," . . . I just took my guitar, a couple of shirts and a pair of pants. I didn't have anything to lose.*
*—Johnny Rodriguez*

# Johnny Rodriguez

TURNER: From what I understand, you have many close friends and family in your audience. Does it give you stage fright when you know they're there?

RODRIGUEZ: Oh, no! I've been in this for a pretty good while now. It just makes me feel good that they would come.

TURNER: Does your family still live in Texas?

RODRIGUEZ: Yeah, my mother lives in a small town down where I grew up in Texas. There are nine of us children, scattered all around the country.

TURNER: Are any of your brothers or sisters in show business?

RODRIGUEZ: No.

TURNER: Do you ever get back to your home town to perform?

RODRIGUEZ: No, I just go back there to visit. I go back to see my old friends about every Christmas or around that season.

TURNER: I will ask you the obvious question. How did you get started in show business?

RODRIGUEZ: I stole a goat.

TURNER: Is this true?

RODRIGUEZ: Yeah. I guess that's the way it really started. It's a funny story. When I was in high school, my friends and I would go down to a state park. Some kids would spend the whole summer down there and some would just go down there and hang out for a week or two. This place is only twenty-seven miles from our home town. It was just great for us. It was right there on a beautiful river. There were all kinds of beautiful, little girls—crowds of them. It was just like heaven for us. We would camp out for a week at a time.

One night we were out having a beer party—we were all under age at that time—and we all got drunk and went out and stole three goats because we wanted to have a barbecue. There were about fifteen or twenty

201

kids out there that night, and we went out and chased those goats out in the mountains in the middle of the night. So we started having a barbecue. We had one goat on the thing when the county deputy drove up. A lot of the guys split, but he caught us. The guy recognized me as I turned around—it was too late for me to run. He recognized me and two other kids. The rest of the kids scattered all through the woods and they couldn't find them.

The deputy took us down to the jail. We figured they would fine us or something like that. But we found out it was a felony for stealing a goat. Like even if you steal a chicken in Texas you can go to prison for it. They explained all of this to us. But before I knew all of this, I took the rap for the goats because I figured it would only take a fine, and we would all throw in together and pay it.

It all wound up so serious. I went to jail for about two and a half or three weeks because I didn't want to tell my folks what had happened. My dad had told me, all the time I was growing up, that if I even got myself into trouble to get out of it myself. It was a pretty good policy, I guess.

TURNER:  You actually spent two weeks in jail?

RODRIGUEZ:  Yeah. That's where the story really starts. Boy, this thing is getting involved. There was this Texas Ranger I knew who had heard me sing before down at the park, but he was on an assignment and wasn't there during the time I was put in jail. When he came back, the sheriff told him he had me in jail, and the Ranger asked the sheriff to let him talk to me. He came up and told me that he knew this guy who might give me a job if I could go out and audition for it. So the Ranger got the sheriff to let me out one day and the Ranger took me himself down to Alamo Village, the place where the movie *The Alamo* was made. To make a long story short, I got the job. But you've got to understand that I had never played with any bands or anything like that, because I didn't like to play in bands. I just liked to play on my guitar and sing for myself and my friends. Most of the kids working there were in college and I was in my last year of school.

I was released from jail and went to work there at the Village that summer. On Labor Day of that year, Tom T. Hall and Bobby Bare came by on their way to Mexico. They heard me sing, then they came back and met me and we talked. Tom T. told me if he ever got a chance he would put me in his band. I figured he was just trying to be nice.

About two years went by and I was working in construction and on a ranch—I lost my father during that time. One day I just said, "Hell I'm just going to go to Nashville and see what I can do for myself." I packed up and went. I just had a few bucks on me because I had just been working on construction jobs.

TURNER: How long did you save up to go to Nashville?

RODRIGUEZ: I just drew a paycheck for the week and left. I just took my guitar, a couple of shirts and a pair of pants. I didn't have anything to lose.

TURNER: What was the least amount of money you ever had in Nashville?

RODRIGUEZ: Well, when I got there, I had eight bucks.

TURNER: Where were you able to find a place to stay?

RODRIGUEZ: I called Bobby Bare, and he was on tour in California, so I couldn't get hold of him. Tom T. had given me his number also, so I called his office and left a message. He called and left a message for me to meet him at a restaurant. I walked over there and he and his bandleader drove up. Boy, he had a big old Cadillac and the whole deal. I thought to myself, "Oh well!" He took me out to his farm with him. He told me I could stay with him for a couple of weeks if I wanted to. After I got to his farm, I listened to his records and I worked around the farmhouse while he was on the road. Then he told me to learn some of his tunes on the guitar. About three or four weeks later he gave me a job playing lead guitar in his band.

TURNER: So you actually played in his band?

RODRIGUEZ: Yeah, I was on the road with him for about a year.

TURNER: Did you ever front for his show?

RODRIGUEZ: Yeah, that's what I did. First I started just playing lead guitar, and after about six months he got me to sing a couple of songs before he would go on. This was before I even tried to get on label or anything like that. Next, he took me by Mercury and I sang a couple of songs for Roy Day. He liked what I did and told me he would sign me to Mercury.

TURNER: Do you find that your approach to a song or to an audience has changed over the years?

RODRIGUEZ: Oh yeah, a lot, because now I'm singing with more confidence. I listen to my records and they're just now getting to sound like I do when I sing around the house to myself.

TURNER: Did you ever have a problem with projecting yourself—were you ever shy or uncomfortable on a stage?

RODRIGUEZ: Oh yeah. I didn't even know how to say hello at first. I'm just now getting to the point where I feel comfortable on stage.

---

❖

More people are just getting turned on to country music—maybe the entertainers aren't changing as much as the people are changing.

❖

---

TURNER: How would you describe your voice and music?

RODRIGUEZ: I don't know. I guess it's country. But some of it has a pop-contemporary sound. I kinda mix things up a bit.

TURNER: Do you mind being labeled a country singer?

RODRIGUEZ: No.

TURNER: There is a lot of controversy about crossover music. Do you have an opinion on this?

RODRIGUEZ: No, I just think that the audiences are growing. I guess they're younger and you get a more progressive listener. More people are just getting turned on to county music—maybe the entertainers aren't changing as much as the people are changing.

TURNER: If you weren't a singer, what would you be doing?

RODRIGUEZ: I would probably be instructing karate. I like karate a lot. I've got a first degree black belt.

TURNER: What do you do for relaxation?

RODRIGUEZ: I guess you would say I do karate because it relaxes my mind.

TURNER: Have you ever done any writing?

RODRIGUEZ: I've been writing since I first met Tom T. I guess I write about forty percent of the material I record.

TURNER: Do you have any favorite songwriters?

RODRIGUEZ: I like Tom T., Willie Nelson, Mickey Newberry, Kris Kristofferson, Billy Joe Shaver, and a lot of other guys.

TURNER: Who picks your material for recording sessions?

RODRIGUEZ: My producer and myself.

TURNER: Does a lot of time go into the selection process?

RODRIGUEZ: Yeah, we have to sit around and listen to all kinds of tapes because you never know when you're going to hear a hit.

June 1977

*I think all I ever want to be in life is a hope and an inspiration for someone who has a dream.*

—*T. G. Sheppard*

CHART-TOPPING singles and electrifying concerts have established T. G. Sheppard as one of the most sought after entertainers in country music today.

Sheppard, a native of Humbolt, Tennessee, attributes his early musical training to his mother, a piano teacher who reserved Sunday afternoon for musical get-togethers. While he was still a teenager, Sheppard moved to Memphis and joined the Travis Womack Band as guitarist and singer. Growing weary of road life, he directed his creative talents to promoting the careers of other young entertainers at the Hotline Distributors and RCA Records.

Later, he formed his own production and promotion company, Umbrella Productions. One of the first people to sign with Umbrella Productions was Robby David, a young songwriter who had written "Devil In A Bottle," a tune Sheppard liked immediately. After the song was turned down by eight record companies, Sheppard decided to record and release the song himself. The record buying public was quick to recognize the talents of Bill Browder and the name and the musical career of T. G. Sheppard was launched.

# T. G. Sheppard

TURNER: Where do you see yourself on the music spectrum?

SHEPPARD: That's a good question; nobody has ever asked me that question before. I still consider myself a newcomer compared to that star status thing people talk about. I don't feel any different now than I did ten years ago. I think we've just started. I have a new album that's just coming out; it's a new direction for us, I think the last nine or ten years have been preparation for some great music, hopefully some great shows.

---

❖

I think country music is definitely the music of today.

❖

---

TURNER: Is this new direction away from country?

SHEPPARD: Good question! I'm country music today. Country music has finally gone down all the different avenues. I don't think it's gone as far in each avenue as it's going to. There's now a contemporary market; there's a bluegrass market; there's a gospel market; there's all types of country music. It will continue to grow in all directions with a lot of new artists coming along. I think country music is definitely the music of today.

TURNER: How would you describe yourself? What kind of image do you want to portray?

SHEPPARD: I think your music portrays your image. If I did truck-driving songs, people would think I was a truck driver. If I did drinking songs, people would think I was a drinker. As a matter of fact, I don't drink. If I did love songs, people would think of me as a sex symbol. I do music that we call country music—a good love song, a contemporary ballad—songs that most all of us could relate to. I can't relate to a truck-driving song because I don't drive a truck. I've got a pickup truck, not an eighteen-wheeler. I can't relate to a drinking song because I don't drink or smoke. To be a sex image-type person is very flattering. *Ok!* Now I was never the guy who got the pretty girl. I'm serious. I was the guy who got made fun of because I was a dreamer. I think all I ever want to be in life is a hope and an inspiration for someone who has a dream. If we share with someone else, they have a chance to have their dream come true. I'm living my dream. If I can be an inspiration to someone else or help them to fulfill their dream, that's all I want.

TURNER: What are your interests and hobbies?

---

> The more a person knows about his business increases his chances of making a livelihood at his chosen profession.

---

SHEPPARD: Stock car racing. And I also enjoy the race horse business. I got my first three horses this week. I went to the auction and bought them. I was able to buy a brother of the world champion horse.

TURNER: Has it been difficult balancing career and family? How do you work it all in?

SHEPPARD: Hopefully you just make enough money to send your kids through school and your wife to Neiman-Marcus. I call my wife every day on the road. I talk to my son every day and get caught up on what's happening in his life to see if he has any problems or whatever. We're really close-knit. We do work a lot. We work very hard in the summertime. During the winter, work will slack down, allowing us to do recordings or do television. Then we go on the road in March or April. It's very difficult to manage family and career. I'm a strong believer that absence does make the heart grow fonder.

TURNER: If you really want to showcase T. G. Sheppard, what type of song would you perform?

SHEPPARD: I'd do pretty much the type of music I've been doing—it's what I call people music or music that you can sink your teeth into.

TURNER: How did your background as a PR person in the music business help you with the entertainment aspect of the business?

SHEPPARD: I think a working knowledge of any industry increases your chances of success in that particular industry. The more a person knows about his business increases his chances of making a livelihood at his chosen profession. The chances of success are a lot greater. On the business side, my knowledge of PR really helped me a lot.

TURNER: Were there doors opened that might not have been opened had you not had your background?

---

❖

I think what I want to do is just to touch people's lives with my music.

❖

---

SHEPPARD: I'm sure! I have to believe in fate and destiny. My performing might have been later or it might have been earlier had it not been for my background—I don't know. I strongly feel that I was destined to do what I'm doing now. Ever since I was twelve or thirteen years old I have always known what I wanted to do. I've had other jobs: I've driven a truck, worked for a bottling company, worked on assembly lines. I know what the common man, the hard-working man, who works eight-ten-twelve hours a day has do to earn a living. I've been there and I know I'm not too good to go back to that if I needed to. I'm not saying I'd like to, but I'm not too good to go back. I do know what a hard day's work is.

TURNER: Of the songs you have recorded, do you have a favorite?

SHEPPARD: There's two or three. "Do You Want To Go To Heaven," which was one of our very first big records when we were on the comeback trail; "If And Forever" became a very good song because its a song most people can relate to. And I must say "Falling" because it is the song everyone requests. I love them all. I really do. I like to do all the songs I sing. It's hard to pick a favorite because they are all like children to you. You find the song, and if you're going to record it, you work on it. You fine-tune it and you grind off the rough edges. You go back and you go back again until you get it just the way you want it. Then you release it. They're sort of like children to you—like babies—they stay in your life forever. They are songs I'll be singing until I'm eighty years old if I'm still performing. Saying I have one favorite song would be hard to do. I love all the music I do.

TURNER: If you could wave a magic wand, what would you want your music to do for your audience?

SHEPPARD: I want my music to do what it's starting to do now. I want to be able to walk on stage and make people oblivious to outside things for that hour or hour and a half. If they're in a car or at home listening to an album, I would like for my music to help them forget their trouble. If you can forget what was troubling you for a few minutes, it can be a mental release. I think what I want to do is just to touch people's lives with my music.

---

> I want to be able to walk on stage and make people oblivious to outside things for that hour or hour and a half.

---

TURNER: You were fortunate to have a close friendship with Elvis. What bit of advice did he give you that has helped you both as an entertainer and as a person?

SHEPPARD: There was only one thing. Don't ever let the ego get so big that you can't tell or laugh at a joke. He never got so famous that he didn't like to eat mashed potatoes, black-eyed peas or cabbage with a slice of meat. But he was a prisoner of his own success. It got to a point where he felt he had to be secluded and couldn't lead a normal life. I'm the kind of guy that if a tour bus came by my house I'd jump on and say hello. I wouldn't run off in the corner and hide. I've worked hard all my life to get where I am. I hope I never get to the point where I feel I need to run and hide.

TURNER: I was impressed with your interaction with the audience and their response to you tonight. How did you develop this talent?

SHEPPARD: Well, that's the way I am. I'm that way off-stage and on the sage. Some people go home and get off in a room and scream their lungs out. I never do that. There's times when you need to be alone. I have all the time I need to relax, watch a movie, read a book, while I ride down the road. This afternoon/tonight I want to be with the people. When I get to the next gig I will want to be with people again. Tomorrow night I might want to be alone.

TURNER: If you were an interviewer with T. G. Sheppard what question would you ask him that I haven't asked?

SHEPPARD: "Is it really worth it? Is all this really worth it?" And I would have to say, "Yes, it's worth it!" To be able to touch people's lives with my music and have them react to me as a person is worth all those years of struggling. Performers are fortunate to be able to touch other people's lives.

October 1983

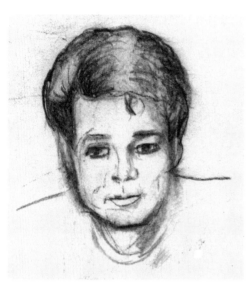

*Music picked me. It's not like I said, "Well I'll learn to play the guitar." It was like, "Hey, give me that guitar; I'm gonna play it."*
*—Doug Stone*

T HEY'RE CALLED THE "new breed" of country music. They are a group of younger, more diverse, and more innovative performers than their predecessors. This new breed is both the product and the cause of the changes in country music in the last few years. Their spirit and force is projected by no one any better than Doug Stone.

Stone burst onto the music scene with his "I'd Be Better Off (In A Pine Box)" from his self-titled debut album, and he has been a regular on the country music charts ever since.

The Georgia native made his singing debut at age seven by opening an Atlanta-area show for Loretta Lynn. The self-confessed "show biz ham" continued to evelop his musical career during his teens and early adult life by performing at local bars and clubs. These varied influences helped to develop his emotionally drenched voice.

The mechanic by day, singer by night was discovered at the VFW Hall in Newnan by a music scout who was so impressed that she immediately pledged to be his link to fame—a link that brought a record deal and national exposure.

# Doug Stone

TURNER: Where do you see yourself on the music spectrum?

STONE: A beginner, I'm a cub scout.

TURNER: T. G. Sheppard once told me that country music is so simple. That's why it is so easy for the emotions to respond to. What are your feelings toward this statement?

---

I don't think country music is simple. I think that it's true life stories—that's what is good about it.

---

STONE: I don't think that country music done right is easy. I've played in every kind of band you could play in. I've played in rock and roll bands and top-forty bands and country bands and to me, anything that you do, if you do it right, you are gonna have to put that extra effort to make it come out right. It doesn't just happen; you go in there and you practice and play together and you talk about it. I don't think country music is simple. I think that it's true life stories—that's what is good about it.

TURNER: You once said that, "When I was younger I could sing a song and I could yank tears from my audience, but yet I didn't know what was bringing those tears, and I didn't really understand that until I started to live." Does life develop a style?

STONE: Life makes you appreciate what you're singing about; it gives you an insight into what you are singing about. Living says it about as hard as it can be said and I've been there where you've felt like that maybe I would be better off there. You don't want to go there but that's the only thing that could be worse than where you are sitting.

TURNER: In another article I read that your parents had a bitter divorce, and part of you wanted to go with your mom and part of you wanted to go with your dad in that he was teaching you things that you needed to learn in life to survive.

STONE: My brothers and I wanted to stay together. I had been working with Daddy since I was twelve years old. He would take us camping and stuff like that, and he was teaching me things that other kids were not learning. The other kids would go home and watch Mickey Mouse. I would go home from school and work on diesel trucks. I figured in the long run you spend eighteen years as a kid, and if you're lucky, you spend forty as an adult. So I'm going to be using what I was learning from Daddy more than I would use watching Mickey Mouse.

❖

> I've had my hard times and I'm sure if I live, I'm gonna have more hard times. But the thing about it is, don't dwell on hard times.

❖

TURNER: Your songs reek with emotion, but in person you are so alive with enthusiasm. Which is the real Doug Stone?

STONE: I'm the whole ball of wax. I've had my hard times and I'm sure if I live, I'm gonna have more hard times. But the thing about it is, don't dwell on hard times. Learn from them and go on and have a good time. The real me right now is definitely as happy as a dead pig in the sunshine.

TURNER: Do you think your quick smile is indicative of the fact that you are satisfied by what you're doing and producing today?

STONE: I don't know; I have always smiled all of my life. As a matter of fact, I usually laugh at things that were not supposed to be laughed at. I've always been able to find a humorous side to a bad story.

TURNER: From all accounts, your live concerts are really an experience; what did your mom teach you about showmanship?

STONE: She taught me how to play guitar and how to sing a song, but as far as showmanship goes, it has to be acquired or learned. The main thing I have found is to be myself. If I feel like jumping, then that is what I do.

That way I'm not putting on an act. It's not something that was prerecorded in the studio; it's the true spontaneity of emotions. When I feel great and the crowd is with me, then I usually do a better show.

TURNER: When you are performing, what do you want your music to do for fans?

STONE: I want them to feel like they are part of it, a part of the whole show, because without them I wouldn't be there and vice versa.

TURNER: What do you get back in return when an audience is receptive to you and your music?

STONE: Well, it's kind of like the guy who builds a statue. He goes in his basement and he gets a rock and starts banging away. Pretty soon he has something that he likes to look at. Then he takes it out to the public and then when they like what he likes, then you think, "Hey I'm doing something right."

TURNER: Is success as sweet as you thought it would be?

STONE: Sure. It's a lot of hours on the road. The worst thing that I've found out about the road is the boredom, because the bigger you get, the more boredom is involved.

TURNER: What do you do to pass some of these idle hours while waiting?

STONE: Well I'm going to put a studio on the bus, hopefully, so I can go in there and record stuff and be creative. I've had several studios in my life. In the studio I can get lost in time and space. Time ceases; I just go in there and I don't think about anything but what I am doing.

TURNER: You have gotten some wonderful reviews; what are you most proud of in these reviews?

STONE: That people are liking what I am doing. They like the show that they are seeing and they like the music they are hearing. And that's all I can expect. That's what I'm after. I am after their appreciation.

TURNER: With all the success that you have achieved, who brings you back down to earth?

STONE: Well, I guess my family. I can go home and talk to Daddy and my brother and my wife and my kids, and they are still planted on earth, and I'm still there too, and so I don't get too far above it.

TURNER: What has been the hardest obstacle or hurdle that you've had to overcome?

STONE: Firing people that I like. It's a business first. You've got friends that you play with, but if they are not doing the job that you think that they should be doing, you have to let them go.

❖

> I'm just trying to do the best songs that I can find. Whether I write them or if John Bell writes them.

❖

TURNER: What measures are you weaving into your career today to ensure that you are going to be around for years to come?

STONE: I'm just trying to do the best songs that I can find. Whether I write them or if John Bell writes them. I think it's like Conway Twitty said, "It's the song; they can find plenty of people to sing it." So when I look, I look for hit songs: something that I can feel like I can be a part of.

TURNER: You know Jean Shepherd, she told me one time that there are a lot of people out there hoping to make it, and those who do make it seem to have something special. What do you think has been your special something?

STONE: Music picked me. It's not like I said, "Well I'll learn to play the guitar." It was like, "Hey, give me that guitar; I'm gonna play it."

TURNER: Who taught you how to play the guitar?

STONE: My mother, she taught me the basic chords, and everybody that I would get around would show me something new. The guitar is something that I don't think anybody has mastered yet until you see Stanley Jordan play two of them at a time—and play them fluently. And there is Chet Atkins; the guy is great. I know that I'll never be a guitar player. I don't even worry about it anymore.

TURNER: When things were bad for you, what kept you going?

STONE: I went so far as to lose my house and my dump truck. Then I bought a five hundred-dollar trailer and anywhere you stepped you might break a leg going through the floor. I had one air conditioner and a TV. It was comfortable. I poured seven hundred dollars into a truck and I was happy. Being happy in any state you are in at a particular time is important. It doesn't matter whether you have a mansion or a shack; if you are happy then you are rich.

---

It doesn't matter whether you have a mansion or a shack; if you are happy then you are rich.

---

TURNER: If you really want to showcase the talent of Doug Stone, what song would you do?

STONE: I am real prejudiced of the first album. Every song on it was well-picked and well-thought-out before we ever started.

TURNER: Do you leave the selection of songs up to another group of people, or do you have a lot of input in the selection of materials?

STONE: I have input into just about everything that I do. I like having other people's opinions. I don't have the last word on anything. Just because I think it is right doesn't mean it is. So the best thing to do is to find other people in the business who have already had success, and ask them about it.

TURNER: What do you see on the horizon for Doug Stone?

STONE: I just want to be able to play. That's what I have wanted to do all of my life, so now that I am here I would like to stay around till I get ready to leave.

TURNER: If I were to look up the name Doug Stone in the encyclopedia, what would it have written after your name?

STONE: Your next-door neighbor.

TURNER: What influence has you mother had on you or your career?

STONE: As far as a career goes, she told me that she always felt that I could do it and that all I had to do was just try. The way I got into the record business was just a chance thing. A lady came and listened to me and then she signed me up and said, "Let's go."

TURNER: In your opinion, what do you like about country music, or what is country music to you?

STONE: It's great. I feel like Alabama was the first group to come out and start the new country sound. We've got a new batch of people doing traditional country with different ideas.

TURNER: What would you tell someone who had never been to one of your concerts to expect?

STONE: A good time and something that you won't be bored with. I am anything but boring. I've noticed myself on stage before, and I feel like I may want to stand still. And then I think, "Well no, I don't want to stand still, I want to walk." I may be dancing from one side of the stage to the other. I love to play a guitar, but I can't play a guitar and do what I want to do. I am also a drummer, a bass player, and a keyboard player. And now I am trying to learn how to play the fiddle.

TURNER: Do you have a song that can showcase all of your talents?

STONE: No, it's kind of hard to get off the drums and do something else. You lose the beat. Unless you have two sets on stage. I am thinking about putting my set of drums up there along with my drummer's set. It is interesting to watch somebody go from one instrument to another. It is like watching a Hank Williams, Jr. concert because he runs around and plays everything.

TURNER: What was your reaction the first time that you opened for a major star?

STONE: "I am going to do the best job that I can do."

TURNER: Who was the first major entertainer that you opened for?

STONE: Ricky Van Shelton and Vern Gosdin I think was the first ones that I opened for. And Vern got up on stage and sang a song with me.

TURNER: If you were doing an interview with Doug Stone, what question would you ask that I haven't asked?

STONE: Why didn't you do it sooner? And I have no answer for that. The timing wasn't right. It falls into place when it is supposed to. If I had gotten the deal that I have right now at twenty, I would've blown it all to pieces because I was ignorant. I'm better able to accept success today than I would have been able to at twenty.

September 1990

*I have had more success than I ever thought I would. I've accomplished more than I ever thought I could. I always dreamed I would, but in the back of my mind I kinda had my doubts because there's a lot of people out there trying to get where I am right now.*
*—George Strait*

George Strait has been acclaimed as the barometer by which all new traditional country artists will be measured. Strait attributes his traditional sound to his early musical influences, Merle Haggard, George Jones, Hank Williams, Sr., and Bob Wills. The desire to sing surfaced after Strait purchased a used guitar during his military stint in Hawaii. He taught himself to play with the help of some old Hank Williams song books. Soon he found himself in demand as a singer, and was assigned full-time duty as an entertainer during his last year in the military.

Upon his discharge from the Army, Strait returned to his native Texas and re-enrolled in Southwest Texas State to pursue an agriculture education degree. He went to school during the day, and played music at night.

Strait, a very popular local entertainer, failed to impress Nashville's elite. Three failed attempts at Nashville bred thoughts of abandoning his musical ambitions.

The big break came when Texas club owner, Erv Woolsey, returned to Nashville to work for MCA Records. Once firmly established in Nashville, Woolsey was in a position to introduce Strait to the right people, which culminated in Strait's being offered a record contract.

Strait's success insures the future of the traditional country sound.

# George Strait

TURNER: If you had to describe your music to someone who had never heard it before, how would you describe it?

STRAIT: I would say it's a kind of contemporary traditional country music. We are doing the more hardcore country stuff. Our stage show is a little different from our album; it's a little more hard country. If I had to describe the music, I'd say "Remember back a long time ago. What we try to do is go back and get the good old songs, the old Texas two-step songs and shuffles.

---

If it wasn't for Haggard, Jones, and people like that, there's no telling where it would be right now, but all I want to do is sing country music.

---

TURNER: One thing that impressed me is the fact that you have a lot of young people in your audience. They seem to be very responsive to the type of music that you are performing; however, very few performers are doing Bob Wills and things like that. Why do you think performers aren't doing his type of music today?

STRAIT: I don't know. Swing music is fun music to play, and once somebody hears it, it's hard not to like the music, so that's a real good question. I really don't know why more people aren't doing it, but we sure enjoy doing it.

TURNER: There are those who believe that country music is going through a transitional period. What role do you see yourself or your music playing in this transition?

STRAIT: I feel that everywhere I go and everybody I talk with puts me in a category with people like John Anderson, Ricky Skaggs, and Reba

McEntire. They say we are all helping to keep country music country. If it wasn't for Haggard, Jones, and people like that, there's no telling where it would be right now, but all I want to do is sing country music. I could care less about having a crossover record—if a record of mine crossed over it would have to be because they liked it. I feel like we are helping to keep the traditional sound in country music.

TURNER: It has been said that you represent the best of the new breed of country singers to hit the market in the last few years. What do you attribute these accolades to?

---

I feel that if you are going to do a video you ought to make it as good as you possibly can.

---

STRAIT: I paid them off to say that! I remember that guy! No, I don't know; that's quite a compliment and I feel good about that. I never thought of myself like that, but I do like to sing.

TURNER: Who would you say has had the greatest influence on your music?

STRAIT: Probably Haggard, Jones, Bob Wills and the Texas Playboys.

TURNER: A lot of people believe that the popularity of country music can be attributed to the fact that it has a beginning, a middle, and an end, and tells a story in three minutes. Do you think this is true?

STRAIT: I am sure that has a lot to do with it. It deals with real things that happen every day that people can relate to. It's not a hard story to understand; most of the stories are easy to figure out. A lot of times the same thing can either run through your mind or has happened to you, so I think it has a lot to do with the success of a song.

TURNER: Music videos are really, really popular right now. What impact is this going to have on country music?

STRAIT: Well! I think it will have a big impact on country music if people start doing videos and really doing them right. You can tell they really put the money into a lot of the videos I see on TV, and you can also tell when they have just done them really fast and as cheap as they can. But I feel that if you are going to do a video you ought to make it as good as you possibly can. I'm all for the videos. I intend to do some more if I feel like the song is good for one.

TURNER: You have experienced a lot of success. How have you been able to keep everything in perspective?

STRAIT: Well, I don't take it all that seriously. I mean, I take it very seriously but I don't let it really get to me. The road is the hardest part about it, being out on the road and being away from home for so long.

TURNER: Do you make music that you like to hear?

STRAIT: Yes, I do.

TURNER: If I were to stop someone on the street in San Marcos, Texas, and I were to say the name "George Strait," what would their reactions and comments be?

STRAIT: I don't know! I hope they would be good. I have a lot of friends down there and I've been living there since 1975.

TURNER: You were raised around that area?

STRAIT: I was raised in Pearsall, Texas, which is about a hundred miles south of there; I went to school there and finished college there. I really do like it. I'd like to say I have a lot of friends there, so hopefully, they wouldn't talk too bad about me.

TURNER: How did your training as an educator help you in the music industry?

STRAIT: Not at all! I was going to school under the GI Bill and wanted to graduate from college. Don't get me wrong, but I went on the GI bill and it allowed me to have time to play music and it didn't tie me down a whole lot, and it was really good for me. I never did intend to teach. I got a degree in agriculture education.

TURNER: If you really want to showcase George Strait, what song or title would you do?

STRAIT: I like doing stuff like "When I Heard You Call My Name." That's a good old song and it's been around for a long time, and I would do some swing and that type of stuff.

TURNER: You mentioned earlier the fact you never really intended to teach. When did you seriously say, "Hey, I want to be a singer"?

STRAIT: When I was about twenty-one, I was in the service at the time and I really just wanted to get a guitar, learn a few songs, and learn how to play it for my own self. One thing led to another and I kept getting more and more serious. Then I started playing in bands.

TURNER: Kenny Rogers once told me that success brings the potential for more success because it opens more doors. What does success mean to you?

STRAIT: I have had more success than I ever thought I would. I've accomplished more than I ever thought I could. I always dreamed I would, but in the back of my mind I kinda had my doubts because there's a lot of people out there trying to get where I am right now. You've got to be very lucky!

TURNER: How important is timing to a performer's career?

STRAIT: Real important. I don't feel that seven or eight years ago this could have happened to me. If it had, I probably would not have been ready for it, and it would have been harder for me to do. I needed those years playing those bars and doing that kind of thing to prepare myself for this.

TURNER: If you had to say one thing about your success, what would you say?

STRAIT: *I love it!*

TURNER: What kind of image would you like to project?

STRAIT: Well, I haven't really thought about it. I think the kind of image I do project is more of a clean-cut type image. I've been called "Mr. Clean" in *People* magazine, you know. I think that's the kind of image I do project. I am into the cowboy scene. I've got a lot of friends in rodeo, and I like that type of thing. My brother and I put on a roping down in Texas every year and it's a real success. I think that's the kind of image that I do project in life.

TURNER: Some trade magazines are trying to project you as a sex symbol. How comfortable are you with this title?

STRAIT: I don't take it too seriously, I really don't. It's kinda funny to me. I would rather be thought of that way than the opposite, so it pleases me pretty much!

TURNER: What do you want for yourself in the future?

STRAIT: Well, I just want to keep having new records, and as long as I can do that, I'll be happy because that's really what I set out to do in the first place. If I can keep doing that I'll be happy.

October 1983

*I see myself as a bit of a bridge between the old timers like Johnny Cash, Ernest Tubb, Lester Flatt, Roy Acuff, Bill Monroe, Grandpa Jones, Jimmy Dickens, and Hank Snow, and today's generation.*
—*Marty Stuart*

MARTY STUART, one of country music's newest sensations, is actually a veteran of more than two decades of playing alongside Music City's most celebrated stars.

Stuart, a Mississippi native, began his professional career at the age of thirteen playing mandolin in Lester Flatt's legendary bluegrass band. Following Flatt's death, Stuart joined the Johnny Cash Band. In 1982, Stuart launched his solo career with the release of "Busy Bee Cafe," thus ending a six-year stint with Cash. His first solo attempt won critical acclaim but met with little commercial success. Four years later, he recorded his first major label release, *Marty Stuart*, which failed to establish Stuart as a major solo contender. As a result of poor record sales he was dropped by CBS Records.

To rejuvenate himself, he returned to his roots: his home in Mississippi. With renewed energy and spirits he soon headed back to Nashville.

Immediately, he signed with MCA Records and recorded such hits as "Hillbilly Rock," "Tempted," and "Western Girl," which met with instant succes and firmly established Stuart as a major solo act.

Stuart, a self-described hillbilly, has a penchant to preserve the history of country music. He collects and surrounds himself with memorabilia of his musical heroes. He owns dozens of sequined costumes that were worn by the great stars of the fifties and sixties, and tours in the bus that was once owned by Ernest Tubb.

# Marty Stuart

TURNER: There was a time when sequins and rhinestone suits were out of fashion. What brought them back in vogue?

STUART: I started wearing them with jeans instead of the whole suit because the suit seemed so serious and I wanted to have fun, but right after that Dwight Yoakam got into them, and the Desert Rose Band started wearing them again, and videos kicked in and it all kind of came back again.

TURNER: Where do you see yourself on the country music spectrum, or the music spectrum totally?

---

I consider myself a hillbilly crusader and
I'm very proud to be doing that.

---

STUART: I have always seen myself as a unique act. The Lester Flatt Show played a lot of colleges and bluegrass festivals, which put us in the rock and roll crowd. For instance, Lester played tours with Gram Parsons, and Emmylou Harris, and the Eagles: that was a pretty rounded show. We played a lot to hippies back then, which are the yuppies today. A lot of people who saw us in concert back then are now driving BMWs; they're the typical yuppies and they still remember us. I see myself as a bit of a bridge between the old-timers like Johnny Cash, Ernest Tubb, Lester Flatt, Roy Acuff, Bill Monroe, Grandpa Jones, Jimmy Dickens, and Hank Snow, and today's generation. They come to me and I go to them with advice, and I feel like I'm the link between the old world of country music and the new world of country music. It's real flattering. For instance, my bus is Ernest Tubb's old bus, and I played poker in this bus when I was a teenager. I consider myself a hillbilly crusader and I'm very proud to be doing that.

TURNER: What is the difference between hillbilly music and country music?

227

STUART: I think it's an attitude! Sometimes I think country music takes itself a little too seriously, that's the only thing. I don't think I am in a position to criticize young entertainers, but I think I can share with other entertainers what I learned from the master. The thing that I don't feel from the new bunch of entertainers is the fraternity and the brotherhood we used to feel when I first started. It's like when Jim Reeves got killed and someone said, "When one gets cut we all bleed." I don't think country music feels that way today. For instance, when Keith Whitley died, I think everybody felt bad about his death, but they were right back on the road Monday morning. Country music is the greatest thing going today. We're not perfect but we're the greatest thing doing. Hillbilly music is a little more catty, a little more of get out on the limb where it's cracked, a little more rock and roll attitude. I consider myself a hillbilly singer.

TURNER: You have been around so many great entertainers and have played with some of the greatest bands in country music. What is the greatest lesson Johnny Cash and some of the others taught you?

STUART: I played with Cash for six years. Johnny inspired me on how and how not to act. Johnny Cash is a great communicator. I remember one time we were at the border of Czechoslovakia and they stopped us and there was all this talk, and the tour manager came in and said, "They will not let us pass until you sing a song." Cash got his guitar out. We went and played some songs for the guards and they let us cross the border. I think with Lester Flatt, I got to see the world through the eyes of a superstar.

The first record I ever had was a Johnny Cash record and a Flatt and Scruggs record was the second one I ever owned. It's ironic that I worked with both of them.

TURNER: You started playing with Lester Flatt when you were twelve or thirteen? Those were real formative years for you. How did he help you make the transition without going astray during that period of time? You probably played a lot of clubs?

STUART: Well, we didn't play clubs, but there were obvious things that happen on the road or were available on the road. Lester was a good moral man. My mother wouldn't have let me tour with the Rolling Stones. I think the reason Lester did so good and was so respected was because he was a total businessman. Lester taught me how to treat an audience. He gave the same show whether there were two people or two million in the audience. My basic rules of show business came from Lester Flatt. He taught me how to have fun when you do what you do. Someone recently gave me a tape of my first night playing mandolin with him, and I really could play. I could see the wheels click in the old man's mind—thinking this kid can really play—old act needs new blood. He was a total businessman.

---

## My basic rules of show business came from Lester Flatt.

---

TURNER: Steve Earle once said country music is a magnet for many artists. Do you find that to be true?

STUART: Very much so; the only problem I have, you know, is that country music is kind of like America. We open up our gates and everybody comes in and then you wind up taking on everyone's problems. I've pretty much got my life dedicated to the Lord and country music and I think that's the finest things you can be dedicated to. If I have two bad years in a row, it doesn't make me stop loving or make me stop playing country music, because from 1987 to 1990 was as bad as you can get commercially for me; I was off the air. I looked around and I saw pop stars that had failing careers coming over to country to try to salvage their careers by doing a TV album, and I hate that. I'm very opposed to that process. Country music rejected some of its own—one being Steve Earle. Steve Earle is one of the most brilliant writers that we have right now. We have writers and we have poets. I think he is a poet for us. Steve's hair did not look right and he didn't go by the mall and buy a cowboy hat. Therefore country music did not accept him. k.d. lang, one of the most important performers we have, was also dubbed by the family of country music. Country music dubbed me for three years. I had to go out and get Ernest Tubb's bus and cut a hillbilly record before they loved me again. I had to do all of this even though I had spent my life performing country music. Johnny Cash gave a good piece of advice. He said, "When Carl, Jerry, Elvis, and I started out we were different. I looked around and Webb Pierce and Carl Smith and all those guys were happening and we used to wonder why we couldn't be like them. Then we finally figured out we were different.

But I figured out how to be a rebel. You don't break the rules; you abide by them and take them a step further—now go out and have yourself a career."

TURNER: Do you find the industry is better poised to accept new acts today?

STUART: Absolutely! The worst years we had musically were the mid seventies to the early eighties. Ricky Skaggs singlehandedly put country music back in order and took out the urban cowboy theme. The only good thing that came out of the urban cowboy movement was that we went from a mom and a pop industry to a blue chip industry. There is so much talent out there until it is staggering. But it remains to be seen who has staying power. I was taught that if you go slow, you can build a foundation, but at times it's frustrating. It takes a little longer. I'm glad we didn't go platinum right out of the box, because if you go platinum right out of the box, then when you start going gold, you're failing. So I'm glad we're having a slow steady climb; I feel like we're building as we go.

TURNER: You mentioned that the industry is becoming a blue chip industry. Has this hampered creativity in Nashville or Music City? The bottom line is M O N E Y, and oftentimes executives step over a lot of talent and creativity. Has this been good or bad for the music industry.

STUART: Well! There are a few producers in town that don't show up for their sessions. If you read a record label it will say produced by blank and the artist. Many times the producers leave it to the artists to produce the record. Oftentimes the producer might make a token appearance, or might not show up at all. Honest to God, some producers have three acts going on at the same time—that's definitely not a hands-on production. Those guys are the pirates as far as I am concerned, and they are just in there for the bucks. There are a handful of guys who still passionately care about the artist and the music. Tony Brown, a brilliant producer, made this statement one time: "I'm trying to build a career, too, and I can't afford a dud." I think Billy Sherill is one of the most brilliant producers in the world, but he won't show up for sessions. He lets George Jones and the engineers cut his records.

TURNER: If I were to look up Marty Stuart in the encyclopedia, what would I find after his name?

STUART: Hillbilly singer, state-of-the-art hillbilly. I think that would pretty much call it right there, hillbilly singer.

TURNER: Huey Lewis once told me that the first thing an entertainer does is get himself into a comfortable position, and then he doesn't try anything else. What are your feelings toward this statement?

STUART: Well, I started playing bluegrass/gospel music, and from there I went to Lester Flatt. I discovered an album call *Sweetheart Of The Rodeo* by the Byrds. I started experimenting with country rock and bluegrass. I played hillbilly jazz and I toured with Bob Dylan and the Rolling Thunder Review. Next I went to work with Johnny Cash, and for the past few years, I've been trying to kick the door down and get some music across to the people. I still have a whole bunch of cards up my sleeve. The minute I get one thing conquered I'm going on to do something else. When I went to work for Lester, he was at the point in his life where he was a statesman and he was enjoying his success. He was a millionaire and he enjoyed walking around being Lester Flatt. He still gave great shows but, as far as learning new chords and songs, that really wasn't his bag. On the other hand, Johnny Cash still gets up every day and works on being Johnny Cash—I know that for a fact.

TURNER: Is there a difference between changing and growing as an artist?

STUART: I think that would be a good question for Bob Dylan. There are two people that I'll never give up on and those are Johnny Cash and Bob Dylan. Sometimes I get angry at Bob Dylan for not having another *Blood On The Tracks* album. But I have to stop and say, "Maybe I'm the guilty party." I think we as an audience want Bob Dylan to be what he was in the sixties, and he's not that anymore. He doesn't have anything to say. He's already said it, and I think the bottom line is you follow your heart and your gut and that's the only way I know to stay out of trouble. It's like western wear—it is not always the most fashionable thing going, but it's always there.

TURNER: How do you think the decade of the nineties will go down?

STUART: Springboard for a lot of new talent and new country. You know, the fifties were the heyday of country talent. There was Kitty Wells and also what was left of Roy Acuff's sparkling career. Then came the hillbillies in Nashville and cowboys like Tex Ritter over in California. Country music was bubbling, man, and the sixties did it. Merle Haggard came in the sixties and revolutionized country music. I think country music is kind of doing that all over again, and that's what is happening now in music.

Country music is real healthy right now. It remains to be seen as to what person can hang in there and go into the twenty-first century. When I bow my head at night and ask for my wishes, I pray to be one of the persons to carry some of real goods from the pioneers that invented the rules around Nashville into the twenty-first century. Music is my soul and I have to consider it my duty to carry it into the next century.

TURNER: To you, what is success?

STUART: There are two dimensions to success. Number one is on a material plane. I've got a closet full of boots. I've got my hero, Lester Flatt's, guitar which I play on stage every night. I've got Ernest Tubb's bus, I've got a great band, and I've got people screaming and hollering. That is number one. I mean, on a shallow level, that is success. Success to me is having people care about my music, really care. True success is after all is said and done when I go home and get in my Jeep and go out in the woods and shut the gate. There is still peace in my heart and I'm very content. I know if I stop and don't play another note, I've had a sparkling career as a young man, and the light is just now coming on for me, and there are no regrets, and there's peace in my heart, and I sleep real good at night. I think that is success.

TURNER: How have you been able to keep it all together like this?

STUART: I've had a good support system. I call them my advisers. My mom is incredible. She's not a stage mother. My sister works where they make these clothes. And she is just as proud of her as she is of me. I have a morally fine family. My family has always been there. It has been a family trip. People like Jack Clement, a legendary producer in Nashville, is another one of my supporters. To this day, if I wake up in wonder, I call Johnny Cash. I've had access to a lot of the masters. I feel like I've been a fortunate child. I've kept people with me that I wouldn't be ashamed of and the council of heaven wouldn't be ashamed of: people who walk it instead of talking it.

TURNER: Of all your accomplishments, which are you the proudest?

STUART: The first summer I was on the road I met a man named Jerry Sullivan. He was a voice in the wilderness, that's what I call him. He and his daughters Tammy and Stephanie and a little mandolin player from Cherokee Creek, Louisiana, would go from one Pentecostal church to another and from schoolhouse to schoolhouse, and to bluegrass festivals on weekends to play their music. They made very little money but they are the happiest people I know. The Sullivans play some of the best string music that I've ever heard. They are rare people. He's one of the greatest songwriters that I've ever heard. I'm talking about standards like "Amazing Grace," "Old Rugged Cross" kind of hymnbook songs. We've written some fifty songs together. My proudest accomplishment is that I turned the Country Music Hall of Fame on the Sullivans and they're gonna publish their songs in a song book. Also, they're about to release the album that I recorded with them. We recorded this album over a year ago, and I've been waiting for it to be released. We're gonna do a video on them so the masses will finally get to see the Sullivans. Oftentimes when I do shows in Nashville I bring the Sullivans out and showcase them to the industry, hoping to turn the industry on to them. I enjoy playing acoustic music with them. When I want to escape my electric world and get away from everything, I go to my acoustic world and play with the Sullivans. If you will remember when you were in college and you saw Lester Flatt and you would say, "That's very nice," then it became fashionable to like those people. The same thing is happening with the Sullivans today. My work with the Sullivans probably makes me happier than anything I've ever done.

TURNER: If you were an interviewer doing an interview with Marty Stuart, what question would you ask that I haven't asked?

STUART: I guess it would be, "Why do you do what you do? Why do you eat at truck stops? Why do you get out and hug people with no teeth? Why do you let them grab you and pull at your clothes and squeeze on your body?" It's because I know I have a light inside of me, that makes me light up and shine. If I can make people forget that they have problems— if they had a fight before they came here, or if the IRS is on them or whatever the problem—if I can lift the problem off of the for forty-five minutes and let them go home to the problem with a little more cha cha cha to deal with it. Then that's why I do what I do.

September 1990

RICKY VAN SHELTON has established himself as one of the major forces in country music today. It is hard to believe that just a short time ago he was a blue collar worker in his native Grit, Virginia.

Van Shelton, a product of a devout Pentecostal upbringing, has a sincere concern for his fans. The often misquoted entertainer goes togreat lengths to rectify any negative images that can result from such inaccuracies. The congenial, young entertainer recently appeared eager to share his view on a wide variety of topics.

*. . . my dream has always been music and I guess I'll be playing till I die. I never wanted to be a star. It just comes with the music.*
*—Ricky Van Shelton*

# Ricky Van Shelton

TURNER: Where do you see yourself on the music spectrum?

VAN SHELTON: That is a tough question. I don't plainly know where I see myself. I just concentrate on the albums and the tours. I don't want to see myself one way or the other.

TURNER: So many artists are having crossover hits: Are artists crossing over or are fans crossing over to Country Music?

VAN SHELTON: Both! The artists are crossing over the fans are also crossing over. We are going one way and they are going the other way. I like it. I wish there was no such thing as a country music station or a rock and roll station. I wish they played everything on the same station like they used to do. I thought that was a great format.

TURNER: Ronnie Milsap once told me that if you are going to be a leader you must take risks. What risks has Ricky Van Shelton taken with his music?

VAN SHELTON: Well I haven't taken much risk. I want to but I've kinda been subdued because the record companies were afraid. We concentrate on what a radio station will or will not play. Record companies pretty much know what types of songs are hits and what types of song can't get airplay. You are bound to work within these lines. I would like to do all kinds of stuff. I have to take risks sometimes.

TURNER: You had such a big hit with "Simple Man." How accurate is that a description of Ricky Van Shelton?

VAN SHELTON: Real accurate! I am just a simple man. That is what I told them last night. At the end of the show I said, "I'm going home—I'm just a simple man."

TURNER: In the song it says, "All I need is a piece of land" and so forth. What does Ricky Van Shelton need?

VAN SHELTON: Well, I need the happiness that God brings. I used to think, "Boy if I had money, I'd have everything."

TURNER: Have your ambitions of today changed much from your young ambitions?

VAN SHELTON: No, my dream has always been music, and I guess I'll be playing till I die. I never wanted to be a star. It just comes with the music. Being a star is a big job because of the time element and all that is demanded of you. It's an incredible amount of pressure. There are lots of things people want out of you and a lot of stuff people want out of you. It just drains the life out of you if you will let it. It is real easy to get wrapped up in awards, glitter, glamour, if that's what you're after. Thank goodness I'm like the song "Simple Man." I don't care about all that stuff.

❖

Well, I need the happiness that God brings. I used to think, "Boy if I had money, I'd have everything."

❖

TURNER: After all of the lights go down and the applause dies, where does Ricky Van Shelton go for inspiration?

VAN SHELTON: To God! I've got my Bible right here on the table.

TURNER: Are performers some of the most misunderstood people?

VAN SHELTON: I think so, because it's hard for us to really get our feelings and thoughts across to other people because we get asked so many questions. If you answer them the same way over and over and over, then one day you realize actually there is something else I want to add to what I've been telling people. You try to be real careful with what you say because sometimes it is not going to be printed right. Someone's going to take away or add to what you said. If someone only prints part of what you said, it can be interpreted totally different from what you had originally intended to convey or say. That happens all the time with newspapers. They have a minimum amount of space and they print a little part of a quote and that can make you sound like something you are not. So, yeah, we are misunderstood. Musicians are just people like everybody else. We want to get in our car and go home like everyone else does after the show. Musicians have got what I call the curse. If you really start searching you'll find that musicians have a reputation of not being trustworthy or reputable. Oftentimes they won't hold a regular job and you can't depend on them. They want . . . want . . . want. But what it is, they've got so much music inside of them that they don't care about anything else. That's the curse and that's the way musicians are. I couldn't quit singing if I wanted to. I guess it's a blessing in a way, but I couldn't quit singing if I wanted to. You know.

---

> If someone only prints part of what you said, it can be interpreted totally different from what you had originally intended to convey or say.

---

TURNER: Who instilled this in you?

VAN SHELTON: What? The music?

TURNER: Right! The drive!

VAN SHELTON: Well, the desire to sing has always been there as long as I can remember.

TURNER: From the moment you arrived in Nashville you have had the reputation of being such a nice guy and a real gentleman. What doors were opened as a result of this reputation?

VAN SHELTON: Well, I really don't know how to answer that question. I'm glad that they hear that about me. I try to be nice—I go out of my way to be nice to people because I believe you reap what you sow. I believe in respecting other people. That's the way I was raised and I do try to be nice to people. I have no ideas about what doors have been opened by what I do, or what I say, or what people thought I said.

TURNER: What advice did veteran performers such as Roy Acuff give you when you started out in Nashville?

VAN SHELTON: Keep it up, boy. Keep it clean. You know the thing about it is I've never had a lot of time to spend with any of the old timers. I've never had the opportunity to sit down and talk in depth with any of them—time is so limited. I see them at the Opry, but backstage there are so many fans and people running around—when I'm coming they're going and vice versa. Yeah, it takes time to get to know people, and that's something I don't have a lot of these days.

TURNER: People create images on stage and off stage and oftentimes they feel caged or trapped by these images. Have you found this to be true?

VAN SHELTON: Yeah. People put you up on a pedestal. You know, you can't get up there by yourself. Somebody might think that you can, but you can't. I don't want to be a pedestal. I don't want to be a star. The image is created when you are seen on TV, or read about in magazines. People think you are famous. They think you are somebody—you are somebody just like them. You're no different than anybody else. I don't try to create an image. I just get up there and sing and people think I'm just a well-known country singer. Off stage I like to be just like everybody else. Being a star is a strange thing!

TURNER: You have established yourself as a real reputable singer, and you are approaching the heartthrob status. Does this concern you?

VAN SHELTON: No! That just goes along with the music. A live show is exciting. There's a lot of electricity in the air. It's fun. It's an atmosphere of fun. Everybody is having fun clapping their hands and stomping their feet and having a big time. They get all wrapped up in themselves and they think they're pretty. But if you weren't famous they wouldn't think that you're pretty. It just goes along with being a famous person.

TURNER: Did you have that much success with women in high school and early adulthood?

VAN SHELTON: Oh! I had a little bit but nothing like this.

TURNER: You are a multitalented person: you write, you perform, and you paint. Is being multitalented a blessing, or does it breed a lot of frustration?

VAN SHELTON: No, being able to be creative or being able to do things is great. It's a blessing. I love to paint. It's very gratifying. I love to garden. That's a real art. Believe me, growing flowers in a house is a real art. Keeping plants alive and healthy in a house is a real art. My wife and I have a lot of plants in the house and we plant stuff around in the yard. I just love to garden. It's gratifying to see plants grow. Gardening is also a talent you have to cultivate, if I may use the word. Everybody has talents of some sort. Some people are good listeners. I think that is one of the most important talents a person can possess. You know what I'm saying? I'm the first person to admit that I'm not a good listener. But everybody loves to talk to somebody that will listen. There are people who are just great listeners. And you love those people. You are drawn to them. It is a talent to be able to keep your mouth shut and listen and be interested in what people are saying. So everybody has got talents. I don't like to feel I'm special, I just want to think that I've got talents. I know that I can paint and I can sing. But I don't like to think they're anything special because they're not. They're just something that I have cultivated. They're God-given talents that I love and I have cultivated. It's nothing special.

❖

> I'm hardheaded; if I think I'm right you can beat me but you ain't gonna change my mind.

❖

TURNER: In painting you must conceptualize and project in your mind how something is going to look before you paint it. How has this enhanced your music and your videos?

VAN SHELTON: Well, I can visualize how something should look. If you can see something in your mind, you can tell people what you want. Like when I built a new set for my show, I had to tell these guys what I wanted. I drew it out on paper, just rough sketches, but I could see it all plain in my mind and once we got everything all back together, professional proofs and all that, it was just like I saw it in my mind. It helps.

TURNER: What thread of creativity do you weave through all of your endeavors?

VAN SHELTON: Well, I guess the thread of creativity that I weave through all of my endeavors is the thread of perseverance. I'm hardheaded; if I think I'm right you can beat me but you ain't gonna change my mind. This may sound strange, but this is just something I have inside of me.

TURNER: You had a very successful duet and video with Dolly. How were two perfectionists able to work together so successfully?

VAN SHELTON: Well, when Dolly gave me the song I listened to it and I liked it immediately. I took the tape of her singing and I listened to it, word for word, and all of her inflections. Then I went back and sang some harmonies with the tape. I followed her every word—if she went up on a note, I went up on the note, and when she put little wiggles on the word I put the same wiggle on the word. I was prepared when I walked into the studio. I remember I went to the studio that morning and I met her and we went through it and she looked at me and grinned and said, "Somebody did their homework." I just smiled and we cut the record. I knew the chemistry would be right, because you create your chemistry if you can sing in the same ranges, and I knew I could sing in her range because I had sung with the tape. If your ranges aren't equal, then there is no chemistry. It is kind of like luck, people say you're lucky or I'm lucky—there is no such animal as luck; things happen for a reason. A person has to make things happen. I wouldn't be here talking to you, nor would I have had a record deal if I hadn't moved to Nashville. Nobody would have discovered me in my hometown. Once I moved to Nashville, I never would have met the right people had I not gone looking for them. If they had found me and I wasn't prepared, I wouldn't have gotten a record deal. You see what I'm saying. Everything in life is relative. There ain't no such a thing as luck. People are fooling themselves when they say you're lucky or I'm lucky.

TURNER: Johnny Rodriguez told me that success is how a person feels about themselves. Do you find this statement to be true?

VAN SHELTON: Yes! Success is how you feel about yourself. If you go through a period and you don't think things are going good and you don't like yourself, and you are unhappy, you ain't gonna be successful. Success is your state of being.

TURNER: What prompted you to write your highly successful children's books?

VAN SHELTON: I don't know. I never dreamed of being an author. I remember it was early one morning and I was on a day layover in Detroit and I was sitting there bored, looking around the room thinking, "What am I going to do with myself all day long?" Then all of a sudden it was like God just tapped me on top of the head and said sit down and write. I grabbed a piece of paper and I started writing and there came the first Quacker story. I didn't sit there and think about it, or does this rhyme with this, but I'm sure I must have though about the rhyme. I write my songs the same way. I never sit down to write unless I feel a song coming. It is like God is standing there with open hands and he is pouring it out and then he closes it up and that's it. I get it when I can. As strange as it may sound I can feel a song coming. It's just like—here it comes. I can feel it. What I'm saying is I'm inspired when I write. The next story came the same way. About two weeks ago, I was on the road. I was lying there in bed that morning, wasn't thinking about writing, and all of a sudden I felt inspired. I guess it's like the feeling when you've got to go to the bathroom: you have to get up and go. I felt it coming so I reached over and grabbed a piece of paper and I started writing and I wrote the third part of the story. The next day, the same thing happened again. I wasn't thinking about it; the stuff was coming on again. I was talking to my wife and I told her that I've got to get off the phone, baby, and I started writing. That's inspiration.

TURNER: You said none of this would happen had you not moved to Nashville. What was the story that took you to Nashville?

VAN SHELTON: It was my love of music. I wanted to be in Nashville. I felt I should be in Nashville because that's where it was all happening so I wanted to go. I didn't want to leave my home, my family, my friends, and where I lived. But I knew if I were ever going to make it in the music business I needed to be in Nashville, therefore I wanted to go. We gathered everything in a van and moved to Nashville when we got out of debt and got the opportunity.

TURNER: I understand you like cars a lot. What is the love affair between country stars, country music, racing, and automobiles?

VAN SHELTON: I don't know but country music and racing really go hand in hand. I guess racers are really country music fans and vice versa. I don't know. They go together like soup and sandwiches. I don't know the words to say.

TURNER: If you were an interviewer doing an interview with Ricky Van Shelton, what question would you ask him that I haven't asked?

VAN SHELTON: I have no idea.

March 1993

BILLY JOE THOMAS climbed the ladder of success the hard way. He reached the top of the music business with hit songs like "Raindrops Keep Falling On My Head," only to crash back to the bottom. At the height of his career, Thomas had sold millions of records, with his hits appearing on both pop and country music charts. But drugs left him bankrupt and burned out, and his career hit rock bottom. Drugs were his downfall, but religion is helping him achieve stardom a second time around.

With the help of his wife, the Texas-born singer found God and started making music history again.

*. . . being a Christian, you feel a responsibility to your music. . . . I just try to make sure my music is positive, of a positive nature. I try not to do any real negative songs or songs that advocate drugs or whatever, I just try to keep my music in a positive vein.*

*—B. J. Thomas*

# B. J. Thomas

TURNER: Recently I heard Michael Douglas, a product of the sixties, talking and he said that the sixties generation is coming around and once again are finding happiness in the institution of marriage, family, and religion. Do you agree with this statement?

THOMAS: Well, I don't know if I really agree with that statement, but I really think that there is a definite movement toward marriage and some of the old-time morals. I really think there is definitely a trend toward religion.

---

## I feel that the Lord commissions me to tell the people about Jesus Christ.

---

TURNER: Do you feel that in your music you have a mission to carry this to the masses of the people?

THOMAS: Well, I think being a Christian, I feel that the Lord commissions me to tell the people about Jesus Christ. But, I don't really feel obligated, so to speak, I mean this is really hard to phrase. I don't really feel called from the Lord to preach or testify for Jesus Christ. What I really try to do is to give my show in a Christian manner. Of course I always say something about being a Christian—I don't feel called to preach or anything. But, I do feel that since I am a Christian, I should. I have a responsibility to do my show in a very Christian-like manner.

TURNER: A lot of people in the music industry who have been born again feel that in selecting their material they have to be very careful about music and lyrics because of suggestive words and titles. Do you have to go through and sort or censor some of your material?

THOMAS: Yeah, you know I would not do any suggestive things when I was not a Christian. Again, being a Christian, you feel a responsibility to your music. I don't really try to cull out too many songs, I just try to make sure that my music is positive, of a positive nature. I try not to do any real negative songs or songs that advocate drugs or whatever—I just try to keep my music in a positive vein.

TURNER: You have been very successful and you have made lots of money for record companies. Have you found any rejection on the part of record officials now that you want to record different types of music?

THOMAS: Well, I guess up to about three to five years ago there was some kind of rejection, but as of now, I have just made a new deal with MCA records, my record company. They want to go into the gospel music business. They see that one out of every four Americans is a Christian or professes to be a Christian, so there has to be some gospel music out there for these people. I'm going to start cutting pop music for MCA again for the first time in a couple of years, but they have really embraced my gospel music. I'm going to produce eight albums for them in the next two years. And I'm going to make two gospel albums for them. There is a movement even on the executive branch for record companies toward gospel music. I think it is going to be a Bible music force one day—at least I hope so.

TURNER: A lot of people believe that the music industry is full of promiscuity. Is the industry as bad as some of the people believe it is?

THOMAS: It's not . . . no it's not necessarily that way. I think a person could be promiscuous anywhere. I think there is some of that which goes on but no more than in the political or medical fields or whatever. I know there is a lot of promiscuity out here. I don't think it's all that bad. It's hard for me to place any blame on the music business, even if there were a lot of promiscuities, because it's up to the individual. I, myself, take my music, my show, as a job. When I go on the road I go into training. I don't party all night. I don't booze it up. I try to get a lot of rest. Really, I take it as a job. I think most musicians and most entertainers who have stuck around for a long time and who are established take their careers as a profession. You can play around on the road and party for two or three years, but after a while as a professional musician you need to be satisfied in a musical sense, so you have to cut out all the partying and try to make your music good.

TURNER: Do you feel that the music you are recording is the real B. J. Thomas?

THOMAS: I think my gospel music is the real me in the personal sense. It gives me a great satisfaction. Hopefully, my gospel music is the real me.

And hopefully we can carry it over into the pop/country music and maybe songs that my Christian following can also accept in the secular field.

TURNER: How have you been able to avoid all labels?

THOMAS: You know, I really don't know. I have had big pop records and I have had big country records. I have been up and down. I have managed to sell millions of records and the Lord has really blessed me. So we have been successful. I'm glad that I'm not being labeled because I believe the strong thing about B. J. Thomas is the sound in my voice and the particular style that I have. It is not that I have more talent or less talent then anybody else. It's just that there's a sound and there's a style and I'm glad it is not labeled. I think I could label it soft rock/contemporary pop/country.

TURNER: Is your voice in better shape now that you are off drugs and everything?

THOMAS: Well yeah, yeah much more so, much better shape now. Used to I could only go two or three days at a time and then I would have to stop and let my voice get back in shape. I don't really have much trouble with that anymore.

TURNER: What does the future hold for B. J. Thomas?

THOMAS: Hopefully, next year I will be able to tour the first and last part of the year and take more time off next year. I have just made a great new deal with my record company. Like I said, I'm going to produce light gospel records for them over the next two years. So I'm excited about that project. Hopefully, I'm moving into a different area of the music business. I'm older now and I need to move more into the office, I guess. It's not that I ever want to get off the road or stop making records. But I have been doing it for twenty-something years and I really feel moved to stay home more. I'm going try to do that next year.

TURNER: Do you have any area that you feel the press misrepresents you in?

THOMAS: No, I don't think so. I'm a fairly low-key individual, so really the press does not have a whole lot to work with.

June 1979

AFTER PURSUING SUCCESS in the music world for twelve years, Gene Watson burst onto the country scene in 1975 with "Love In The Hot Afternoon". Since then, he hasn't made an album that didn't climb the national charts or contain at least one hit song.

Back in Palestine, Texas, where Watson was raised, he worked on cars all day and played clubs at night. Success was only a dream.

Now that he has achieved stardom, the one thing Watson is adamant about is never doing anything remotely mechanical to a car again.

*I do the kind of music I do because I love it and that's what my fans expect out of me . . . I'm just country and I know that. And that's what I'm going to continue to be doing.*

—Gene Watson

# Gene Watson

TURNER: In doing research, I read that you are very particular in selecting material for new records. You like to do your own material and you will not delegate this task to someone else. Is this statement true?

WATSON: Well, I don't do my own writing, because I don't have enough time to write anymore. I choose my materials from other writers. But yes, I have the last word in the selection of my material. Let's face it, I'm an idiot. I turned down "The Gambler." I've turned down a lot of good songs because I didn't feel like they were my songs. I try to pick the material that I think I can sell to my public.

TURNER: What do you look for in a song?

WATSON: I can't say; it's just something that comes from the guts—gut feelings. I think I basically know what my public wants out of me, and that's what I look for. I never know where I'm going to get it until I find it. We have been pretty lucky.

TURNER: From what I see and read, there seems to be a revival in traditional country music. When I think of traditional country music, I think of you and three or four other artists who are leading this revival. How do you feel about this?

WATSON: I really don't know how to answer that question. As far as being solid, straight country, I think the only ones left are me and Moe Bandy.

TURNER: Both your careers seem to be going so good. Do you think people consider you a maverick sticking with traditional country music?

WATSON: Well, I'll tell you right out front. I do the kind of music I do because I love it and that's what my fans expect out of me. I'm just country. There is no way I could jump out there and do "Stardust" with a bunch of strings and all that stuff. I'm just country and I know that. And that's what I'm going to continue to be doing.

TURNER: Is it hard to find the traditional type of country music being written today?

WATSON: No! I would say there is an abundance of it. Man, we have boxes full of tapes that some of the finest writers in the business have sent us. We've got the whole catalogue from Acuff-Rose. So we are bound to be doing something right. I don't know what it is. Again, no, we don't have to look for it. Now I can remember when I first started on independent labels and everything, man, we could not buy a good song. Now we have risen above that and we've got some of the best writers in the business sending songs to us. A writer usually knows what style of music a certain singer does, so I have the guys who are really pros sending me stuff they know that I sing.

TURNER: Once you have made a name for yourself, they come to you rather than your having to go to them.

WATSON: Well, that's the name of the game. I'm really proud, I guarantee you.

TURNER: How did you get your start back in Texas?

WATSON: I worked at a car dealership in Houston when it all started. We were recording for a small label that Lewis, my manager, owned, and we just got lucky and came out with "Love In The Hot Afternoon." Then I signed with Capitol Records. I've been singing all my life.

TURNER: When you first started and it was hard to find material and dates, how did you keep from getting discouraged and giving up?

WATSON: I did get discouraged lots of times. There were people who had a lot of faith in me and kept me going. I mean people who would put a few dollars in me. I was just a country boy who didn't have nothing—you know I was just working on cars. But my friends had enough faith in me, so I hung in there.

TURNER: Do you still work on cars as a hobby?

WATSON: No I don't! Man, I haven't touched a car since I quit Southwest Lincoln-Mercury.

TURNER: What can we expect from Gene Watson in the future?

WATSON: I have a brand new album coming out. We're just looking around, looking for gold records. I have reached a lot of goals with the help of my fans.

TURNER: You give me the impression that you are a "fans" person—you recognize the importance of your fans.

WATSON: I definitely am.

TURNER: Do you feel obligated to continue on the same avenues you have taken in the past?

WATSON: Yes.

TURNER: Fans of some performers will not let them do different types of material or music. How do you feel about expanding?

WATSON: I feel like if it wasn't for them, the fans, I wouldn't be here. I don't think they get enough appreciation, I really don't.

TURNER: Do you think people are a fan of a particular song or a fan of the performer?

WATSON: I think they start out as a fan of a song. Because I'm just now getting things worked in so they are recognizing my name. When "Love In The Hot Afternoon" or "This Dream's On Me" came out, everybody loved the songs, but they said, "Who is Gene Watson?" Name recognition is a big thing you have to go through. I think people are associating me with the songs today. And that is one of the hardest hills to climb you have ever seen in your life.

TURNER: If you were an interviewer doing an interview with Gene Watson, what questions do you think should be covered?

WATSON: (LAUGHS) I really don't know. I'm one of those "you ask the questions" guys, and I will answer them if I can. No, I will tell you we've been working real hard. We've just finished a tour and we're real tired. But that's the life. You get a wink of sleep when you can and you just gear yourself up for the next job. If you are sick you do it anyway, get out there and smile. Everybody thinks you are feeling real fine even if you have a temperature of 104 degrees. It has taken me several years to realize that your feelings are not your own. No matter what you feel like, the people are depending on you; you get out there whether you feel like it or not. You just do it.

August 1982

*I've always loved country music, but I haven't really agreed with the way a whole lot of people choose to make country music.*

—Don Williams

**D**ON WILLIAMS has almost slipped up on the country music world. The tall, soft-spoken Texan had been almost ignored by Nashville during the early years of his music career. Then came his now-famous tour of Europe in 1976 when he was mobbed at the International Festival of Country Music in London and had crowds all over the continent screaming for encores.

When Williams returned home, he found an invitation to join the Grand Ole Opry in his mail. Don Williams had arrived. Or more accurately, the "biggies" in the business had been shaken into realizing that this deep, rich voice and the laid-back, simple man who sang good country songs with it were to be reckoned with.

# Don Williams

TURNER: I've asked some of my friends if they like country music, and they've said, no, but I like Waylon Jennings, Willie Nelson, and Don Williams. What puts you in that category? What is your universal appeal?

WILLIAMS: Oh, I don't know. I've always loved country music, but I haven't really agreed with the way a whole lot of people choose to make country music. I guess as far as Waylon and Willie and me, I guess the three of us in particular, we all came out of Texas, and Texas has its own kind of music that's popular in Texas and isn't exposed to the rest of the world. And there are artists that really get big in Texas that the rest of the world doesn't know anything about. I guess that's probably part of it. I think the three of us just make music the way we feel it and believe it, regardless of how anybody else is doing it. That's the only thing I could say, really.

TURNER: Back in the sixties, I remember you came to our college and performed. How much of the folk is carried over into today's Don Williams?

WILLIAMS: Well, that's really hard to say. I've always been into lyrics. And that's just right square where folk music always was. But it really hasn't made any difference to me what the form of music was. I listen to the lyrics first, you know. So it would really be hard to say how much.

TURNER: When you write a song, do you write the lyrics first and then put the music to it?

WILLIAMS: It all happens at the same time.

TURNER: Can you visualize how a song is going to sound before you get it down on paper?

WILLIAMS: Well, of sorts, yeah.

TURNER: If you were writing a book and it had the name, Don Williams, followed by two blank lines, how would you fill in those lines?

WILLIAMS: I don't know, that's throwing it at me pretty fast.

251

TURNER: Have you got a philosophy or motto that has carried you through life?

WILLIAMS: Well, the way I feel is that I want to do the best I can with any given situation and be as fair and honest with whoever I'm dealing with as I can.

---

❖

I want to do the best I can with any given situation and be as fair and honest with whoever I'm dealing with as I can.

❖

---

TURNER: Are there any drawbacks to being a recognizable star?

WILLIAMS: Well, there are drawbacks to anything you do. Sure there's plenty of drawbacks, but you just try to assess them and deal with them as best you can.

TURNER: Tell me about your hat. Where did you get it?

WILLIAMS: I got it when I was making a movie with Burt Reynolds— *W. W. and the Dixie Dance Kings*. Prior to that, I hadn't really worn a hat very much and I just little by little wore it more and more until it's just kind of part of my clothes.

TURNER: How did you like moviemaking?

WILLIAMS: Well, it was a real experience. It was my first and only experience at moviemaking. We had some good times, but it was a lot of work.

TURNER: Do you ever worry about your creativity in writing songs ever drying up?

WILLIAMS: Oh, yes!

TURNER: When you are on stage performing, your rapport with the audience is great. What do you attribute this to?

WILLIAMS: Well, audiences to me are like talking to people. It's just like sitting down and talking to one person. If you meet someone that you've never met before and they're very outgoing and they help you, say, whatever, then it's an easy situation. I've run into audiences that I've literally not said a word to, because in that respect I'm not an entertainer.

TURNER: In foreign countries you have tremendous appeal also. Do you like performing in these foreign countries?

---

❖

> I've run into audiences that I've literally not said a word to, because in that respect I'm not an entertainer.

❖

---

WILLIAMS: Well, I've gone back to England a lot and I've been to Ireland now about three times. It's a long ways from home, but really the only reason that I keep going back is because the people are so fantastic.

TURNER: Have you ever performed for an audience who did not understand English?

WILLIAMS: Yes.

TURNER: Do they just understand the music?

WILLIAMS: Well, they understand. See, all of your people in Europe understand enough English that in a song they can get what you're singing. Now, you can't stand up there and try to tell them a joke or something that they can't really follow that quick. They can all understand it and speak it, of course. But they're not able to just sit down and talk to you.

TURNER: What aspect of your career do you find the most fulfilling? Writing? Performing?

WILLIAMS: They all give you something that the others can't. On an average, I would say that songwriting is probably the most fulfilling. But on those special occasions when you record a song that you just know— there on the spot—that that's a special event, and then when you have an audience that's really a special audience. It's really gratifying.

TURNER: What makes up an ideal audience?

WILLIAMS: The audience that I had on the first show tonight.

August 1981

*I just want to be playing twenty years from now. I want to be able to go out and do a concert somewhere—not necessarily make money but break even. Just be able to perform and let people have a good time and have a good time myself.*

—*Tom Wopat*

Tom Wopat, better known as Luke Duke, rode to fame aboard the General Lee in the hit TV series *The Dukes of Hazzard*. However, Wopat was singing long before he envisioned a career in television.

Wopat grew up on a dairy farm in Lodi, Wisconsin, along with six brothers and a sister. During this time, he was perfecting his singing and acting talents by appearing regularly in school musicals. Immediately upon graduation from high school, Wopat enrolled as a music major at the University of Wisconsin in Madison. After a brief stint as a college student, Wopat left the university and joined a local rock band as lead singer and trombone player. To appease the acting bug, Wopat left the band and returned to the university to pursue acting in college and civic musicals.

Two very successful seasons performing summer stock in Michigan prepared Wopat for the move to the Big Apple, where his talents were readily recognized. In a matter of weeks, he was appearing off-Broadway in the musical, "A Bistro Car," which in turn led to a role on Broadway in Si Coleman's production of "I Love My Wife."

The desire for financial security led Wopat to audition for *The Dukes of Hazzard*, a series he and John Schneider parlayed into a hit and a financial bonanza. The financial success of the hit TV series has afforded Wopat the opportunity to pursue his first love, music, which he hopes will insure his longevity in the entertainment industry.

# Tom Wopat

TURNER: How did you get interested in acting and music?

WOPAT: Well, way back in junior high, or before then, actually, I started to do little musical comedies in school. I got very involved in it and one thing led to another and I did them all through high school. Then I got interested in a musical and followed it up at the University of Wisconsin. I was majoring in music there, and I did a lot of musical comedy and one thing led to another. I ended up doing summer stock in Michigan and getting my Equity card. I then went to New York and on to Broadway, in both music and acting. *The Dukes* came after that.

---
❖
---

I think in music a lot of the imagery is kind of subconscious, built by the beat and the volume of the music.

---
❖
---

TURNER: How do you think the theater prepared you for a career in singing?

WOPAT: Well, it gives you stage presence. You have an idea of what is going on, and what is necessary to get by, as far as being able to pull something off. I don't know; the more kinds of things you do like that, where you have to take the stage and be the focal point, the easier it gets.

TURNER: A lot of people feel that acting and music are related in the fact that acting is creating a visual image, whereas in singing you are painting an imaginary picture. How do you feel about this theory?

WOPAT: That sounds pretty accurate. I think in music a lot of the imagery is kind of subconscious, built by the beat and the volume of the music. Acting is a little more naked. You don't have as many things to hide behind.

TURNER: Did you just walk in one day and say, "Hey I think I would like a singing contract"? Was it all that easy?

WOPAT: No it wasn't quite that easy. I had wanted to record for a long time. Actually it was something I had dreamed about. Three years ago we started talking with Post and consequently was heard. We talked to Post about the possibilities of me recording, and he seemed to think there was a possibility. So we went ahead and I spent my own money for the first four songs that we recorded. We then took them around and finally Electra Sound was willing to sign. It was something we went about step by step, but it wasn't a whim and it isn't a whim. It is something that I want to see fulfilled. I want to carry it out as far as I can.

TURNER: Were record executives and program directors of radio stations hesitant to play the records of actors who cross over to singing?

WOPAT: Yes, I have run into some of that. I think that most of the people who have heard the album and those who have taken the time to listen to it are favorably impressed.

TURNER: Do you think that you had to work harder to prove that you had substance as a singer than you would have had you not been an actor first?

WOPAT: Possibly, I don't know. I still haven't proven anything yet.

TURNER: It is out and it is getting good reviews.

WOPAT: Yes, in that sense, I feel a little vindicated, but it hasn't sold; it hasn't caught on yet. The jury is still out on it. I don't feel discouraged or anything. I'm not counting my chickens before they hatch or anything.

TURNER: Where do you see yourself on the music spectrum?

WOPAT: How do you mean?

TURNER: do you see yourself as a country, western, etc.?

WOPAT: I would say, if it is anything, it is kind of West Coast country music—kind of a country rock.

TURNER: You think that differs from the Nashville sound?

WOPAT: I think somewhat. You are not going to find a lot of violins on my album. I think it's going to be pretty much guitar-oriented with a lot of vocals. I think maybe in future stuff I may try to put a little more of a bluegrass sound into it.

TURNER: Herb Peterson has a great admiration for bluegrass music. How much influence did he have over the album?

WOPAT:  He had a lot of influence over the album. I would say the vocals show a lot of the influence of Herb Peterson. I think my personal style has reflected a lot of his influences, and I'm happy with that. I admire him greatly.

TURNER:  A lot of country music performers grow up listening to the Grand Ole Opry and are influenced by the greats. Who were you influenced by?

---

❖

to be perfectly honest, I was not a big country and western fan when I was younger.

❖

---

WOPAT:  Well, to be perfectly honest, I was not a big country and western fan when I was younger. I listened to some of the Hank Williams music. and as I got into my teens I listened to Willie and Waylon. Mainly the people that I listen to are Dobie Grey and Ronnie Milsap and singers like that.

TURNER:  What do you look for when you select material for a Tom Wopat album?

WOPAT:  Well, I try to look for a song that I can sing and believe in. It has to have something that makes it valid, like the song, "We Had It All." What a great song! That is a great song.

TURNER:  Oftentimes we do find actors and singers going into different areas to conquer. Why do you think they turn to other creative aspects of the profession?

WOPAT:  I think a lot of times you see people kind of inflicting their tastes on the performers—you know, like producers, writers, and directors. A lot of times when you are an actor or a performer you feel shackled by that. You feel like someone else is inflicting their taste on your performance because you have to do what they give you to do. I think that a lot of the things that I felt had value seemed to work pretty well on a day-to-day basis.

TURNER: Recently you were in the news about a contractual dispute with television. A lot of it was over creativity—not so much money. What kind of artistic control or creative control do you have on your record contracts?

WOPAT: Contractually, not that much. As it worked out I ended up having a pretty fair amount of control as far as the live shows—more than I do on the TV things.

TURNER: *The Dukes of Hazzard* has been very kind to country music stars in casting them in key roles. Have the people of the country music community supported you in your recording endeavors?

WOPAT: They have been very supportive. They have been very nice. On a personal level I am fairly good friends with Waylon, and I saw him a couple of weeks ago, and he had nothing but good things to say about the album.

TURNER: You were very successful as an actor. Did you prepare yourself for the fact that you might not be successful as a singer and how it would affect you?

WOPAT: I am not looking to be an overnight sensation. I enjoy performing a lot. The recording part is real nice. It would be nice to have a hit album or a hit single and get that kind of exposure. However, it wouldn't discourage me too much if this album doesn't sell very well. I think I will still go on and record another album, even if I have to produce it myself or whatever. It gives me personal satisfaction to perform music and I think the musicians I have assembled for the live act have done a good job. It has been real satisfying for me.

TURNER: Have you been satisfied with the reaction you have gotten from your fans?

WOPAT: Yes, people don't go wild about it. We always get a good reaction when we go live. It is a situation, I think, that if there was a hit involved it would be different. I am satisfied so far.

TURNER: Don't you think that today's music is a throwback into an earlier era and that we are moving in a nostalgic direction?

WOPAT: Oh, I think so. That is part of the satisfaction in doing an album, also the live act is the same way. These are the things that I enjoy. It is the good lyrics and the good songs.

TURNER: Where would you want your music to take you?

WOPAT: I just want to be playing twenty years from now. I want to be able to go out and do a concert somewhere—not necessarily make money but break even. Just be able to perform and let people have a good time and have a good time myself.

TURNER: What kind of a song do you feel most comfortable with?

WOPAT: Well, there are a couple of things. Right now in the live action, in our performance, we are doing a Chuck Berry song, "Living in U.S.A." I feel pretty comfortable with that and we also do a version of "If I Were a Carpenter." It's just a great song. It's one of my favorite songs to sing.

TURNER: What can an audience expect from a Tom Wopat concert?

WOPAT: Mostly up-tempo stuff and a couple of ballads, a lot of vocal harmony, a lot of vocals, and a lot of guitars. It isn't real loud—it sounds like country rock.

TURNER: You had name and face recognition when you started to record. I would think that this would prevent you from mingling with the fans at concerts. Do you think this has hindered your singing career?

WOPAT: No, I don't really think so. I don't really have too much trouble with that. It has never gotten to the point where it has been dangerous or anything. I can still go out to places and listen to bands and stuff and not get hassled too much.

TURNER: What aspect of your career do you find most fulfilling?

WOPAT: I would say right now the musical thing. I directed a *Dukes of Hazzard* episode and that was really satisfying and challenging.

TURNER: If you were an interviewer doing a Tom Wopat interview, what would be one question you would ask that I haven't asked?

WOPAT: I have no idea.

May 1983

# About the Author

WILLIAM TURNER, A SUCCESSFUL FREE-lance newspaper columnist, has interviewed dozens of leading country entertainers (a few of whom rarely grant interviews) since his writing career began in 1975. His columns have appeared regularly in newspapers and magazines throughout the southeast.

With a detailed knowledge of the country music scene and skillful questioning and listening techniques, Turner elicited responses of warmth and candor. Turner has transcribed the audiotaped interviews and written introductory material for each profile to produce a diary of interviews. The diary of interviews with country superstars of the 70's, 80's and 90's chronicles the growth and explosion of country music.